8 4   39.34

8 9

Social Policy and Social Welfare

Social Policy
and
Social Welfare
Structure and Applications

Thomas M. Meenaghan
and
Robert O. Washington

THE FREE PRESS
A Division of Macmillan Publishing Co., Inc.
NEW YORK

Collier Macmillan Publishers
LONDON

The Free Press
A Division of Macmillan Publishing Co., Inc.
866 Third Avenue, New York, N.Y. 10022

Collier Macmillan Canada, Ltd.

Library of Congress Catalog Card Number: 79-54669

Printed in the United States of America

printing number
2 3 4 5 6 7 8 9 10

Library of Congress Cataloging in Publication Data

Meenaghan, Thomas M
    Social policy and social welfare.

    Bibliography: p.
    Includes index.
    1. Social service. 2. Social service--United
States. 3. Public welfare--United States.
4. Social security--United States. 5. Social
policy. I. Washington, Robert O., joint author.
II. Title.
HV40.M457   361'.973   79-54669
ISBN 0-02-920750-9

Contents

Preface

As recently as 1973 Alfred Kahn, referring to the future of social welfare in the United States, said that "given its affluence the society has more institutional and programmatic choices before it . . . than ever before."[1] We have written this book to explicate those choices in the context of the social welfare institution. However it is also our purpose to delineate the varieties of constraints that impinge upon choices within a societal context.

We have selected several areas of choice for this analysis. At the highest level is the basic choice of how to look at—and define— social welfare as an institution within the context of society. Should we, for example, stress cultural perspectives or special group interests? If we focus on cultural perspectives, which values should dominate and which appear to be dysfunctional for achieving a viable social welfare institution? Then, on another level, there are the choices concerning the purposes of social policy, particularly the programs and services that are tied to policy decisions. A third choice involves the way in which we as a society see, explore, and eventually attempt to solve social problems. Is there a single way for us to look at problems? And, if not, what are some of the conceptual options available? Related to this choice are the more specific alternatives afforded us in the concepts, models, and strategies of intervention suggested by the social and behavioral sciences. To what degree do we feel that sociology, economics, and political science constructs can help us make informed analyses of people and their experiences? Also inherent to this choice area is the question: To what degree shall we continue to see the problems that people experience as tied to personality and personal causation, rather than to society and structural elements?

In exploring these choice areas several objectives have been uppermost in our minds. One is to try to communicate to human service professionals that their activities and their professional careers are continuously shaped by the institution of social welfare. That is, the institution of social welfare is the context that helps, limits, and shapes the way in which we can deal with people who are in trouble. We feel that it is naïve and incomplete, as well as professionally derelict, to consider social policy as an area of concern for others but not for the human service worker. It is our concern, like it or not.

Just as human service professionals carry out their activities within the broad context of social welfare, so social welfare itself is shaped by what has occurred and is occurring in society. As a result another objective of this book is to examine how society's ongoing choices in areas other than welfare can and do shape social welfare responses.

Finally, we have emphasized critical thinking as a necessary component of human service training and orientation—that is, the need to ask the important questions, canvass the range of existing answers, assess their validity, and offer prescriptive alternatives. If this critical posture is adopted, we will be more likely to achieve an understanding of the parameters and supports for current policies and programs and develop a tentative guide to the areas in which social change should occur. And pursuit of change can, of course, become a subsequent practice goal for human practitioners. What we are suggesting is that critical analysis is the essential precedent both for constructive practice decisions by human service professionals and for relevant "institutional and programmatic" choices by society.

Before considering the topic of social welfare in detail, let us identify some of the themes that the reader will be encountering in this book—themes that should be seen as part of the contextual fabric in which analysis and choices will occur. They include *conflicts* in our society in terms of norms, values, and interests, which have often led to *pragmatic solutions; interinstitutional relations* between the major structural components of our society (e.g., the economy, government, family, etc.); the battles and tensions among the basic concepts of *need, rights, and paternalism* and among the concepts of *fairness, equality of opportunity, and equality*. A list of these themes has helped us in putting together the book, and we hope that it can serve the reader in a functional fashion.

Structurally the book is divided into several sections. The first two chapters, which comprise the first section, introduce the cultural and power perspectives and relate them to the issue of how to approach the study of social welfare in society. Attention is given to how society's major institutions can relate to each other and how such relations can and do influence social welfare. In focusing upon interinstitutional relations, the concepts of social welfare policy and social welfare programs are presented in the context of the functions of social welfare and types of program options.

In the next section of the book, Chapters 3–5, we discuss the concept of a social problem and the interplay of the social sciences and possible societal definitions of social problems. We stress two particular disciplines: sociology and economics. Each is described in terms of some of the major schools of thought within these disciplines. This section concludes with a discussion of how the various concepts and theories within the social sciences can structure the perception of appropriate policy–program responses.

In the third section of the book we examine how three of our society's major cultural–interest items have influenced social welfare. Chapter 6 reviews the role of work in shaping social welfare. Chapter 7 discusses the role of individualism and collectivism in affecting caring responses within society. Throughout these two chapters is the recurring theme of how the economy and government interact with each other in operationalizing social welfare. This section concludes, in Chapter 8, with a delineation of many of the options within the social welfare institution concerning populations to be covered, types of benefits, modes of service delivery, and sources of support.

The fourth section, Chapters 9–13, looks at policy-specific areas in light of the material already presented in the book. Chapter 9 serves as a bridge to this section by presenting a framework for the discussion and analysis of policy–program products.

Chapter 14 concludes the book with some reflections on the future direction of social welfare. Areas of concern that might be stressed, as well as intervention strategies, are cited.

Acknowledgments

In preparing this book, we have had the support and assistance of a number of persons whom we wish to thank. First is our families, especially our wives, Kathleen and Mary, for all their continued encouragement. We would also like to acknowledge Ms. Becky Rutter's many outstanding contributions to the preparation of the manuscript. And we would like to thank our students for their informal study and critical reactions to our thinking. Without the assistance of all these people, this book would not have been possible.

Note

1. Alfred Kahn, ed., *Shaping the New Social Work* (New York: Columbia University Press, 1973), p. 6.

Chapter 1

An Introduction to Social Welfare: Cultural and Power Perspectives

IN STUDYING AN AREA as broad as that of social welfare, one of the very first issues that has to be explored is, What is social welfare and how does it relate to our society? Among the many possible answers, this chapter focuses upon some of them. For preliminary purposes it may be said that there are two broad types of answers—one that stresses cultural elements and one that stresses relative differences in power and interests among various groups in the society.

Cultural Perspectives and Social Welfare

Generally culture has been defined as a way of looking at the basic questions and needs of people and of mapping out routinized ways of solving these problems.[1] These basic issues involve the ways in which people are to worship, to mate, to raise their children, and so on. A question of particular interest to us is, How are people within a society to relate to and care for each other? Anthropologists would say that each culture tends to develop a particular set of answers to these questions and concerns and that these answers get expressed in specific, routinized ways

1

of acting that are supported and justified by norms and values. Simply put, the norms are the correct ways to act, the procedures and rules that guide the behavior of those who live in a given culture. But people act relative to some purposes, ends, beliefs. These we call the values of a society.[2] Both the values and norms are the answers, the choices of society's members regarding how to live with one another and how to solve the basic questions and issues.

Obviously each society, and even groups within a given society, will have somewhat different answers to these basic issues, so that societies and subcultures will differ, that is, be somewhat distinctive, by virtue of the content of their cultural answers. Further, the cultural answers tend to endure over time as long as they are perceived as functionally relevant to a society's basic questions.

NORMS AND VALUES

When society, by virtue of its culture, shapes and influences behavior relative to certain rules (norms) and values (ends), the behavior in question is characterized as institutionalized behavior. For example, in the past American society has tended, by virtue of its dominant culture, to state that sex relations should be confined to married people, that marriage should be related to reproduction, and that there should be a specific division of labor between spouses. These societal expectations collectively produced the institution of American marriage and in so doing structured the behavior of many actors within society.

This example suggests several points. One is that the society's will and expectations are imposed upon the actor. Another is the apparent fact that in many cases a given actor will want to do what the society expects him or her to do. And third, in recent times, many people have come to believe that some of their needs may not be met, or adequately met, within the prevailing institution. In short, institutionalized behavior tends to remain stable only if actors perceive that the prevailing behavior forms meet their needs. This last characteristic can lead to cultural change.

This cluster of factors is certainly not limited to the institution of marriage. Other areas of society such as religion (the purpose of life and the role of the deity(ies); government (the way in which people are to be bound to each other); and the economy (the way in which goods are to be produced, distributed, and owned/shared) have sets of distinctive answers. In all these areas the shaping of actors' behavior by the culture is apparent. This phenomenon is often discussed within the specific context of role behavior.

ROLES

Roles are packages of behavior involving certain rights and responsibilities that fall within the overall guidelines established by the society's dominant culture. Ideally every act of a society member is tied to, and justified by, the role cluster in which he or she is to operate.[3] That role cluster in turn is justified by the norms and values dominating a given area, such as family, religion, education, and so on. For example, the isolated acts of a young woman toward her infant child are not usually idiosyncratic and purely creative. Rather, such acts are shaped by what the society says a mother should be and how she should behave. Similarly, the way in which a parent reprimands a child is shaped by society's expectations regarding the role of parent.

The overall relation between culture and the given act of a society's members can be shown schematically, as in Figure 1-1.

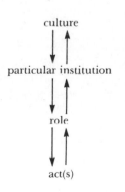

FIGURE 1.1

culture	ends (values) & roles (norms)
particular institution	(specific content in norms & values)
role	(the acting out of sanctioned norms & values)
act(s)	(behavior in situation, directly or indirectly tied to role)

4

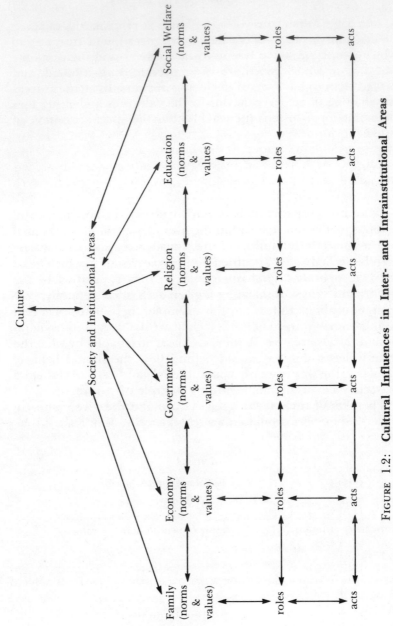

FIGURE 1.2: **Cultural Influences in Inter- and Intrainstitutional Areas**

When one sees given acts as influenced by culture and more specific role packages, it is also possible to see that the repetition of specific acts tends to reinforce and maintain both the culture and the role package(s). When there is a large amount of activity in accordance with assigned roles and overall norms and values, several effects are produced. The culture endures; the actors reflect the culture in a predictable way; and there is a level of consensus produced within the society and a level of satisfaction or harmony within actors. In short, many people begin to see life through these norms and values, expect others to act in accord with these norms and values, and may even see solutions to problems in terms of these norms and values.

Moving from our looking at activity within one area of society to looking at all the acts within the society, we can see, in Figure 1-2, how culture can influence inter- and intrainstitutional areas. However, the model also raises the point of how the respective institutions relate to each other. Are they all equal, or do some disproportionately influence others? If so, in what ways; with what effects?

Analytical Framework

Our book focuses on a single institutional area, namely, that of social welfare. We would expect that the acts of a given social worker will be influenced by the norms and values inherent within the social welfare institution, especially as they are operationalized in job assignments and job descriptions. But perhaps of more immediate concern is the issue of what is the nature of those norms and values. Are the norms and values of social welfare peculiar to social welfare, or are they heavily influenced by the norms and values of other institutions?

It appears that there are at least three concepts that shape possible answers to the question of what the social welfare institution is in our society. These are (1) equity, (2) primacy, and (3) dependency. In discussing these concepts it will be well to keep in mind that they embody fundamentally different views of the nature of man and the nature of contemporary society.

1. *Equity.* The basic argument here is that social welfare is on
equal footing with other institutions in society. Put another way,
social welfare has distinct norms and values that are not borrowed from other institutions; it is not shaped excessively by
other institutions' needs or norms and values. Generally, the
institution of social welfare would suggest, through its norms
and values, that the well-being of all of society's members is
important and socially desirable.[4]

This view of social welfare is embraced by the constitutional
mandate, "to promote the general welfare." The underlying
value frame of reference implies that man is social, is good, and
thus is entitled to a wide range of services, programs, and benefits that would contribute to his human existence and social nature. It recognizes that in a complex society such as ours all
people at some point will have needs that go beyond the individual in terms of their causation and their solution.

The concept of equity in social welfare also calls attention to a
value frame of reference in society that holds that society has
some responsibility for the plight of its members. In other
words, it gives credence to the proposition that public funds
should be used to assist people who have lost their ability to be
self-sufficient or who have lived all their lives under conditions
of hardships. Dyckman (1966) suggests that the whole complex
of welfare services in our society as it has developed is a device to
compensate for the wastage and breakage in a competitive,
individual-serving, industrial society. These services exist, according to Dyckman, to cushion the blows of the competitive
struggle for those so disadvantaged as to be unable to compete
effectively.[5]

On the basis of these considerations, the social welfare institution would have three distinct properties: *comprehensiveness, universalism,* and *prevention. Comprehensiveness* speaks to a wide
range of services—from day care to recreation, from clinical
services to programs that promote participation and reduce
alienation, from social services to programs that are geared to
man's aesthetic needs. *Universal coverage* means that everyone is
entitled to certain services and programs. *Prevention* recognizes
that many needs are predictable and therefore that the society

should do something either to prevent the need or to plan for how best to meet it when it occurs.

In a classic discussion of this kind of social welfare institution, Wilensky and Lebeaux (1965) state that social welfare is, "the organized system of social services and institutions, designed to aid individuals and groups to attain satisfying standards of life and health . . . which permit individuals the fullest development of their capacities."[6] Their statement clearly stresses a societal choice concerning man and society and a degree of importance for social welfare. When a society makes a choice, through its culture, to relate to its members in accord with the concept of equity, social welfare would be seen as one of the basic institutions in that society.

2. *Primacy.* Just as a society can choose to make social welfare needs paramount agenda items, it is at least conceivable to go one step further and say that those needs of man should take precedence over other areas of the society. Although equity suggests that social welfare is just as important as, say, the maximal development of a free-enterprise economy, the concept of primacy suggests that, if people's social welfare needs are being jeopardized by the way in which an economy is operating, then the economy (or government or education) should be adjusted to meet these basic (most important) needs. Such a society would have a set of norms and values relative to social welfare that would shape and influence both the norms and values of the other institutions and behavior within such institutional areas.

As in the case of equity, this type of social welfare is a choice—a choice in culture that would affect interinstitutional relationships.

3. *Dependency.* This concept is the converse of primacy. In this cultural option social welfare would be seen as an institution that operates in time and importance after the other institutions. Further, its content (that is, the norms and values of social welfare) would be derived from the values found in other institutions. It suggests that, after the person had demonstrated the existence of a problem and incapacity to solve it, either personally or through family, then the social welfare institution could respond. But the response would take place in the context of an

assumption that, if the person had acted appropriately, relative to some other institutions, there would be no problem. Thus, when the social welfare institution offers help, the values and norms associated with other institutions are often stressed, in the belief that many of the major institutions in society, especially the family and the economy (as well as the person), can and should be the front line of defense in meeting individual needs.[7]

Again Wilensky and Lebeaux speak to this type of social welfare, stating "that social welfare institutions should come into play only when the normal structures of supply, the family and the market, break down."[8] This cultural option is often referred to as the residual conception of social welfare.

Several characteristics of this alternative are worth noting. First, the social welfare institution will tend to relate to selected individuals and groups—those who clearly demonstrate specific problems and an inability to solve such problems. Not all people or all problems will necessarily be covered. Second, what help or service is provided is ideally provided for fixed (often limited) periods of time to ensure that the individual and/or the front line institutions of the family and the economy can effectively deal with the problem. Third, it implies some judgment concerning the ability of the recipient to act responsibly. Such a judgment can lead to stigma concerning character, moral, and personality failure of a recipient. Finally, this type of welfare does not have much conceptual appreciation for the notions of prevention, that is, for helping people to remain free of potential problems. In a sense, it acknowledges the fact that individuals experience the effects of certain arrangements in our society, but it lacks a corresponding appreciation that individuals are not the main causes of such effects.

In the dependency model of social welfare, the social welfare institution is seen as intimately related to the way in which the other institutions function. First, social welfare steps in only after the other institutions appear to have been unable to solve demonstrated problems that people have. Second, social welfare in its response often reflects the values, norms, and purposes of these other institutions. In a very real sense, the institutions of the economy and the family can shape the timing, scope, and content of social welfare responses.

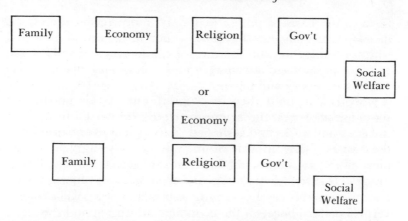

FIGURE 1.3: **Dependency Conception of Social Welfare in Society**

If a society chooses to emphasize this alternative, the major institutions may be arranged relative to one another as shown in Figure 1-3. In both instances of the dependency type, the positioning of social welfare suggests that it is influenced by the other institutions more than it influences them. When cultural perspectives are seen within this context, it becomes useful to introduce a second relevant perspective in an attempt to determine how and why societies select certain social welfare alternatives; how and why certain norms and values come to dominate our care responses within social welfare; and how and why certain types of care responses are maintained over time.

The Power and Interest Perspectives

This perspective is greatly influenced by the analysis originally developed by Marx and elaborated upon by conflict theorists. It stresses the role that individual and group self-interest can play in shaping society and society's major institutions. Central to this perspective is the assumption that whatever values tend to dominate in a social arrangement may be mere rationalizations of the needs and interests of the more powerful segments of the society. Although Marx focused exclusively upon property relations as the basis of power in society, more recent theoretical developments suggest that it is economic interests interacting with a complex network of race, sex, and ethnic variables that produce positions of advantage/disadvantage and differences in terms of interests and needs.[9]

Nonetheless, most theorists coming out of this perspective focus initially upon the interests directly connected to the way the economy works and is shaped. So central is the institution of the economy that this line of analysis strongly suggests that almost all relationships within a society are affected by the special interests that tend to dominate the economic institution. By definition, then, this perspective suggests that societies will exhibit a vertical pattern between the economic institution and the other institutions, and between the needs and interests in the economic sector and those elsewhere in the society.[10]

Some examples might clarify the direction and content of these relationships. The needs of an industrialized society can greatly influence the size of the family, the mobility of family units, the relations that people have with extended family members, the content of socialization about the primacy of career work, the content and focus of formal education, and so on. Thus, economics can shape family and educational institutions. Similarly, government can either blatantly reflect economic and corporate interests, as in a fascist state, or, more routinely, may be staffed and operated in the context of the value that its role is to assist and encourage free-market devices in the economy, on the assumption that over the long haul the economy can produce enough benefits for the majority of the populace.

In the latter instance government may not even question the primacy afforded the economy; rather, it may take as a given its position as a support instrument of the economy. In this type of situation, appropriate change may be very hard to achieve as it is difficult to perceive the actual power of economic interests.

From another vantage point this perspective suggests that the dominant forces and interests within the economic institution can have a major stake in preventing other groups within the society from questioning prevailing interinstitutional relations. It obviously would be concerned with those groups whose needs and interests are inadequately served by current patterns of institutional functioning and, as a result, have a greater potential for valuing basic changes in the society. More specifically, this perspective suggests that a variety of strategies and processes might be pursued to prevent the least fulfilled members of society from aggressively seeking solutions to their unmet needs and interests. It is within this context that some conflict or power analysts have suggested that the major function of current social welfare responses is the social control of selected populations.[11]

The range of social control responses, as Meenaghan has indicated elsewhere, includes the processes of separation, containment, and resocialization.[12] *Separation* refers to isolating problematic populations that are at variance with the dominant societal expectations and are most prone to engage in nonconforming behavior. It could be accomplished in jails and state hospitals as well as in ghettoes and other segregated social areas. *Containment* refers to benefit provisions that would ameliorate the living conditions of these separated populations so that they would not have a great incentive to challenge their separation. *Resocialization* refers to the effort to reabsorb the populations in question into the expectations of the dominant society, by means of education, assimilation, therapy, and the like.

Surrounding these control processes is the dominant society's continual stress upon goods, or what Mills has called the "fetish of consumerism," the importance of fitting into and adjusting to the range of positions and statuses available to members of the society and selective exemption (tokenism) and limited upward mobility for those members of populations who generally do not have many of their interests met.[13]

Schematically, analysts approaching social welfare from this perspective tend to see society as depicted in Figure 1-4. As shown the institution of social welfare basically supplements the economic institution, either by deflecting concern away from the basic force in society and social relations—the economy—or by fitting peoples and groups into the other institutions in the society in such a way that the needs of the dominant economic institution are legitimated.

We are not suggesting that narrow definitions of interests—that is, those group and self-interests directly associated with the

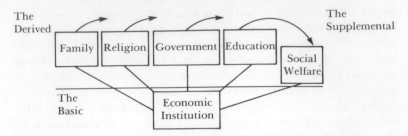

FIGURE 1.4:   **A Marxist-Conflict Conception of Society**

private economy—are the only interests that influence society and social welfare responses, although they are extremely important. Other interest groups are always at work within a society or, at least, are perceived by political decision makers as groups to which the society has to respond. Normally, interest groups associated with certain age, ethnic, and religious categories have been characterized as having significant input into specific areas of social life within our society.[14] In addition to these kinds of groups, there is increasing recognition of the role of organized professional groups in influencing perceptions of problems and solutions of problems. Such influence attempts are often directly and positively associated with the rewards (income and prestige) afforded such professionals.

It appears to us that the social welfare aspect of our social life is influenced by these interest perspectives as well by the interests directly associated with the economy. Subsequent chapters will explore the possible connections between dominant economic interests and the less global special interests of selected groups. This relation may be synergistic, in the sense that certain interest groups, in pursuing their goals, may actually be contributing to the interests of key economic groups.

Synthesis of Culture and Power

From the foregoing remarks it may appear that analysis of society's alternatives relative to social welfare leads to two somewhat contradictory perspectives. We do not regard this as a correct conclusion. Rather, we seek to show that both culture and power perspectives are potentially valid and relevant frames of reference. In attempting to do so we will look at social welfare as basically shaped by cultural norms, values, tradition, mere habit, experience, and routinized activities. However, in looking at how these cultural elements can and do influence social welfare alternatives and social welfare programs, we will always be asking an additional question: *Why* does this particular package of culture appear to be involved? Is it functional to some specific interest groups? Is it dysfunctional to and possibly controlling of other interest groups?

In trying to synthesize these two perspectives it would be useful to introduce and explore one of the specific dynamic elements in a society that triggers and reflects the particular welfare alternative that dominates in a society. This triggering device is the area of social policy, the topic of Chapter 2. In reading that chapter, and all subsequent ones in the book, it will be useful to reflect upon the implicit conceptions of man and society that appear to underlie social choice.

Summary

In this chapter we have examined two apparently contending perspectives concerning the role of the social welfare institution in society. One perspective stresses the importance of culture, especially its normative and value components, in structuring social welfare. The second perspective stresses the role of power and group interests in influencing how social welfare operates. It was suggested that the two perspectives became somewhat compatible if one asked why certain norms and values exist in social welfare and whose interests they serve.

In discussing the concept of social welfare, the importance of viewing it within an interinstitutional context was emphasized. Much of the remainder of this book will focus upon the impact of society's major institutions on social welfare.

Notes

1. For the classic discussion of culture, see Talcott Parsons, Edward Shils, et al, eds., *Theories of Society* (New York: Free Press, 1961), pp. 963–993; C. H. Anderson, *Toward a New Sociology; A Critical View* (Homewood, Ill.: Dorsey Press, 1971), pp. 29–62.

2. Talcott Parsons, *Societies: Evolutionary and Comparative Perspectives* (Englewood Cliffs: N. J.: Prentice-Hall, 1966), pp. 18–19.

3. *Ibid.*

4. The first explicit discussion of this social welfare option is to be found in Harold Wilensky and Charles Lebeaux, *Industrial Society and Social Welfare* (New York: Free Press, 1965).

5. John Dyckman, "Social Planning, Social Planners and Planned Societies," *American Institute of Planners Journal*, 32 (March 1966), 66–76.

6. Wilenskey and Lebeaux, *op. cit.*, p. 139.

7. *Ibid.*

8. *Ibid.*

9. David Gordon, *Theories of Poverty and Underemployment* (Lexington: Mass.: D. C. Heath, 1972), pp. 53–85; Ralf Dahrendorf, *Class and Class Conflict in Industrial Society* (New York: Free Press, 1963), esp. chap. 5; John Horton, "Order and Conflict Theories of Social Problems as Competing Ideologies," *American Journal of Sociology*, 71 (May 1966), 701–713; T. B. Bottomore, *Classes in Modern Society* (New York: Random House, 1968).

10. Irving L. Horowitz, *Power, Politics, and People* (New York: Ballantine Books, 1965), pp. 405–599.

11. The most influential discussion of this point is to be found in Frances Fox Piven and Richard A. Cloward, *Regulating the Poor: The Functions of Public Welfare* (New York: Pantheon, 1971).

12. Thomas M. Meenaghan, "Specifying Sociological Options and Social Welfare Strategies," *Journal of Sociology and Social Welfare* (forthcoming).

13. *Ibid.*

14. Thomas Dye, *Understanding Public Policy* (Englewood Cliffs, N.J.: Prentice-Hall, 1978).

Chapter 2
Policy and Program Alternatives

IN THE FIRST CHAPTER we presented a broad picture of how social welfare as an institution may be analyzed and structured in a societal context. In this chapter we will examine some of the specific ways in which social welfare becomes operationalized and made specific. To begin our analysis of social welfare in action, we will examine two interrelated topics: social welfare policy and social welfare services. Inherent in the discussion of each is the topic of choices for change and constraints against change.

Social Policy and Social Services

To enter into an honest discussion of social policy, it is useful to admit at the outset that there does not appear to be any universally agreed upon definition of the term. In great part, social policy definitions are clouded by unresolved issues associated with a more basic question, What is public policy?

In the most general terms, public policy may be construed as statements of what ought to be (normative). Because these statements occur in a social context, they are obviously influenced by the values operating within the society. However, as

15

was suggested in Chapter 1, they may also be influenced by the interests operating within the society. In a pluralistic society, a society with an internally varying cluster of beliefs, backgrounds, and interests, it is not surprising to observe that not everyone will agree upon statements of what is or what should be for the society. In short, public policy statements are apt to produce some significant levels of disagreement in such areas as the purpose or end of a given policy, the population or problem to be covered (or not covered), and the standards influencing the production of the policy or the evaluation of ways in which a policy is implemented (we call this a program). Further, the political nature of public policy may also be inferred if we consider that there are rarely, if ever, enough resources to meet every group's preferences and interests. The very process of jockeying by diverse groups to gain access to scarce resources frequently makes the area of public policy a political process.

If we move to a specific area of policy, namely, social welfare policy, we find that the previous remarks related to the definition of policy and its quite political character are quite relevant. On a definitional level, nearly universal agreement is found only in the rather vague statement that social welfare policy is concerned with declarations that relate to the "general welfare" of society's members. As such, social policy could be construed as the central point and activating thrust of the social welfare institution. In a very real sense it is a reflection of how a society has chosen to solve some of the problems in functioning that beset its members. It is in precisely this vein that Richard Titmuss, the British policy analyst, has written that the area of social policy speaks to all those societal declarations of ought to be that structure "activities which serve a common purpose related to the welfare needs of a society."[1]

On one level this kind of statement is merely vague; on another level, it suggests that the area of social welfare policy is politically variable. It is political because groups (e.g., the elderly, medical groups, religious organizations, and business and manufacturers associations) can and often do attempt to operationalize and produce specific declarations of ought to be that attempt to project their relatively narrow interests, values, and needs as those of society at large. It is variable in the sense that societies have several options regarding the *functions or purposes of social policy* and the *nature of coverage* of *social policy* (which problems, what populations, in what ways, up to what levels).[2]

Social Policy as Options in Perspective, Purpose, and Coverage

If we take the purpose and function of social welfare first, Rein has provided a very useful framework to explicate social welfare policy alternatives. He has stated that social welfare policy can be construed in terms of one or more of the following perspectives: (1) as burden, (2) as handmaiden, (3) as interdependence, and (4) as instrument of social stability.[3]

If social welfare is perceived from a *burden* perspective, then it would be logical to assume that statements of what ought to be for people's well-being would be seen as actual depressants to the free-enterprise system in that they would drain dollars from the economy and reduce individual initiative, especially within the free-market system. And yet there would be the recognition that some groups and individuals just have to be helped. These groups and individuals could be children, the blind, the disabled, the elderly, or whatever other persons the society chose to legitimate as having "worthy needs" that the society has to meet. This conception of social welfare policy suggests a predictable tension between free-market processes and legitimate welfare needs. The tension is probably best reflected in the question, How much welfare can you have without overburdening the economy?

Inherent in this concept of the purpose of social welfare is the assumption that welfare objectives have to operate within the constraints of higher-ranked economic purposes. More specifically, a smoothly functioning economic institution cannot and should not be compromised excessively to promote the purposes of social welfare.[4] Welfare policy and derived welfare services should play a role only when it is clearly demonstrable that free-market processes do not ensure the necessary benefits for valued populations. This notion of the purpose of social welfare policy is one in which the operationalizing of a *dependency conception of social welfare* is actually produced. Such a product in turn limits drastically what subsequent welfare responses can and should be made relative to the range of services (narrow rather than comprehensive) and populations covered (selective rather than universal).

A second perspective concerning welfare policy construes social welfare as a very useful way in which to meet a variety of society's other institutional objectives. This perspective suggests that welfare can be a supplement or handmaiden to the other institutions. In a sense an investment in such areas as unemployment benefits not only helps the recipient but ensures that local economies will continue to have potential customers. Thus, an investment in nonproductivity for a temporary period can help ensure continued stability among economic sectors of the society. Viewed in light of another example, payments to dependent children via a parent in a sense are a potentially good investment relative to the current costs of institutionalization of children or to future costs of the effects of malnutrition, poor health, and the like.[5] Although the handmaiden conception of social welfare recognizes the possible interplay among different interests and institutional sectors in a society, it is circumscribed by the major consideration that the type of social welfare that should be pursued is the one that has positive side effects for some key nonwelfare audience. It also suggests the converse proposition that welfare proposals that do not have explicit, positive effects for such audiences might not be pursued.

A third perspective is the logical extension of the handmaiden concept of social welfare. This perspective says that *certain activities can interdependently serve the needs of at least two institutional sectors and that each sector's needs are vitally important.*[6] For example, the policy objective of full employment not only might meet many of the needs of the economic institution in the area of productivity, but also would have clear and positive consequences in such welfare areas as level of family income and cohesion and level of socially induced stress. However, the converse of the example is also worth noting. That is, economic goals that have clearly negative human welfare implications are goals that should not be pursued. From this perspective, human welfare objectives are so significant that they help shape economic functioning so that welfare benefits are predictably ensured and consciously sought after. Unlike the supplement/handmaiden perspective, this perspective suggests that social welfare may influence the parameters of other institutions, rather than vice versa.

The last perspective relative to social welfare sees welfare as a means whereby *social stability* is maintained and problematic behavior is changed, minimized, or separated from the dominant society. From this perspective a major function of social welfare policy is to serve as a pragmatic means (cost) to an end (stability); it is not a valued end in itself. Ideally, such a cost–investment strategy produces benefits to the dominant society that are not necessarily limited to the economic sector. Cloward and Piven, in stressing this conception of the function of social welfare, have suggested that, when civil disturbances increase, public welfare increases. They have also suggested that, when controlled populations are in states of quiescence, then contraction or stagnation of welfare is likely to occur. For them the triggering factor in welfare responses is not the "objective" needs of potential recipients, but rather the perceived need of the dominant society for minimal social unrest.[7]

Societies tend to evolve a social welfare policy that reflects varying combinations of these four perspectives. In terms of the purposes of welfare, choice also occurs within the context of several other areas that we have referred to as the *coverage of social policy.*

Societies do not automatically respond to every problem—in fact, some problems are not even recognized by the dominant society. For example, for many years the implications of our excessive use of natural resources were not conceptualized as one of America's problems. Then we started experiencing some major dysfunctions, for example, inconveniences, costs, and loss of balance of economic power to other countries among others. This process of direct experience of dysfunctions appears to be central to society's choices of which social problems it legitimates as areas to be addressed. Again, in recent years our society has increasingly recognized the problems associated with physical health, advancing age, crime, mental illness, and unemployment. Once there is recognition and legitimation of areas of concern, there can be a corresponding process of *ranking these problems*. Is crime to be considered more of a problem than the concerns of the elderly or vice versa? Are they both more or less important than unemployment? These are not easy decisions for a society, nor are they always made deliberately and systemically. Yet such decisions do occur in a society.[8]

When they occur still more decisions have to be made concerning the populations to be served. For example, if unemployment is considered a priority concern, should equal attention be given to all the unemployed, or should special attention be given to the young (or middle aged), to inner-city or suburban populations, to white or nonwhite populations? If the area of health is selected, should everyone be the concern of welfare policy, or should policy be developed to handle those with catastropic illness (and costs)?

Actual social choices in these areas often occur in the context of some prevailing thinking about what is causing the problem—for example, the personalities of the people who experience the problem, their use of resources, lack of skills, and so on or the blocked opportunity structures, unequal distribution of resources, and other social forces. The prevailing notions of causation direct societies in their decisions as to how specific problems and populations should be served.

Service has to do with program types and the nature of benefits. Rein, Wolins, and others have attempted to delineate typologies of programs and benefits.[9] For Rein, social welfare programs can be seen as *substitutes, preparatory devices, and alterations of existing environments* and as *providing a set of amenities* related to human development.[10]

Substitution programs are those designed to take the place of normal institutional structures developed to handle needs. For example, if serious illness strikes a parent of young children, homemaking or foster care may be a program response to fill a gap and meet children's and household needs. If a worker becomes unemployed because of factory layoffs and as a result there are financial shortages in the family, unemployment benefits may be provided to meet some of the financial needs that the private economy, through jobs and wages, normally handles. In these examples, needs that were initially met by the institutions of the family and the private economy come to be handled by social welfare responses. Such responses take place after the problem occurs. The strong implication is that they are temporary, to be applied only until the normal functioning of major institutions resumes.

Substitution programs and benefits usually meet some package of needs and often at the same time attempt to head off major economic and social costs and consequences. Homemaker and foster care programs, for example, not only serve various family members but may also prevent major costs associated with institutionalization. Unemployment benefits can help a family or a person to survive economically, but they may also help banks protect their loans on houses and cars and ensure that businessmen will continue to have customers to purchase items.

Preparation programs are specific attempts to help clients be more responsive and adaptive to the range of activities possible in the society. In many cases clients need only limited help of a specific nature. A prime example of this would be information concerning the availability and location of day care, job-training programs, and the like. In other instances, what clients want and need may involve more than information and referral. They may need advice, counseling, help in mapping out future courses of action, and so on. In both types of examples, the intent is clear. Services are geared to allow people to maximize the nonwelfare sectors of the society in the short run. Again, a time-limited response and a somewhat selective recipient population are suggested by this type of program.

More complex programs are those designed to alter the environment that certain populations face. *Support programs,* as they are often called, are more complex than preparation programs because they operate on the assumption that many clients are in situations that apparently do not directly lend themselves to personal solutions. Because of this it is assumed that society may have to provide incentives and supports to the population in question so that the cycle of entrapment may be broken. For example, as long as a single parent has to provide direct care to his or her children, there is often little hope that he or she can become anything other than a welfare-assisted parent. Support programs in this case would operate on the basis that perhaps day care should be initiated (environment) so that this parent can receive a job or a job-training experience. Because of the cost of environmental alteration, these programs may be quite expensive; but, theoretically at least, they are investments in the subsequent reduction of welfare costs through maximization of individual responsibility.

It should also be noted that these programs are increasingly numerous and vary considerably in terms of purpose and function. Can one say that support programs for the blind and for veterans (i.e., stipends for living expenses during periods of education) are designed for the same reason with a similar context of benefit provision as, say, training programs covered by work–incentive arrangements in the public welfare sector? The issue of "worthy" recipients and the corresponding purposes of welfare will be discussed in Chapter 6, which concerns welfare responses and cultural determinants.

The last type of program to be described is one geared directly to people as people, to help them develop their abilities and to enhance the quality of life they experience (*amenities*). This program presupposes a broad range of human attributes, needs, and potential. It assumes that people, by virtue of being human beings, are entitled to programs in such basic areas as nutrition, health, education, work, and housing to name a few. However people may also be seen as entitled to programs in the areas of art, music, and other areas related to man's aesthetic and creative nature. Such programs can be almost limitless, only bound by man's imagination. Viewed collectively, programs geared to a humanistic conception of society's members reflect a core of values that includes universalism (people are entitled as people), comprehensiveness (related to all man's facets and needs), and a particular conception of social rights and social responsibility.

As you move through the discussion of these types of programs and program coverage, you may already be concluding that these types of programs are not totally free decisions or options within a society. Many factors influence program-type decisions, but the most proximate influence upon coverage decisions appears to be the prevailing conception of the purposes and functions social welfare should serve. Should welfare's purpose be primarily geared to handling some conception of worthy clients (burden); to helping achieve objectives in other institutional sectors (handmaiden); to promoting and stressing social welfare values as legitimate ends that might influence other institutional sectors (balanced interdependence); to achieving some desirable measure of social stability in the society? Answers to these basic questions concerning purpose can influence the range and emphasis of program types selected and stressed.

Figure 2-1 outlines some of the major topics introduced in Chapters 1 and 2. Those topics include *conceptions of the social welfare institution* (equity/primacy or dependency), *policy purposes* (burden, handmaiden, promotion of equitable interinstitutional relations, promotion of social stability) and types of *program options* (substitution, preparation, support, amenities). As a society collectively approaches these choice areas, it begins to answer in more specific terms how and why we relate to and care for each other.

FIGURE 2.1: **Systemic Conception of Society's Choices for the Social Welfare Institution, Social Policy, Social Programs**

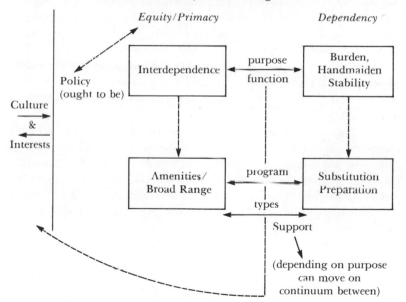

Welfare in Action: Services and Professions

In examining Figure 2-1, you may notice that one major ingredient in social welfare seems to be missing—those people who receive and those who provide services. Where do they fit in? The answer is both simple and complex. The simple answer is that both recipients and providers come together and interact in the context of programs and services. It is the provider, especially the professional provider, who is responsible for carrying out the specific activities required by a program designed to meet certain objectives. It is the client to whom and with whom the provider works so as to attempt to meet some legitimate definition of need. Many welfare analysts have characterized this interaction as part of the distinctive nature of the social work profession; that is, it is the profession that takes as its basic responsibility the running, dispensing, and managing of social services. Friedlander, in a classic introductory book on social work, has stated that "social work is a professional service, based upon scientific knowledge and skill in human relations, which assists individuals, alone or in groups, to obtain social and personal satisfaction and independence."[11] In addition, social work professionals have a body of distinctive values that stress broad human conceptions of clients, and ideally these values impact qualitatively upon their interaction with clients within program settings.

This last statement leads into some comments related to the complex answer of where people fit into social welfare, especially the professional provider. The complex answer starts with the same assertion—in a program designed for some set of objectives and client needs. But it also involves some choice areas upon which the professional provider can reflect. These areas include the following issues:

1. How does the program in which I am involved reflect some social welfare purpose? What is that purpose? Is that purpose in keeping with my professional values?

2. How can the professional, whatever the range of purposes behind the program, broaden the service response so as to make it more compatible with human rights and professional values?
3. How can the professional constructively use experience and collected information in the program to modify and extend the relevance of the program to clients?
4. How can the professional recognize that current program limitations may be not merely program limitations but may also be tied to social policy formulations?
5. How can the professional in conjunction with colleagues in the field have input into the policy process operating in the society?
6. Finally, if social change is to occur, what are some of the specific relations and strategies possible, and how might they involve some division of labor between professionals, lawmakers, clients, and other constituencies?

These matters do not have readily available, or easy, answers. But reflection upon these areas is a necessary prelude to relevant, value-oriented professional activity. Social work professionals admittedly have many external, both societal and organizational, constraints imposed upon them. Yet they perhaps have some degree of freedom as well. Enumeration of the areas just listed plus a true understanding of possible professional orientations to conceptions of social problems, the influence of prevailing culture, and the specific ingredients of certain welfare programs in our society may suggest what those degrees of freedom actually entail for the professional.

In Chapter 3 we will explore ways in which social problems can be viewed by both society and professionals. In Chapters 4 and 5 we will examine some of the major constructs within social sciences as they may relate to social problems and possible solutions through policy and program responses.

In approaching these chapters, it is useful to keep in mind the premise that concepts and theory, especially social science theory, affect the possible meaning(s) of social facts and, hence, the definitions of social problems that might be addressed by social welfare policy and programs within society. Concepts and

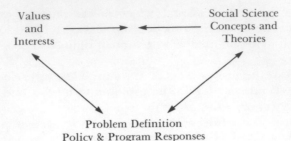

FIGURE 2.2:   **Forces Impinging upon Policy and Program**

theory, in turn, may be affected by various values and interests operating within a society. Some of the major value–interest influences upon social welfare will be discussed in Chapters 6 through 8.

Figure 2-2 depicts the organizing scheme behind the next several chapters, stressing the possible interactive and reinforcing processes operating within society.

Summary

In this chapter we have examined the political realities of social welfare policy and social welfare services in relation to the possible alternative purposes of policy and types of benefits and programs. It was suggested that certain policy–program options tend to operationalize a dependent type of social welfare institution, whereas other options tend to operationalize a more vital social welfare institution. In both instances, culture and interests are seen as sources of influence on policy and program choices.

Notes

1. Richard Titmuss, *Essays on the Welfare State* (New Haven, Conn.: Yale University Press, 1959), p. 42.

2. Martin Rein, *Social Policy: Issues of Choice and Change* (New York: Random House, 1970), pp. 21-41.

3. *Ibid.*, pp. 24-27.

4. For a classic statement of social welfare policy reflecting this purpose, see Eveline Burns, "The Financing of Social Welfare," in Cora Kasius, ed., *New Directions in Social Work* (New York: Harper, 1954), pp. 131-158.

5. Rein, *op. cit.*, p. 26; Theodore Schultz, "Reflections on Investment in Man," *Journal of Political Economy*, 70 (Supplement 1962), 1-8.

6. Rein, *op. cit.*, p. 26; David Donnison "Social Work and Social Change." *British Journal of Psychiatric Social Work*, 8 (November 1966), 3-9.

7. Frances Fox Piven and Richard A. Cloward, *Regulating the Poor: The Functions of Public Welfare* (New York: Pantheon, 1971).

8. See Neil Gilbert and Harry Specht, *Dimensions of Social Welfare Policy* (Englewood Cliffs, N. J.: Prentice Hall, 1974), for a discussion of problems to be addressed and the ways to address them.

9. Rein, *op. cit.*, p. 17; Martin Wolins, "The Societal Function of Social Welfare," *New Perspectives*, 1 (Spring 1967), 5.

10. Rein, *op. cit.*, pp. 17-19.

11. Walter A. Friedlander, *Introduction to Social Welfare* (Englewood Cliffs, N. J.: Prentice-Hall, 1966), p. 4.

Chapter 3

Society, Social Sciences, and Social Problems

IN THE FIRST TWO CHAPTERS we spoke about how a society may choose to conceive its institutions, especially its social welfare institution. We also spoke about how and why a society may institute certain social welfare policies and programs. Implicit in that discussion was the notion that social welfare policies and programs exist as vehicles to deal with people and, more specifically, with problems that people have or may have. In a sense the welfare policies and programs created by a society presuppose some specific conceptions of the problems in a society.

A society's conceptions of social problems are heavily influenced by the prevailing social science concepts and categories within the society and the major features of the culture dominating the society. This is because concepts and values are interconnected, and both are related to the proposition that "social facts do not organize themselves into a coherent framework simply by being observed."[1] While these two influence factors forcefully interact with each other, each plays a unique role in triggering the process of problem definition, causal explanation, and social welfare policy–program response. The focus of this chapter is upon the general influence of concepts and categories from the social sciences on the problem–definition options open to a society. In Chapters 4 and 5 we deal with the conceptual varieties within sociology and economics as they structure and influence social policy and program responses.

In an ideal sense, certain conceptions of social problems should lead to certain policy–program responses. Others should ideally lead to different policy–program responses. Thus, policy–program responses may be construed as structured by-products of how society choses to view problems and people.

Before turning to a discussion of the varied concepts of social problems within a society, let us state very clearly that the general topic is fraught with many debatable and unresolvable issues, stemming largely from controversy regarding the role of perception in knowledge building. This general topic, in turn, produces variation, incompatibility, and even conflict within and among disciplines in the selection and use of concepts and theories concerning aspects of the external world, their possible meaning, and the appropriate policy–program strategies to deal with deficiencies in the social world.

Knowledge Sequences in Social Problems

A fundamental philosophical issue concerning man and society is the following question: How do you relate to, and deal with, the external world? As with most philosophical issues, this one is important because its ramifications spill over into many areas, including the world of social welfare. In relatively simplistic terms, the question points to the human problem of knowing and, more recently, of rationally solving problems in the world in which we live.

Historically, the process of knowledge building has produced two grand schools of thought. For a long time one position stressed that there was a manifest, intrinsic meaning in the external world and that any informed observer could extrapolate that meaning through the use of the senses and the intellect. Knowledge that was produced was in a sense a product of extrapolation by the observer.

With the rise of science and counterpositions in philosophy, a different school of thought emerged. This view suggested that the process of knowledge building was tied to trying out "meanings," creating meaning for the external world. Such meaning products ideally were implanted on the external world, which suggested, first, that observers created different realities by virtue of how they chose to think about external phenomena and, second, that the concepts selected and used by any observer were crucial to derived knowledge about the external world. Also, it suggested a possible role for both science and volitional commitment (will)—science in the sense that, if meanings of phenomena were to be subscribed to, there should be some external, objective check upon the meaning product. Logically, this was to be the role of science and empirical testing—will in the sense that some meanings were not testable (e.g., the meaning of death) or that, given the absence of universally accepted criteria, different people chose to subscribe, even commit themselves, to different meaning products.[2]

America, as a modern society, reflects the principles of both science and volitional commitment. Perhaps in no area is this duality more apparent than in the area of social problems. Our society produces, in part through its social sciences and their activities (theory and research), a great variety of ways to look at problems in our society. Yet no single explanation of social problems is subscribed to by all of a society's members or by all the members of any social science discipline. Scholarly and scientific activity seems to coexist with large amounts of willed beliefs concerning the nature of, and the solutions to, social problems. The obvious questions to raise at this point, are, What is the basis for certain conceptions of problems dominating in our society? Do they reflect and reinforce certain values and interest positions? How do they affect the policy–program responses operating within the society?

If we move to specific areas, perhaps we can more readily perceive the options available for both society and analyst concerning problem perception and meaning. For illustrative purposes, let us evaluate a physical structure called a concert hall and a social phenomenon that we will call crime. With respect to a concert hall, a sound engineer and a lighting engineer may see the auditorium in completely different ways. Both in turn may see the auditorium differently from the ticket sales manager. Each of the three functionaries has his own type of concepts—acoustics, lighting, seating—that he applies to the same external phenomena. The three see different facets of the same physical structure and may have different evaluations of the structure. In fact, if deficiencies are perceived, each, by virtue of the relatively narrow range of concepts and criteria used, may be able to prescribe a solution to make the concert hall "better." Critical thought by each craftsman can structure several subsequent activities.

If we now shift to the complex social phenomenon of crime, we can see that some similar processes of thought and analysis are present. However, we will also see, because of the complex phenomenon in question, the great amount of choice and variability open to the analyst and by extension to the society.

Just as with the perception and evaluation of the concert hall, the analyst of social phenomenon relics upon the following:

1. Selection of the area to be studied.
2. Selection of the concepts to be employed.
3. Relation of the concepts to one's training and experience.
4. The possible role of testing or checking out perceptions—either under structured procedures or by trial and error.

Once having identified these common features in knowing about a phenomenon (physical or social), we can move quickly to the major area of difference between the two types of phenomenon. That difference is the great amount of latitude, call it choice or subjectivity, afforded the analyst in the area of social phenomena.

Let's start with the area to be studied. Here are just a few of the choices possible:

—Do I study the *behavior* of people judged to be criminal?
—Do I study the *judging process* (behavior) of noncriminals?
—Do I study the *person* in physical terms—that is, who is criminal?
—Do I study the *personality* of the criminal? If so, do I focus on personality as a product of early childhood or of current stress sources? If the latter, is stress environmental or personally induced?

—Do I study the *context* and *situations* in which crime is conducted?

—Do I study the *social structure* possibly affecting the criminal—his or her roles and statuses, the nature of roles relating to him or her, the dynamics of organizational relations, and the manner in which the institutions designed to link him or her into the society are functioning?

—Do I study the *culture of the actor,* his or her norms, values, behavioral intentions, and so on as they relate to certain behavioral forms?

—Do I study the *costs*—physical, economic, and otherwise—of crime?

These are but a few of the choices available to the analyst in studying the social phenomenon referred to as crime. Fortunately for society and the analyst, the choices are structured by several factors. One is the selection of concepts and categories to be used in the study. In science, ideally the role of concepts and theory (linking concepts together) is to assist the analyst in looking at selected facets of phenomena and then making testable statements concerning the relations between and among specific aspects. Thus, one of the major roles of concepts is to facilitate, even structure, the selective perception process. Ideally, as indicated earlier, scientific inquiry suggests that conclusions and meaning should be tested. But, if meaning is not tested or is incapable of being tested by commonly held criteria, then the selective perception product can become akin to a belief product to which one commits oneself by will.

Now, just as any analyst's frame of reference is structured somewhat by available concepts and theories, such concepts and theories do not exist in a vacuum. Rather, disciplines, such as psychology, sociology, and economics, are the domains within which many concepts and theory products concerning social phenomena are generated. Thus a given analyst is structured into looking at any phenomenon, especially a complex social phenomenon, by exposure to a selected, unrepresentative range of concepts and theories presented through the formal education process in his or her discipline.

Clearly, several implications present themselves. If analysts were suddenly separated from the concepts and theories that they normally use and if these were replaced with alternates, there is a good likelihood that the original social phenomenon being studied would mean something different to them. Further, if subsequent intervention into any social phenomenon is to occur, then its appropriateness is in part a function of how such intervention relates to the original perception and meaning of the phenomenon. Put another way, if there are choices concerning what we perceive and how we perceive and think about it, then this variability in the meaning of social phenomena is likely to produce variability in subsequent intervention designs. This point of view is very much related to our earlier comment that social policy and program responses in a society are logically designed to relate to certain problems and/or populations with problems. If choice, discretion, and belief as well as science and possible variability have a role in our understanding of the external world, then these same factors must be understood as having an influence on social welfare policy and program responses.

As John Seeley notes, when anyone "recognizes a problem it is a revolutionary thing because the definition [of the problem] affects attitudes and behavior."[3] In fact, as he also notes, "Description by categories and concepts is implicit intervention."[4]

Basic Social Choices in Social Problems

"Public Issues" and "Private Troubles"

If we move now to some of the specific options available to a society in looking at social problems, the writings of C. Wright Mills probably provide the greatest insight. For Mills, all human behavior and the subsequent social problems that people have should be understood in the context of biography intersecting with history, the person interacting with the world in which he or she lives. In *The Sociological Imagination* Mills argued that there is a tendency in contemporary society not to see that the well-being or problems of people are affected by the social patterns of their lives, including the reality of institutions affecting them and the developments over time within society, including the structural transformations of the society.[5] He suggested that in a very real sense social problems involve not just the personality of given actors but the culture in which they live and the structure of social arrangements in their society. The tendency in contemporary society not to recognize all three components led Mills to conclude that we erroneously confuse "public issues," which for him were true social problems, with "private troubles." In so doing, we adopt a societal definition of the meaning of social problems that is narrow and inappropriate, as is our policy–program response.

For Mills a "private trouble" involves something "within the character of the person, and the range of immediate relations to others."[6] To define something in this way is to see biography without history or the social world. Normally "private trouble" is experienced by relatively few people in the society. Mills further stated that the notion of social problems as the arithmetical summation of private troubles is most likely to occur "if a society believes in the role of moral, biological or psychological explanations tied to the person."[7] When these types of belief patterns are present, there is a real possibility of the logical fallacy of confusing effect (the person or group experiencing a problem) with cause.

For Mills and many other sociologists,[8] a social problem is a "public issue" that has a distinct set of characteristics, as follows:

—*Size and extent*—some considerable number of people within a society share a particular effect.
—*Endemic*—that is, common to or disproportionately found in some group, such as age, sex, or racial groups.
—*Relatively permanent*—the effects have been present for some continued period of years.
—*Institution(s) malfunctioning*—the effect, while it is experienced by particular people, is not necessarily caused by these same people but may originate in how major institutions such as government, economy, education, and health relate to those who experience the effect. In a sense institutions are central to understanding the causation of problems in people.

Whereas the "private trouble" perspective speaks to intervention by policy and programs in the lives of people affected, the "public issue" perspective requires consideration of structural change in the very institutional fabric of the society, including roles, norms and values, and the interests disproportionately influencing such cultural items. One perspective suggests personal reform; the other perspective suggests structural change in the society.

Both social science perspectives, however, can generate social welfare policy and program responses. The private trouble perspective is likely to produce a social welfare policy–program response when some important value and/or norm of the majority (i.e., those without the problem) is threatened and/or dysfunctions and costs as a result of private troubles are experienced by the majority as well as by those with the private trouble. (Some sociologists would refer to the latter condition as strains in the society.)

When one or both of these conditions are present, the majority may conclude that a social problem exists (although possibly in an arithmetic summation fashion) and that something should be done. Why? To meet some of the needs of those members of society who do not have a particular private trouble. In this process the very policy–program product can help the dominant portion of the society to reassert their preferred value–norm packages and/or reduce possible sources of social and political instability within the society. In addition to basic choices within this area, several derived choices are discussed in the following paragraphs.

PATTERNS

In addition to the choices involved in whether problems are or are not perceived by society, and whether they are perceived as "private troubles" or "public issues," society has additional choices related to options within the social sciences. One choice is whether to recognize that many problems occurring in a social context are heavily associated with particular groups—age, social class, racial–ethnic groups, and so on. If a given problem is disproportionately experienced by some social entity, the choice that society has is whether to take the patterned variations as the phenomenon to be dealt with and, if so, whether to explore the social processes affecting certain groups as groups or to perceive, and perhaps deal with, individual members of the social groups as if their social attachments were not involved in the problem.

However this choice is made, there are potential costs. To deal with the people who have problems as if their group attachments are not significant probably ensures an after-the-fact (dependency) social welfare response. This delayed response almost always results in the maintenance, over time, of the pattern of problems.

On the other hand, for society to intervene in the quality of the relation between the broader society and some particular group(s) within it logically suggests changes on the part of the dominant society. This choice perspective may be especially difficult for many members of society who have been conditioned to equate the cause and the effect of problems. Given this mind set, it would be difficult for the majority to perceive how problems affecting others could be resolved by modification of those who do not have the problems or of structures that seem to adequately serve the needs of people without problems.

SEPARATE AND UNANTICIPATED CONSEQUENCES

A second area of social choice is whether society perceives specific social problems as simply negative conditions or as potentially tied to socially preferred conditions. In other words, is mental illness a problem that society faces? Or is it, as considerable evidence seems to suggest, an unanticipated consequence of the attainment of a desired state of a technologically oriented mass society? In a similar vein, it is possible to see or not see that some problems are intimately related to the process of social solutions. For example, in the areas of abortion and discrimination by race and gender, "one group's social problem tends to be another group's solution, just as, sequentially, one group's solution becomes defined as another group's problem."[9]

Again, in selecting the former position, society basically opts for a problem perception that has limited, if any, implications for structural modification of the society. In the perception in which desired states are intimately tied to social problems, there is clear recognition that to solve the social problem, the desired state also has to be examined and perhaps modified.

INTERRELATIONS OF SOCIAL PROBLEMS

A third area that the society might have to confront in dealing with its problems is the way in which it choses to perceive social problems with respect to each other. Are the problems and the populations affected to be seen as discrete social phenomena? Or is there an appreciation that some social problems are highly related to each other and to certain populations within the social structure? If the former is chosen, there is the possibility that the problems selected for subsequent intervention activities may be quite unrepresentative of social conditions in a society. In fact, such problems might be addressed largely because of the dysfunction that they induce for some key groups in the dominant society or to meet the needs of certain interest groups (i.e., professionals and human service organizations). If the latter is chosen, is there a tendency for the society to see two or more social problems as possibly covarying together, or is there a strong tendency for the society to try to attribute a causal connection between these problems?

If a systemic view reflects the principle of covariation, then perhaps the problems of poverty, mental illness, and deviancy are seen as related effects of some structural feature(s) of the society—for example, limited opportunity for social and economic mobility. Policy and program responses relative to these problems would then involve expanding opportunities, as well as providing direct services to populations exhibiting problems and problematical behavior.

If a systemic view does not reflect covariation but, rather, attempts to relate the problems to each other causally, the society might evolve a different policy–program response. Thus, if, say, mental illness is seen as causally related to poverty and deviancy, then policy–program responses to all three areas would be heavily laden with psychiatric and person reform strategies. In short, in opting for a systemic, interrelated conception of social problems, society in no way assures that there is movement away from a "private trouble" perspective. This point is even more significant when one also considers that society, given its limited resources and the interests and influences of helping organizations, often has to select some limited number of social problems as a wedge into the nexus of social problems present in a society. Such a selection, though rather arbitrary, does have implications for reinforcing causal connections between and among problems.

CAUSAL EXPLANATIONS

The last area of social choice to be discussed is inherent in much of the foregoing discussion. That area involves the types of causal explanation and etiology perspectives to be stressed by a society as it confronts social problems. If we were to examine any given social problem developmentally, we would see that the social sciences have been productive and imaginative in offering a variety of explanations. For example, the problem of crime and juvenile delinquency has been explained as a result of "defective physique, climate, feeble-mindedness, poverty, mental illness, lack of recreation, and a host of other factors."[10] Note that it is the explanation of crime, not crime itself, that tends to vary over time and, further, that each explanation has been offered as *the* explanation. Just as any cultural product exists because it is functional, so various causal explanations of social problems have existed and even flourished within society because they too have been judged valid and functional to some members of society at different times.

In contemporary society the range of available causal explanations appears to be broad. We have the dominant person-oriented psychological explanation (ranging from neo–Freudian theories to behavior–stimulus explanations); collective person-oriented explanations (i.e., culture-of-poverty explanations); social stress explanations; and explanations focusing upon basic institutional malfunctioning (e.g., the economy). In later chapters we will explore how these explanations relate to specific social problem phenomena and policy–program responses. For now, it is sufficient to indicate that just as volitional elements—in the broad sense, call them subjective and political—are intimately involved in problem categorization and description, so such elements are also involved in looking for the reasons behind social problems. Causation analysis is obviously contaminated by the very concepts selected in the original problem description. For example, if the definition of the problem of income deficiency heavily stresses the skills, behavior, attitudes, and motivations of poor people, then there is a great likelihood that the attributed cause of income deficiency is going to emphasize individual and cultural deficiencies. However, if initial assessment of the problem stresses the nature of the job markets available to people, there is a probability that the society will stress opportunity structures and barriers to economic mobility in "explaining" the social problem. Thus the relationship between problem definition and causal explanations is dynamic in nature, and this basic relationship in turn heavily influences subsequent intervention strategies in the areas of social welfare policy and program responses.

Analysis of Social Problems in a Social Context

In this chapter we have introduced the topic of social problems and society's choices. This topic is central to social welfare policy analysis because social problems are the focal concerns of social welfare policy and program products. In a very real sense, how a society and its analysts come to approach social problems heavily structures the welfare institution.

It was suggested that society in part relies upon prevailing concepts and theories to describe external problem phenomena, to give them meaning, and to infer causal explanations. How the society relies upon such concepts and theories is not automatic. Rather, society has before it a variety of contending social sci-

ence concepts and explanations from which it can choose. Enmeshed in this choice process is the very basic choice of whether
to perceive social problems as "private troubles" or as "public
issues." Table 3–1 suggests possible interrelations of the several
choice areas society has in approaching social problems.

Society's choices in these areas, largely involving the selection
and use of social science tools, are not necessarily rational or
unstructured. Rather, the actual use of social science constructs
is probably heavily influenced by the nature of the society's dominant cultural package and by the role of particular interests
operating in that society.

Let us conclude this chapter by at least identifying some of the
normatively preferred elements that should be in a preliminary
social problem definition:

—Those who bear the effects of the problem.
—Size of problem, its extent.
—History and duration of problem.
—Any patterns within the population directly affected by the
    problem, especially in terms of correlation between/among ra-
    cial, sex, ethnic, age, social class groups and the social prob-
    lem. This process will identify patterns within the general
    problem, and in so doing you will be identifying groups at
    risk.
—Trends or changes in those directly experiencing the effects of
    the problem, with special attention to whether identified pat-
    terns are chronic or temporary. Are identified patterns stable,
    diminishing, or intensifying over time?
—Exploration of possible causal factors:

    1. person/culture of those with problem
    2. opportunity structures
    3. institutional arrangements

—Examination of prior policy–program efforts (if any)—their
    effects, their relation to identifying problem patterns; the ap-
    parent causal explanations inherent in the policy program re-
    sponse.
—Those whose values/interests in broader society are being af-
    fected negatively by the social problem.

TABLE 3-1. **Social Choices in Problem Perception**

	"PUBLIC" (INDIVIDUAL/GROUP/INSTITUTIONS)	"PRIVATE" (INDIVIDUAL/GROUP)
Area of concern Social context	Patterns of variation *Strong*—problems possibly tied to other social good and/or social solution	Discrete individuals/group *Weak*—problems more apt to be seen as a discrete negative
Problem inter- relation	Systemic, covariation, explore common structural cause	Nonsystemic or tendency to look for causal connections between problems (effects)
Causation	Social stress and structural dysfunctioning	Person and/or subculture influence

41

—Those whose values/interests in broader society are affected positively by the persistence of the social problem.

—The way in which the problem in question relates to other social problems in the society, with special attention to similarities and differences in groups affected by problems, and socially perceived connections between the problems—Do they mutually stem from some other problem or factor, or are they seen in a causal relationship with each other? If so, which is seen as causing which?

In the next two chapters, we present some of the major specific conceptual options afforded society in its attempts to structure the social welfare institution. In Chapter 4 we focus on options suggested in contemporary sociology, and in Chapter 5 we discuss welfare options suggested by the discipline of economics. Both chapters, implicitly at least, refer to the continuing influence of psychological perspectives.

Summary

Social welfare policy and programs are responses to the social problems existing in a society. But the way in which social problems are viewed and defined by society helps structure the nature of policy and program efforts. The material in this chapter has indicated that society can approach problems as being private (person) or public (social) in character. Further, we have suggested that society ought to be aware of the choices that it has relative to the role of social context, the interrelations of social problems, and causal explanations. It was suggested that the different social sciences may, in part, help society make its choices concerning what is a social problem and what policy and programs are appropriate.

Notes

1. Neil Gilbert and Harry Specht, *Dimensions of Social Welfare Policy* (Englewood Cliffs, N.J.: Prentice Hall, 1974).

2. This perspective is compatible with the phenomenological perspective of knowledge. See Thomas Kuhn, *The Structure of Scientific Revolution* (Chicago: University of Chicago, 1970).

3. John Seeley, "Social Science? Some Probative Problems," in Maurice Stein and Arthur Vidich, eds., *Sociology on Trial* (Englewood Cliffs, N.J.: Prentice Hall, 1963), p. 61.

4. *Ibid.*, p. 63.

5. C. Wright Mills, *The Sociological Imagination* (New York: Oxford University Press, 1959), chap. 1, esp. pp. 1–18.

6. *Ibid.*, p. 8.

7. *Ibid.*

8. See, for example, Robert Merton and Robert Nisbet, eds., *Contemporary Social Problems* (New York: Harcourt Brace Jovanovich, 1976), pp. 7–21; Ritchie Lowry, *Social Problems: A Critical Analysis of Theories and Public Policies* (Lexington, Mass.: D. C. Heath, 1976), pp. 3–18.

9. Merton and Nisbet, *op. cit.*, p. 10.

10. See John M. Martin, and Joseph P. Fitzpatrick, *Delinquent Behavior: A Redefinition of the Problem* (New York: Random House, 1966), p. 31.

Chapter 4

Sociology and Social Welfare Within Society

A. McLung Lee recently spoke to the possible relations between sociology and social welfare. In doing so he focused upon a shared base of humanism and stated, "I take the position that it is the kind of sociology—roughly called 'humanist'—that will make a lot of social work as currently practiced a thing of the past."[1] We would like to look at the same relationship within the societal context and in terms of the mediating role of social theory, conceptions of social change, and the derived parameters of the social welfare institution. To focus such a discussion, it might be useful to emphasize three distinct but highly related choice areas: (1) *the nature of social arrangements* and how sociologists and social welfare personnel might choose to conceptualize social arrangements, (2) *the preferred versus the actual state of the welfare institution* in light of organizational theory and behavior, and (3) *the status and role relations* of professionals and consumers *in applied social change efforts*.

Conceptions of the Social Arrangement

In broad social theory, there are two general contending points of view, namely, order theory and conflict theory. Order

44

theory basically proceeds from the conceptual question of how cohesion, stability, and identity are achieved in a society. In answering this question there is a derived conceptual emphasis upon the major concepts of values and norms. More specifically any social arrangement is said to be produced when actors reflect, through their behavior, consensual acceptance of the norms and values.[2] Stemming from this type of theory, there is a conceptual tendency to perceive and expect cohesion among disparate actors and groups. In fact, through the use of systems theory, there is a conceptual expectation that various structures in the social system can and should mesh, that is, be integrated, to produce the stable social arrangement.

Several consequences, quite relevant to social welfare, are logically produced. One has to do with the conception of the social arrangement as a system analogous to the physical system or body. In the physical system, when there is a health problem in one or more members, there is a recognition that the well-being of the entire body may be affected. Further the fields that relate to the diagnosis and treatment of the physical basically attempt to move from symptoms to meaning to logical solutions. Often in order theory there is an attempt to proceed in a similar fashion when given behavioral forms and/or groups appear to disrupt the dominant flow of social relations within the social system. Thus behavior, or social functioning, that is at variance with the dominant norms and value structures is defined as deviant or, when such deviance is extensive, as a social problem—a problem precisely because it produces a threat to the identity and integrity of the social body.[3]

Related to this is a second consequence for social welfare, namely, that dominant norm–value structures are the standards for health and pathology on individual and group levels. This in turn tends to produce a conceptual appreciation in the helping fields for such order concepts as sickness, social and personal disorganization, anomie, stress, and weakened social control.[4]

If concepts such as norms and values in turn tend to influence the use of such explanatory concepts as sickness, disorganization, anomie, then these latter concepts heavily influence the logic and selection of intervention strategies involving policy and program responses available within social welfare. More specifically, when there are strains operating within a social system, order theory tends to suggest that boundary maintenance processes should operate. Such processes, given the prior conceptual focus upon cohesion, basically should operate to remove or reduce the problematic behavior or, if necessary, to absorb the variation within the social system in the least disruptive manner.[5]

Shattuck has suggested that boundary maintenance tends to involve three distinct stages: the stage of separation, the stage of containment, and the stage of (re)socialization.[6] Separation basically means removing, in diverse ways, the problematical actors and behavioral forms from the normal range of interaction in a social system. Such separations have historically produced jails, concentration camps, death, ghettoes, or "deviant" areas within communities. Containment is the corollary process that attempts to minimize the potential strength and power that problematic populations, once concentrated, have by virtue of their density. This can involve the deployment of armed guards, pacification rewards and services for compliance, and the conditioning of groups not to expect anything more than what they experience. Socialization is the attempt to inculcate in contained populations behavioral expectations that are functional to the broader social system. Devices such as education, training, and therapy are perceived as functional to producing more appropriate behavioral adjustments.

Obviously, the actors delegated by the social system to facilitate effective boundary maintenance processes often include members of the social work profession.[7] In using order theory concepts the latent function of social welfare efforts, often not perceived by the helpers, is to control people and behavior, whereas the manifest purpose is often a professional and personal motivation to improve social functioning and help deprived populations. In short there can be a discrepancy between individual and system purposes. The net result of the relation between order theory and social welfare is that society, through the activities of social workers, often does not address itself to significant structural change but, rather, chooses to perceive intervention through the nonstructural prism of mental health.

Conflict, or coercion, theory is a relatively systematic attempt to look at society by way of the conceptual question of how change (rather than cohesion) is produced.[8] Generally this perspective sees values and norms as far less important than the concept of interests. In fact norms and values are assumed to be extensions of selected interests. Thus social arrangements are fluidly produced by the process through which some groups and interests manage to coerce others. Because some groups and interests have coercion possibilities, that is, power resources, this perspective suggests that vertical relationships will characterize the social arrangements.[9] These relationships of inequity at times produce behavioral struggles by the power inferiors in the role relationships. In fact it is precisely because of these power inequities and prior differences in interests and behavior that change occurs and is predictable in social arrangements. Given this conceptual reasoning, dissent in thought and behavioral forms is not only predictable, but can also be normal.[10]

When society and social welfare are influenced by this type of social theory, relevant concepts for assessing people and behavior do not necessarily emphasize sickness, anomie, and the like. Rather, there is conceptual appreciation for assessing the conditions of organization, power inequities, incompatibility of interests, and degree of alienation.[11] Further there is a conceptual willingness to entertain the possibility that behavioral change struggles are constructive and that existing dominant norms and values may be, to use Goodman's phrase, "absurd."[12] Viewed another way, policy and program responses within social welfare are cognizant of and reflect a concern with structural change and the manner in which institutions function.

This social perspective does not stress a preoccupation with boundary maintenance processes. Rather, it suggests that policy and program responses within society, especially within social welfare, should relate to encouraging, facilitating, and promoting a positive sense of group interests and group solidarity.[13] Such group solidarity can be a way of producing greater collective power that is seen as functional to the group's sense of self and as a vehicle for engaging in trade-off processes with dominant society. In place of intervening with the person or group, conflict theory suggests change of the current social structure by the group. In that way functioning perceived as relevant to group interests and needs is stressed. Obviously this perspective is quite compatible with recent trends, to be discussed in the following paragraphs, to replace narrow individual client dependency upon professionals with collective consumerism.

Ultimately social theory, which speaks to a view of society as based upon consensus, has to rely on the concepts discussed by Weber, that is, tradition, charismatic leaders, and reason.[14] Normally, contemporary developed societies achieve the degree of consensus that they have largely by virtue of reason. But to produce consensual agreement such systems have to have significant participation by all, including the weak and problematic. Such participation could breed evaluation and criticism of and dissent from the existing social arrangement. The choice for the members of society, and certainly for the professional in the social welfare institution, is, How much stability and how much variation is desirable? The way in which the society and the social welfare institution relate to the types of social theory discussed seems to suggest varying conceptual approaches to the content and purpose of social welfare policy and programs.

The Preferred and Actual Social Welfare Institution: Belief Versus Behavior in Organizations

In Chapter 1 we introduced the social choice of which type of social welfare institution should operate in a society as well as the various classifications that spoke to social welfare as being in positions of primacy, equity, and dependency relative to other institutions.[15] A dependent social welfare institution was characterized as an institution that was excessively influenced by other institutions such as the economy and family. The primacy/equity conceptions of social welfare suggested distinctive ends and values that denoted universal and comprehensive programs, stressing developmental and preventive components.

Those of us who are directly associated with the helping fields will readily profess a value–belief commitment to the primacy/equity conception of social welfare. To do otherwise would mean some cognitive acceptance of the dominant antiwelfare values and how they are peculiarly operationalized in America. These values include work, economic individualism, localism, private over public, and a rather minimal role for government (these will be discussed in later chapters). Intellectually we recognize that a dependency conception of welfare logically means seeing welfare expenditures as a drain on the gross national product. Such expenditures could be orchestrated to reinforce the dominant economic model of organization and generally to mediate between selected economic and community interests and culture. A preference for a dependency conception of welfare suggests minimal, if any, appreciation for the role of the structural and economic factors associated with "American society as a social problem"[16]—a suggestion that our contemporary professional conditioning, that is, formal training, largely precludes.

Yet behavior within organizations often seems to reflect the fact that the way in which welfare is distributed is at variance with beliefs inculcated in professional formal training and quite in line with the dependent conception of welfare. The obvious question, given this discrepancy between beliefs and behavior, is, Why do beliefs of professionals have such little impact on their behavior? In general terms the answer, in part, involves the area within sociology known as complex or formal organizations which speaks to the interactive role of the professional and his/her organization within society.

Social welfare as an institution is heavily associated with and influenced by the choices that can be made by key interest groups within society concerning the dynamics of formal organizations. The key interest group that we will consider is the human service professional within social welfare. Specifically two of the choice areas such professionals have include (1) how they will relate to their own organizational contexts and (2) whether they will stress continued reliance upon monopolistic arrangements within bureaucratic service structures.[17]

PROFESSIONALS IN FORMAL ORGANIZATIONS

On one level, human service professionals can participate actively in promoting the characteristics of formal organizations. These include greater amounts of specialization in service delivery, more managerial and operations-oriented functions, greater reliance upon formal training and licensing requirements, designing relatively uniform procedures to handle cases and clients, and activities generally geared to promotion of organizational stability and constancy. On the other hand, professions can focus more upon the possible dysfunctions of complex organizations within social welfare. These would include excessive specialization producing lack of services and lost cases, lack of innovation and adaptability to changing clients or clients' needs, insensitivity to human need produced by routinized use of uniform procedures, and the general possibility that organization needs, for example, image, efficiency, and stability, may take precedence over client needs.

On another level the choices have to do with how to handle the loss of autonomy faced by professionals within complex organizations. Finch has indicated that a central concern of bureaucrats who are professionals is how to maximize and achieve personal autonomy from various bureaucratic controls.[18] In fact, according to Finch, trends in specialized service systems suggest that professional bureaucrats can anticipate less autonomy over time.[19] Related to the dilemma of personal autonomy versus bureaucratic control is a second concern associated with professional autonomy, namely, How do workers routinely act out professional beliefs, preferences, and service objectives and yet function in terms of organizational needs? Green has suggested that these two types of concern often lead to various personal and professional adjustments.[20] One type of adjustment involves, over time, the scaling down of service objectives by professionals. This type of adjustment is best explained by Blau's assertion that there often is an inverse relation between experience in a bureaucratic setting and professional motivation to provide service.[21] Thus, young and inexperienced professionals, fresh from formal training settings and armed with primary institution ideals of service, are often unable to negotiate bureaucratic settings to meet client needs. On the other hand, more experienced professionals could theoretically be of more service to clients, but the experience differential is vitiated by the long period of functioning within the bureaucratic setting, which tends to produce diminished motivations to serve. Thus many professionals can become jobholders who are professionals rather than vice versa.

Still another type of adjustment for professionals is to seek out and collectively create areas of high personal control in their work. One way for this to occur is to accept certain kinds of internal control in particular areas in exchange for minimal controls in other areas. For example in most social service systems there is an increasing reliance upon staff accountability via fiscal audits, PERT, PPBS, MBO. Formal training facilities now widely include this accounting orientation in their programs. But note that the type of control, and accountability, that is produced is often within the context of business criteria, such as efficiency and economy—criteria that Gouldner, Blau, and others state intrinsically may have little to do with service objectives and more to do with dominant political and economic interests.[22] In return for this type of control, professionals are often able to create some degree of internal autonomy and control over daily service provision. As a result the actual specifics of programming are largely subject to professional peer control, within the context of the economic and political interests of the broader community. The bottom line often is that professionals are willing to trade primary institution service ideals for some narrow degree of professional autonomy. The trade-off is often so unbalanced that the broader community and economic interests do not perceive that they have traded anything significant. Put another way, professionals often achieve autonomy to create and provide rather irrelevant programming. The group that pays for the trade-off, of course, consists of clients/consumers, who are effectively denied any possibility of witnessing a primary institution of social welfare. To test this latter conclusion only two questions have to be asked: Are the excessively business-oriented criteria used the criteria that recipient populations would routinely select? Are the produced services, to which the criteria are being applied, necessarily preferred by consumers?[23]

Although our discussion strongly suggests a powerful and possibly negative interaction between complex organizations and human service professionals, the professional certainly has options. The options speak to how much the normative expectations derived from professional affiliations will be compromised, for what purposes, for what rewards, relative to what reference groups.

MONOPOLISTIC STRUCTURE OF SOCIAL SERVICES

The tendency for organizational and professional self-interests at times to take precedence over client/consumer interests is a rather natural consequence of the monopolistic nature of the structure of social services. Monopoly in social service speaks to two interrelated characteristics: the dominance of nonmarket mechanisms, with little actual emphasis upon supply–demand dynamics, and little or no accountability to primary consumers (clients), with principal accountability to peer interests (professionals) and secondary consumers (economic interests, contributors, and politicians). Central to these two characteristics is the passive and dependent role of the consumer.

Inherent in the current structure of services is the fact that many agencies, because they are specialized and few in number relative to potential demand, do not really need primary consumers. In fact agencies often are oversubscribed, and providers can be somewhat selective in whom they serve, with what kind of services, under what requirements or conditions. Consumers in many service areas are needed only in the sense of providing documentation to fiscal monitors that the service being provided is necessary.[24] The net result of this tends to follow Reid's analysis that, "the primary consumers cannot reward organizations providing social services which they consider good. Seldom do they have an opportunity to choose openly . . . among agencies. . . . An agency finds little advantage in pleasing a customer."[25] This becomes even more of a problem for the poor because many of the types of services that they need are not directly supported by primary consumers, so that the poor really cannot reward or influence the range of service provision.

Several rather disturbing effects are possible within such a structural arrangement. First, as Safretti-Larson suggests, professionals can manipulate market mechanisms so as to promote their positions of advantage, for example, wages, location of services, and the like.[26] Second, resources for services are not necessarily allocated on the basis òf consumer-perceived needs. The simple reason for this is that consumers do not have current positions of power, whereas professionals and others do. Third, some consumers, given the possibility of incongruence between actual consumer needs and service provision, may have difficulty in presenting their needs and adjusting their attitudes and behavior to fit into provided services. This situation gives professionals even more license to judge some consumers as problem clients, hard to serve or manifesting maladaptive behavior. In short, structurally there is set up a perception of the "good" client as one who reflects congruence and acceptance of organizational–professional expectations. Fourth, in some cases the dynamic suggested in the third point can put workers and consumers into an adversary position that in turn can lead to withdrawal and even greater personal and programmatic insulation from certain consumer types and social areas. If this occurs, obviously even greater discretion is afforded professionals relative to need definition and program provision. Again, the choice presented involves whether society and professionals stress monopolistic patterns with possible side effects or service strategies that attempt to prevent such side effects stemming from complex organizations.

Social Change Efforts

The last sociological area we comment upon involves the concept of social change. Mayer has suggested that social change basically involves realignment of preexisting status, role, and membership patterns.[27] Obviously the first choice before society and its human service professionals is whether or not social change is really desired. The second choice, assuming that change is desired, has to do with both the manner in which it will be pursued and the appropriate policy perspective supporting such change. Specht and Meenaghan have suggested that, when proposals in social welfare involve significant change in current status–role patterns, the strategy of intervention that is most likely to be relevant is the one that presupposes an special interest or conflict orientation by the change group.[28]

Running somewhat parallel to these change discussions is Reid's assertion that there are basically three types of policy perspectives that can influence change.[29] They are the planning or technical model, the community action model, and the competitive market model. The first model involves professionals who have significant say in how and what should be changed. From the preceding discussion it would appear that the type of structural change that would be produced, if any, would be minimal. Organizational factors previously discussed, as well as the disproportionate number of professionals and administrators who are clinically trained and oriented, suggest that this may not be a viable option to promote structural change. The second type of change speaks to organizing and mobilizing consumers and would-be customers to exercise collective and political power upon organizations. Although this is definitely relevant to promoting organizational responses, the resources of such a group would largely be tied to their numbers and the consumer's ability to disrupt "normal" processes within organizations. Such consumer groups however would still be at the mercy of supply and demand mechanisms. The third model suggests that, if funding mechanisms, via vouchers, would bypass organizations and professionals and distribute benefit purchasing power directly to consumers, current supply–demand mechanisms could be affected. The reason for this would be that benefits might be used for more relevant, more accessible, and cheaper services. If this were to occur, the nature and amount of services could be positively affected. One of the limitations of this model involves the probable insensitivity of the current service arrangement to the individual consumer using voucher benefits. Another has to do with the matter of why benefits should be distributed directly to consumers in the first place without prior use of collective consumer power. It would appear that models 2 and 3 would have to be combined if there is to be some likelihood that significant structural change would occur.

Even without a corresponding policy change involving benefit distribution, consumers, if they are organized, could negotiate more significant kinds of involvement in service provision. Some of these include (1) collective presentation of service expectations, type and amount; (2) introduction of contract relations between providers and consumers; (3) direct involvement in the planning of services or treatment for family members; (4) evaluation, official or unofficial, of current services; (5) collective presentation of information, including consumer evaluations, to funders and boards of agencies; (6) participation in the screening of prospective staff and administrators; and (7) in some service areas, negotiation by former consumers to provide service to current or would-be consumers facing similar situations.[30]

Changes such as these, which involve new status and role positions for consumers, may be desirable for many reasons. First, they are in keeping with many current conceptions of health that speak to the need for an active role on the part of clients. Second, they are compatible with role theory that says that the role of recipient does not exhaust the set of role possibilities open to people. Third, because of needs and experiences, consumers can often be more motivated than professionals to extend services and, in many cases, to relate to fellow consumers. Finally, significant involvement of consumers could increase the degree of fit between service needs and service provision.

Summary

In this chapter we have explored the possible relations in society between selected aspects of sociology and social welfare. The aspects discussed focused upon the options or variants in sociological theory, approaches to formal organizations, and types of social change.

The discussion suggested considerable room for choice and action by society and the human service professional. One possible combination of choices stresses order theory, sickness or personality variables, and the promotion of selected organizational characteristics within a relatively monopolistic service structure. In a combination such as this, fairly traditional conceptions of client dependency prevail. A second possible combination of sociological choices, called conflict theory, stresses interest groups and power variables, the possible dysfunctions of formal organizations in social welfare, and the need for more conscious pursuit of social change strategies, including those utilizing consumers.

We are not suggesting that either sociological combination exists in pure form in our society, but we do feel that many prevailing welfare practices are compatible with the first combination. In Chapter 5 we stress some of the major schools of economic thought and what each suggests for social welfare policy and programs.

Notes

1. Alfred McClung Lee, "What Kind of Sociology Is Useful to Social Workers?," *Journal of Sociology and Social Welfare*, 4 (September 1976), 9.

2. Generally functionalism as a type of order theory stresses the recurrent social processes that maintain the society or group and generally emanates from Emile Durkheim. See Emile Durkheim, "The Normal and Pathological," in *The Rules of the Sociological Method* (New York: Macmillan, 1966), pp. 65–73.

3. See Talcott Parsons, "Definitions of Health and Illness in the Light of American Values and Social Structures," in E. Gartley Jaco, ed., *Patients, Physicians, and Illness.* (Glencoe, Ill.: Free Press, 1963), p. 176.

4. John Horton, "Order and Conflict Theories of Social Problems as Competing Ideologies," *American Journal of Sociology*, 71 (May 1966), 701–713.

5. Talcott Parsons, *The Social System* (New York: Free Press, 1951), chaps. 7 and 9; Talcott Parsons, Edward Shils, et al., *Theories of Society* (New York: Free Press, 1961), vol. 1, pp. 70–79.

6. Gerald Shattuck and John Martin, "New Professional Work Roles and Their Integration into a Social Agency Structure," *Social Work*, 14, (July 1969), 18–19.

7. Herbert Gans, *The Urban Villagers* (New York: Free Press, 1962).

8. Ralf Dahrendorf, *Class and Class Conflict in Industrial Society* (New York: Free Press, 1963), chap. 5.

9. Horton, *op. cit.*, pp. 703–707.

10. *Ibid.*

11. *Ibid.*

12. Paul Goodman, *Growing Up Absurd* (New York: Random House, 1960), p. 11.

13. Robert Knickmeyer, "A Marxist Approach to Social Work," *Social Work*, 17 (July 1972), 58–65, for a discussion of positive assertion of the special interests of low-income groups.

14. Max Weber, *Basic Concepts in Sociology* (New York: Citadel Press, 1966), pp. 67–81.

15. Harold L. Wilensky and Charles N. Lebeaux, *Industrial Society and Social Welfare* (New York: Free Press, 1967), pp. 138–140.

16. Term borrowed from Robert Gliner, *American Society as a Social Problem* (New York: Free Press, 1973).

17. Until recently there has been a beginning awareness of the two factors as disparate points, but little attention has been given to analyzing their functional interrelation.

18. Wilbur A. Finch, Jr., "Social Workers versus Bureaucracy," *Social Work*, 21 (September 1976), 370–376.

19. *Ibid.*

20. A. S. Green, "The Professional Worker in the Bureaucracy," *Social Service Review*, 40 (March 1966), 71ff.

21. Peter Blau, "Orientation toward Clients in a Public Welfare Agency," in Peter Blau, ed., *On the Nature of Organizations* (New York: Wiley, 1974), pp. 170–186.

22. Peter Blau and Marshall Meyer, *Bureaucracy in Modern Society* (New York: Random House, 1971).

23. These questions are suggested by Nelson Reid, "Reforming the Service Monopoly," *Social Work*, 17 (November 1972), 44–54.

24. Thomas M. Meenaghan, "Role Changes for the Parents of the Mentally Retarded," *Journal of Mental Retardation*, 12 (June 1974), 48–49.

25. Reid, *op. cit.*, p. 47.

26. Based on a conversation with M. Sarfretti-Larson relevant to a forthcoming book, as yet untitled, on the role of professions.

27. Robert R. Mayer, *Social Planning and Social Change* (Englewood Cliffs, N.J.: Prentice-Hall, 1973).

28. Harry Specht, "Disruptive Tactics," *Social Work*, 14 (April 1969),

5-16; Thomas Meenaghan, "Clues about Community Power Structures," *Social Work*, 21 (March 1976), 126-131.

29. Reid, *op. cit.*, pp. 50-54.
30. Meenaghan, *op. cit.*, pp. 48-49; Edward J. Pawlak, "Organizational Tinkering," *Social Work*, 21 (March 1976), 376-381.

Chapter 5

Economic Thought and Social Welfare Responses

IN 1977 ALFRED PAGE COMMENTED, "The influence of social work, with respect to public policy, can be strengthened by restoring its natural ties to the field of economics."[1] Although Page's position has its supporters, not all agree with his notion of what the nature of that fusion should be. In fact, Aigner and Simons, reflecting upon the specifics of Page's point of view, state, "We will argue . . . that the value base of social work . . . is antagonistic to and not congruent with the pure competition model of microeconomic theory."[2] In this chapter we explore the areas of specific congruence and incongruence between selected aspects of social welfare—not just social work—and specific and differing theories within economics.

Basic Issues in Economics and Societal Options

Admittedly economics, as with any of the social sciences, is beset with issues associated with the relation of the human assessor to his or her field of inquiry and external phenomena. Some of these issues are metaeconomic, whereas others stem

from the scientific process. More specifically, an economist, as
with any scientist approaching an area of study, has to create
some bridges between himself or herself and the external world.
In an ontological sense, assessor and external phenomena are
separate and discrete. Yet, through the creation and/or continued use of concepts and theoretical schema, attempts are continuously made to reduce the separation. When this process is
set in motion, the economist selectively creates "meaning packages" for selected aspects of the external world. Produced
"meaning packages" can dynamically interact with the values,
beliefs, and preferences of the given economist.[3] They can also
relate to how the economist characterizes problems in economic
terms and, at least implicitly, may induce a possible range of
solutions to problems. Needless to say, some "meaning packages" created by economists can be judged by selected aspects of
the broader society as being right (or wrong) and relevant (or
irrelevant).

Fortunately, the canons of empirical inquiry can assist both
the economist and others in the society in their acceptance of
specific "meaning packages." Ideally, the scientific process is
deemed a functional vehicle by which to test the validity of
created meaning packages. Realistically, however, both
economists and the broader society never fully escape the issues
that impinge upon scientific testing of meaning packages. Such
issues include economists' assumptions, selection of indicators,
conditioning within economic schools of thought and corollary
methodological approaches, and the economists' socially situated
position. Because of such issues, plus the absence of universally
agreed upon criteria of assessing meaning packages even within
the discipline of economics, it appears that economics and the
dominant society will continue to be open to elements of volition
and ideology.[4] The interplay of theory and testing in economics,
as in the other social sciences, helps protect all of us from many
indefensible meaning packages, but also seems to produce a
plethora of variable, somewhat defensible, meaning packages
concerning our economic life.

It is within the context of these issues that the constraints and
potential options for social welfare suggested by economics have
to be examined.[5] Specific attention should be given to how

selected economic concepts influence the study and assessment of people and problems, as well as the subsequent policy and program responses logically derived from such concepts.

Fusing Selected Economic Theories to Social Welfare Policy and Program Options

To begin an exploration of relations between economics and social welfare, it might be useful to identify a process that might facilitate the identification of areas of compatibility. That process is as follows:

1. *Selection of an area* (or dependent variable) that appears *germane* to the inclusive field of *economics* and to the social welfare institution.
2. *Specification of some broad concepts* that are conventionally used, in varying degrees, *across the social sciences*, including economics and the helping (social welfare) professions in defining problems—such specification should logically structure a range of ideal types of solutions to social problems.
3. Examination of *specific major theories in economics* and what each, by virtue of its use of concepts, seems to suggest in terms of solutions to a given problem.
4. *Synthesis of compatible areas of social welfare strategies and specific economic theories as they may relate to public policy and program responses.*

SELECTION OF A GERMANE AREA

The social welfare institution throughout its history has been concerned with relating to disadvantaged people. Perhaps the most frequently used subset of "disadvantaged" has been poverty or income deficiency. Admittedly, many poor people are seen by professionals within the social welfare institution through intervening prisms such as mental illness, problematical behavior, and the like. Nonetheless, the dependent variable for the social welfare institution has often been how to deal with, and help, people who have limited financial resources.[6]

Economics, as a discipline, attempts to study many things, but central to it is a concern with explaining the production and distribution of income and wealth.[7] All schools of economic thought recognize that in our society distribution of financial rewards is never fully equal.

Thus it appears that the operations of the social welfare institution have traditionally oriented themselves in part to a given population (income deficient), whereas economics has a special concern with the distributional processes that affect that population. The area of income deficiency would therefore appear to be germane to both economics and social welfare. As such certain societal options are available. The most basic one is how we choose to map out, by concept selection, the specific meaning of income deficiency.

SPECIFICATIONS OF CONCEPTS

Throughout the social sciences, there are broad concepts that are conventionally used in approaching areas of study or in describing problems. Broadly speaking, they are the following:

—*Person*—I.Q., skill levels, race, age, sex, current, and past situations and experiences.

—*Personality*—attitudes, motivational packages, stress levels, as well as gross levels of mental functioning (neurosis, psychosis, ego functioning, etc.).

—*Culture*—norms, values, beliefs, life-styles, socialization patterns, and so on.

—*Structure*—role relations among members of different groups, opportunities for economic and political mobility, quality of relations between society's institutions and different types of social actors, and the degree of vertical separation among classes.

The "meaning packages" that are produced by any theory in studying some area or derived from describing a problem are essentially produced by the selective use of some combination of specific concepts subsumed under one or more of the broad concepts just cited. Not surprisingly, these solutions can deal with person(ality) modifications, cultural change, or significant structural and institutional adjustments.

ECONOMIC THEORIES

In this chapter we will examine three major perspectives in economics in light of actual concept application within the germane area of income deficiency: (1) orthodox economic theory, (2) dual labor theory, and (3) radical economic theory.

1. *Orthodox economic theory* explains income distribution in a relatively simple manner.[8] Basically, employers distribute wages on the basis of (1) assessment of a given worker's ability to produce at some level (degree of marginal productivity) and (2) the prevailing dynamics of supply–demand for labor. Inherent in these two principles is the assumption that there is (or should be) sufficient competition behind actual supply–demand processes.

The prospective employer attempts to assess marginal productivity by specific criteria (indicators), including physical dexterity, and/or mental aptitude, and/or educational level, and/or previous work experience. Use of these criteria ideally allows the employer to make a judgment concerning the probable marginal productivity level of the workers. In addition, the employer, in arriving at a wage level, makes an assessment of the nature of the supply of labor available. Specifically, this refers to the gross numbers of prospective workers and the distribution of their various skills and abilities.

Workers, for their part, enter the labor market at least intuitively recognizing that there are a fixed number of job possibilities and that the most financially rewarding positions are liable to be found in positions where employer demand for productive personnel outstrips supply of relevant labor. Therefore, the prospective worker, to ensure high economic rewards, must take steps to present himself or herself in the best possible light. This usually means making a series of interrelated decisions concerning amount of education, accretion of certain skills, and exposure to reinforcing work experiences.

Obviously, the "meaning package" that is produced in this line of analysis, which focuses on differences in individual characteristics, is heavily laden with person(al) causation. As Thurow has stated, "if an individual's income is too low, his (her) productivity is too low."[9] Quite logically, ideal solutions to income deficiency would focus upon Thurow's additional observation that "income can be increased only if his (her) productivity can be raised."[10]

To minimize dysfunctional differences in individual characteristics, two general types of solutions are suggested relative to the problem of income deficiency. One type would focus upon some particular changes in the set of characteristics a worker brings into the marketplace. This could range from increased skills through more education and training to helping workers through counseling and related approaches to defer gratifications, make constructive career decisions, and generally develop better appreciation of the role of individual responsibility for derived income. The other type could move to the social context around certain individuals—loosely referred to as the "culture of poverty." In focusing upon this, there might be a sensitivity to the notion that the income deficient often have distinctive life-styles that produce a self-generating cycle of individual failure in the marketplace.

If society and its social welfare institution gravitate to this general meaning package, the role of counseling strategies is strongly suggested. Further the social welfare institution would emphasize prospective workers' upgrading themselves and the provision of job-training and educational programs. The collective role of the manpower-training programs would seem quite compatible with the meaning package derived from orthodox economic theory. Similarly, social welfare's recent preoccupation with preschool programs and developmental approaches, which have characterized much of the "War on Poverty" programs, at least suggests that factors other than prevention and early detection are at work. More specifically, it would appear that many elements within the social welfare institution have accepted, consciously or not, the normative position inherent in orthodox theory that assimilation into working-class and middle-class values and behavior patterns is the route for redressing income deficiencies.

As a derivative of the meaning package suggested by orthodox economic theory, it is the social welfare professional who often becomes the "caretaker" of the labor market failures.[11] It is social work and social welfare, largely through public assistance services, that have the responsibility of providing substitute means for those not capable of producing income through the labor market. Not surprisingly, the level of support that is produced usually reflects the concept of "less eligibility." Such a concept, of course, has been criticized by many as a continuing stimulus to the maintenance of low-paying jobs and, hence, a continuation of income deficiency for many people.[12]

Thus, it would appear that, when society and social welfare workers allow themselves to be influenced by this economic perspective, or commit themselves to it, areas of convergence between social welfare and economics are

—A preoccupation with the individual.
—An implicit assessment that cultural properties of poor people are dysfunctional.
—A judgment that person/personality/cultural change should occur when services are dispensed.
—The belief that the existing market structures are relative constants.

In short, clinical orientations by social welfare professionals may unwittingly be supported, even manipulated, by those who have a stake in the continued dominance of orthodox theory.

2. *Dual labor theory* uses a different set of concepts relative to income distribution, and hence the meaning package that is produced for both economists and social welfare leads to different perceptions of problems, solutions, and strategies of change.[13] Fundamentally, this perspective focuses upon income deficiency, unemployment, and underemployment as interrelated phenomena.

Specifically, these conditions stem from the peculiar interplay of the nature of current job structures and the selected social and background characteristics of workers as perceived by prospective employers. The most relevant of these background characteristics—age, sex, and race—are not economic but have profound economic implications. This meaning package differs substantially from orthodox theory that uses a narrow range of economic concepts (e.g., productivity and supply and demand) to explain economic consequences for any population group.

As the title of the theory or perspective suggests, the American labor market is dichotomized into a primary and a secondary labor market, which tend to distribute income somewhat differently, to different types of people. In the primary labor market, workers receive fairly satisfactory incomes. Such incomes are distributed to people who are perceived as stable (often male, white, and of a moderate age range) in industries that tend to be unionized and have labor cost pass-on possibilities. Wages are usually tied more to length of service and union-negotiated contracts than to mere productivity levels.

The secondary labor market is often characterized by age, race, and sex minorities, who are perceived as unstable (discontinuous) work force members. This labor market has few unions and often dispenses volume services rather than producing durable items. The businesses and industries within this sector tend to compete with each other in the context of limited labor cost pass-on possibilities. Wages tend to be low, and income can be increased only by workers' expansion of working time (hours), as there are few vertical ladders of economic mobility within this labor market.

A symbiotic relation between low wages and worker instability tends to be produced, but this instability is not necessarily dysfunctional to employers. In fact, as Gordon suggests, there is incentive to employers within this labor market to manipulate the instability as a means to insure a pool of available low-priced, nonunion labor.[14]

Central to this perspective is an appreciation of the relative fixity of certain jobs and certain populations relative to the two labor markets. Because of this consideration, income distribution is significantly tied to issues of limited opportunity for access to given labor markets and limited ability to move from the secondary labor market to the primary labor market.

In attempts to minimize income differentials between labor markets and select populations, logically derived policy solutions focus upon the goals of equal opportunity for access to the primary labor market and more opportunity for vertical mobility from the secondary labor market to the primary labor market. Thus, problem solutions relate to structural considerations as well as to workers' ability to operate at higher marginal productivity levels.

Social welfare that is tied to this perspective would offer social welfare professionals a broad spectrum of options. Obviously, they can work with individuals in the secondary labor market, advising and counseling them. They can serve as a supplemental support system, dispensing services and programs, often through unions and private agencies, to workers in the primary labor market. However, merely to do this suggests a behavior response that does not appear significantly different from the practice options supported by orthodox theory.

Perhaps more important, professionals can begin to address structural issues more directly. Because the basic issue is direct access to the primary labor market, as well as indirect access to it, through educational and training centers as well as unions, a relevant professional social welfare practice option appears to be maximizing the collective power of income-deficient populations by such strategies as organizing and legal action. Such strategies would be aimed at minimizing the role of discrimination in income distribution. Desired policy products could, at minimum, include promotion and expansion of affirmative action programs and minority recruitment and retention in unions and selected industries. Such policies, however, might lead to greater degrees of fairness, but not necessarily to greater equality.[15] The latter objective of social welfare would be considered a structural goal and solution only if one were to combine some of the meaning packages suggested by dual labor theory with the meaning packages suggested by radical economic theory, which follows.

In summary, it appears that, when society and social welfare allow themselves to be influenced by this economic perspective, convergence between social welfare and economics is to be found in the following areas:

—There is more concern for socially shared characteristics (e.g., age, sex, race constraints) as they have implications for opportunities for income deficient populations as well as continued options to engage in practice related to other individual characteristics.

—Solutions to the collective problem of income deficiency are more efficiently pursued when there is concern with the characteristics of the existing social system.

—Existing labor market arrangements are not necessarily fixed constraints within which intervention is to proceed.

3. *Radical economic theory* uses some of the same concepts that dual labor theory uses relative to income distribution.[16] As a result, some of the meaning packages suggested by this perspective are not incongruent with the meaning packages inherent in dual labor theory. However, the radical perspective in examining income deficiency (and, even more so, wealth–asset deficiencies) relies heavily upon the dialectic methodology as it relates to the concept of mode of production. This perspective suggests that prevailing modes of production shape all social and economic relations—including wage relations. Within this context, the concept of class, objective and, possibly, subjective, is developed as a potential dynamism for change in the structures of a society. Change in such areas as ownership of production, control of surplus, and distribution of surplus can occur only if workers perceive their interests as being frustrated by the interests of employers (owners and managers).

To prevent the sequence of collective consciousness leading to basic changes affecting income and wealth, this theory suggests that specific cultural and institutional (superstructure) arrangements will tend to prevail and to deflect basic criticism from the existing mode of production. One central institution that can serve as a vehicle of extending and reinforcing dominant economic interests is the state via its legislation and policing powers.

As with dual labor theory, radical economics perceives the labor market as discontinuous and comprised of two separate labor pools. It also stresses worker stability and perception of worker stability as important to the distribution of income to certain groups at certain levels. However, because of its reliance upon the concept of power—as suggested by the corollary concept of class—it seems that there is a direct correlation between the stability of workers and their respective power. Workers who reflect and exercise power resources are likely to receive a greater wage, whereas those who cannot wield power will be subject to income deficiency.

The difficulty this theory perceives in contemporary American society is that power resources tend to emanate from racial, ethnic, and religious bases rather than from mere class bases. As a result, workers in general tend to compete with each other and become fragmented into the discontinuous labor markets. In fact, within each of the major labor markets there are additional devices to diffuse workers' common perception of interests. Such devices include large amounts of horizontal, as well as vertical, stratification of workers; focus upon education as a substantive difference between blue-collar and white-collar positions (and workers); and reliance upon race and sex differences to perpetuate the separation of blue-collar and secondary labor market workers. The heaviest losers in this process become the groups with the least potent collective resources; as a result, they are most prone to being income deficient.

If and when society and social welfare wish to relate to the meaning packages suggested by this theory, there would appear to be both expanded and restricted options. Clearly, social welfare cannot occupy itself entirely with traditional clinical and quasi-clinical approaches (e.g., teaching budgeting techniques) toward low-income citizens. Furthermore, professions within social welfare would have to become extremely aware of the conceptual differences between the effects of income deficiency (people) and its causes (structure). Assuredly, social welfare professionals can attempt to use consciousness-raising strategies, organizational power, and the courts to promote greater accessibility to the primary labor market.

But these program and practice options appear to be incomplete. In the short run, social welfare professionals would have to reassert their role as advocates of the poor against the contending interests and audiences of public bureaucratic services. In the long run, pragmatic coalition strategies will have to be developed so that policies of a guaranteed income (at a sufficient level) and comprehensive services in the areas of health, housing, food, and day care can be produced. These long-run strategies, political in nature, would be designed to transform the role of the government relative to the economy in terms of tax structure and income distribution. Such long-range strategies are probably not going to occur if social ferment is absent or if voluntary groups organize themselves separately (e.g., women, blacks, etc.).[17] Rather, they will probably occur only if the broad concepts of class and interests are used as umbrella concepts and as the basis for organized political power. Because this is a questionable possibility at best, social welfare professionals (and their clients) will probably have to settle for a combination of strategies focusing upon organization of groups and incremental change.

Fusion of economics and social welfare, as suggested by radical theory, always runs two risks. One involves unrealistic calls of "power to the people"; the other, can lead to reversion to policies and programs that focus only upon personal reform strategies.

Summary

In this chapter we have examined possible areas of integration between the discipline of economics and the institution of social welfare. A central problem facing both fields—income deficiency—was discussed in terms of how the meaning packages suggested by three specific economic theories can structure types of welfare policy and program options. Recognition of such options can force society, its social welfare institution, and its social welfare professions to confront, and perhaps better define, their goals in dealing with people in need.

In this chapter and Chapter 4, we examined a few of the salient options within sociology and raised policy and program possibilities for social welfare. We are suggesting that how and why particular social science options are chosen depends not primarily upon the persuasiveness of schools of social science thought but more upon the compatibility of variants of social science thinking with the dominant interest–value orientations in the society. In Chapters 6 and 7 we will discuss some of the major interest–value orientations in the society.

First let us summarize in Table 5-1 some of the major concep-

TABLE 5.1. Social Sciences Concepts and Social Welfare Implications

	SOCIOLOGY		ECONOMICS		
	Order	*Conflict/Power*	*Orthodox*	*Dual Labor*	*Radical*
Concepts	Norms and values: Separation Containment Resocialization Functions of formal organization Monopolies of Service Traditional role Limited change	Group interests: Separateness Negotiation Bargaining Dysfunction of formal organization Expanded roles Promotion of change	Marginal productivity Ability Experience Training Motivation Personal causation	Discontinuous job Structures Social factors: Age Sex Race Accessibility Opportunity Social discrimination	Mode of production Distribution pattern Ownership pattern Discontinuous job structures Social factors: Age Sex Race Structural deficiencies
Psychological implication	Traditional psychoanalytical/ psychological	Alienation	Traditional psychological, stress of ego functioning	Socially induced stress, individual stress, social psychology	Stress alienation
Policy–program level solution	To the person/ subculture	Maximization of group interests	To the person/ subculture	Promotion of opportunity: affirmative action	Change of economic structure

72   SOCIAL POLICY AND SOCIAL WELFARE

tual options afforded the society by developments in the social
sciences—sociology, economics, and, at least implicitly, psychology. What we are suggesting is that society often operationalizes
the integration of selected concepts from sociology, economics,
and psychology within the context of the dominant interest–
value orientations.

Notes

1. Alfred N. Page, "Economics and Social Work: A Neglected Relationship," *Social Work*, 22 (January 1977), 48.
2. Stephen M. Aigner and Roland L. Simmons, "Social Work and
   Economics: Strange Bedfellows," *Social Work*, 22 (July 1977), 305.
3. For an excellent elaboration of these points, see William P. Mc-
   Ewen, *The Problem of Social-Scientific Knowledge* (Totowa, N.J.: Bedminster Press, 1966).
4. For a discussion of this point, see Thomas S. Kuhn, "Reflections on
   my Critics," in Imre Lakatos and Alan Musgrave, eds., *Criticism and
   the Growth of Knowledge* (Cambridge: Cambridge University Press,
   1970), pp. 48–67.
5. Alfred Page, "Points and Viewpoints: The Myth of Professional
   Purity," *Social Work*, 22 (July 1977), p. 308.
6. Almost any basic introductory text in social work attempts to demonstrate this point. See Neil Gilbert and Harry Specht, *The
   Emergence of Social Welfare and Social Work* (Itasca, Ill.: Peacock,
   1976), esp. part 3 for a critical discussion of social work and social
   welfare.
7. Campbell McConnell, *Economics: Principles, Policy, and Problems*
   (New York: McGraw-Hill, 1976).
8. For example, see Lester Thurow, *Investment in Human Capital* (Los
   Angeles: Wadsworth, 1970); Melvin Reder, "A Partial Survey of the
   Theory of Income Size Distribution," in Lee Soltow, ed., *Six Papers
   on the Size Distribution of Wealth and Income* (New York: National
   Bureau of Economic Research, 1969), pp. 224–239.
9. Lester Thurow, *Poverty and Discrimination* (Washington, D.C.:
   Brookings Institution, 1969), p. 26.
10. *Ibid.*

11. The use of this term is influenced by Gans's concept of caretakers in Herbert Gans, *The Urban Villagers* (New York: Free Press, 1962).

12. Jeffrey Galper, *The Politics of Social Services* (Englewood Cliffs, N.J.: Prentice-Hall, 1975).

13. For example, see Michael J. Piore, "The Dual Labor Market: Theory and Implications," in D. M. Gordon, ed., *Problems in Political Economy: An Urban Perspective* (Lexington, Mass.: D. C. Heath, 1972), pp. 34–61; Peter B. Doeringer and Michael J. Piore, *Internal Labor Markets and Manpower Analysis*, (Lexington, Mass.: Heath Lexington Books, 1972).

14. David M. Gordon, *Theories of Poverty and Underemployment* (Lexington, Mass.: D. C. Heath, 1974), p. 49.

15. See Neil Gilbert and Harry Specht, *Dimensions of Social Welfare Policy* (Englewood Cliffs, N.J.: Prentice-Hall, 1974), pp. 40–41 for a distinction of two concepts.

16. See Stansilaw Ossowski, *Class Structure in the Social Consciousness* (New York: Free Press, 1964); Richard C. Edwards, Michael Reich, and Thomas E. Weisskopf, eds., *The Capitalist System* (Englewood Cliffs, N.J.: Prentice-Hall, 1972).

17. For an excellent discussion of the problems inherent in welfare reform, see New York Research Bureau, "Evaluating a Reform: Welfare," *Catalyst*, 2 (Spring 1978), 18–34.

Chapter 6

A Developmental Analysis of Work and Welfare

IN THE PRECEDING CHAPTERS we have indicated that the way in which a society operationalizes caring relationships, largely through its social welfare responses, involves several interrelated factors. Of great importance is the way in which we as a people tend to define the human within society—Is she or he good, perfectible, and entitled to a range of goods and services? A related factor involves the amount of emphasis to be given to the role of contemporary society itself in affecting the human experience and human needs.

Against the backdrop of these factors, society over time develops statements of what "ought to be" relative to its members' social welfare. These statements, referred to as social welfare policy, can serve a variety of purposes and generate a broad spectrum of program types relative to need. In creating policy–program products, society is heavily influenced by how it chooses to look at problems that people experience. Society's perspective on problems is in turn influenced by many things, not the least of which are prevailing social science constructs. However, the most significant element influencing and initiating the cycle of problem perception → policy product → program response is the long-standing cultural context of the society itself. In this chapter we focus upon a major facet of our cultural

74

context—the work ideology—and show how it influences social welfare perspectives.

The Emergence of the Ideology of Work in Cultural and Group Interest Perspectives

Americans have often criticized each other as lacking a sense of history. Whether this sweeping charge is valid is debatable. However, there does seem to' be considerable validity to the assertion that Americans have a rather myopic view of the concept of work. The current conception appears to be that work, as we know it, is both natural (the way that it is is the way that it was meant to be) and unpleasant, yet required, and as old as man.

Although human effort for the purpose of survival is as old as man, the prevailing conception of work is not ancient, nor is the way work organized necessarily natural. How we relate to work is a product of postfeudal society and is heavily enmeshed with a matrix of other social phenomena, such as the emergence of an entrepreneurial and later a capitalist form of economic organization, the rise of Protestant thought, and basic changes in the structure and role of government. Together, conceptions of work and its purposes, plus the other phenomena mentioned, constitute the main ingredients of contemporary developed industrial states. Put another way, the ideology of work can be understood only within the context of how the major institutions of economy, religion, and government were transformed in modern times, how they interrelate, and how their functioning affects the evolution of the social definition of need and the range of responses to need. Our concept of work is both part of the creation and effect of the institutions of modern society.

To understand the subtle and pervasive role of the ideology of work as it relates to social welfare, it might be useful to specify the institutional fabric of premodern time. In that period, the content and structure of the society were heavily dominated by the institution of religion, specifically the Roman Catholic Church. The church offered society a teleological message, and it offered society a mode of organization that was to be replicated in the economic and governmental sectors of society.[1]

The teleological message stated that humans were bound together through Christ and church. It is also stated that anyone who followed the church's interpretation of Christ's teachings would assuredly merit reward in the next life. The prescription for personal harmony was clear: Follow the church's collective message, and you will always know where you are, where you stand before God. Such a prescription, it could be argued, tended to vitiate against a strong sense of individualism and a strong appetite for things of this world. In addition, the church offered its collective message through a hierarchical form of organization—Pope, to bishop, to cleric, to lay person.

The church's twofold contribution—a collective relationship based on adherence to the church and patterns of leadership associated with vertical inequity in a highly stratified system—was replicated in other institutional sectors. Within government, monarchical forms prevailed, and a pattern of king → lord → common man was typical. The key political leaders were often legitimated by church officials, and the two institutions were often so entwined that it was difficult to delineate temporal and spiritual leadership, government and religious institutions.

Similarly, a vertically differentiated pattern characterized the economy, which could be described as a land economy. The land was owned and/or controlled by a few, while the average person basically worked for a subsistence (nonsurplus) existence. What surplus was produced largely fell to those few in control of the land.

Although inequity was present in government and the economic organization, a collective or social relationship was also present in the society. The notion of brotherhood in Christ, through church, gave bishops and clerics not only special rewards but also special responsibilities. Those under their care were often referred to as the flock.[2] Similarly, in government, rulers had to protect the physical well-being of their subjects, and controllers of land had to be sensitive to the well-being of those who worked their land. In short, this type of society produced role inequity and, concurrently, social responsibilities and social relationships.

Because the value of the social relationship existed within the context of inequity, the latter influenced the very nature of the former. Specifically, the types of relationship between unequals in the society produced the social concepts of paternalism and stewardship.[3] Paternalism, as the word denotes, has to do with a fatherly caring response to those in one's charge. Yet the very act of caring often reinforced the prevailing inequity between the helper and the helped. Stewardship speaks to the selective use of abilities and resources by those in power for their own good and, in part, for the well-being of those in their charge. Stewardship also suggested and reinforced inequity, especially in the definition of need and selected use of resources. However, in ideal form stewardship suggested that those in positions of leadership had private property and possessions, but that such property was not exclusive private property. Theoretically, at least, situations could present themselves whereby role inferiors could ask for, even expect, some access to some portion of the property and resources. Viewed together, the society's dual concepts of paternalism and stewardship suggested inequity and a social conception of man whereby some range of social responsibilities was institutionalized.

With the onset of modern times, certain historical phenomena began to alter the organization of society, the respective roles of the major institutions, and the cultural thrusts operating within the society. Specifically, as the feudal society broke down, towns, and later cities, began to emerge within the context of newly developing national states. As this occurred, new economic and political objectives were defined, and these radically transformed how people began to care for each other.

Most notable of the changes was the movement away from a land- and farming-based economy. Over time, trade and commerce competed with, and subsequently dominated, farming. With the rise of trade and commerce, new economic objectives presented themselves. These objectives related to the need of a surplus for trade, and a surplus that was diversified. To create a surplus, the concept of productivity was salient; to achieve diversification, manufacturing of various goods, in addition to food, was paramount. As history spun itself out in the western world, these twin concepts of productivity and diversified manufacturing were central not just to trade, but to national honor and wealth.

In moving toward these new objectives, clearly the existing concepts of work and the social relationships between economic units—landowner and worker—were obstacles. To produce surplus, productivity, not subsistence, had to be stressed. To achieve efficiency economic units could not continue to have extended, noneconomic relationships.[4] In short, the rise of a new type of society produced new economic and social forms that reinforced the cultural item of inequality but narrowed the cultural concept of social responsibility.

In place of landowners' posssessing disproportionate amounts of resources and power, the new type of society witnessed the production of a new class—the entrepreneur, the manufacturer, and ultimately the capitalist. This group spearheaded the production of diversified items for trade by the selective use of its resources, especially capital. They, the capitalists, in turn, were to receive the greatest level of economic rewards.

Although capital was necessary to start the process of manufacturing, which led to trade and profit, labor was also a necessary ingredient. Initially, at least, the manufacture–trade process was intimately tied to capitalists successfully mobilizing productive workers within the marketplace. It also meant that, if tradable items leading to profit were to be produced, then the cost of labor should be curtailed as much as possible. In a very real sense, central to both trade and profit was the ironic need to have large numbers of motivated, productive workers who would work for relatively stable, low wages. This economic dynamic led to the notion of a wage relationship between capitalist and worker. A wage, an economic construct, said the relationship between capitalist and worker was basically economic in nature. The notion of wage introduced a formal, narrow conception of people's responsibility to each other. Along with the concept of productivity, the wage relationship transformed the nature of work from subsistence in the context of social relationship to one that focused upon surplus within a narrow economic relationship. This cultural transformation was extremely functional to the interests of the new capitalist class or group and severely affected basic caring relationships (social welfare) in society. Extended caring relationships between members of a society could now be dysfunctional to the social and economic forces of change within the society.

Up to now we have handled the question of social change in the western world within the context of economic considerations. In a very real sense, this simplifies and distorts the complex dynamics of change. Both religion and government were influential in the process of change and in turn were influenced by the process of change.

Religious institutions provided a support for economic change, and, once that change was set in motion, they provided a consistency and a rationale for the evolving model of economic organization. Weber, in a classic retrospective analysis, identified the key role of the rise of Protestant thought in triggering the development of capitalist economic forms. Protestant thought, reflected most clearly in the writings of Calvin and Knox, questioned the practices, excesses, and apparent corruption of the dominant Roman Catholic Church. In so doing, it ultimately questioned not just the operations of the church, but its teleological message and its reliance upon a vertical, hierarchical form of organization. Further, the central concepts of free will, individual surrender, and adherence to church doctrine as the basis of salvation were replaced with greater emphasis upon the individual's relation to God and salvation as a gift imposed by God on the elect.

The freeing messages suggested by the reformers, however, produced a religious–psychological problem, a problem that went directly to man's state of harmony with self and with God. That problem revolved around the issue, How do I know if I am saved? It was Weber's thesis that this ultimate question led many, including the newly evolving capitalists in countries heavily influenced by Reform thought, to seek an answer, or at least an indication of an answer, in the external, material world.[5] Very simply put, that answer suggested "God shows this decision relative to the next world by blessing me materially in this world." How do I achieve a blessing in this world? By being economically successful. How can I best be economically successful? By shaping and controlling forces in the marketplace and by having profits accrue from the production and marketing of goods, through the marshalling of a productive and efficient working force.

When this connection was made between the spiritual world and the economic world, the content of both the religious and economic institutions reinforced each other. Thus the value of work was forged indelibly within both institutional sectors; in turn, each institutional sector reinforced the other. Work became a cultural product that set up a prevailing motif within the society and that subsequently influenced other institutional sectors, namely, government and social welfare.

Government and Social Welfare as Residual Institutions

As the work ethic emerged, there were profound effects on the scope and purpose of other institutions as they related to the economy. In the area of government, John Locke developed a theory of property that was functional to the evolving economic order but clearly reduced the parameters within which government might operate. Basically, he suggested that property predated the social arrangement and the body politic and that, therefore, society, via government, had no right to abridge man's property. In a very real sense the issue of individual freedom, relative to government's functioning, began to be fused with property.

The implications of this have been profound. First and foremost, Locke's argument suggested that government could do very little to the economy. Over the years in our own country, this has affected the concepts of taxation and business profits, the hesitancy to accept wage and price controls and the near avoidance of profit controls, and the delay in government's promoting standards concerning the quality and safety of products.

However, the influence of the value and interest of work and the primacy of economy over government and social welfare are best exemplified in a range of social processes that were institutionalized in the western world.[6] These processes or guidelines for behavior were identified as functional to the forces that controlled the new economic model of organization. To some degree these processes worked, and still do, in concert and as a system. Briefly, these processes and factors to which they relate are as follows:

1. *Wages*—keep the wages of workers as low as possible to maximize individual incentive to continue to produce.[7]
2. *Population*—encourage, or at least not discourage, the production of large pools of available laborers to as to maximize the competition of workers with each other, so that the price of labor will be bid down.[8]
3. *Imbalance of potential workers and employment opportunities*— make little concerted effort to ensure availability of jobs while continuing to stress the importance of a work ethic.[9]
4. *Level of unemployment*—tolerate significant percentages of unemployment and underemployment, so as to maximize intralabor market competition.[10]
5. *Ethic of mobility*—socially stress the possibility of individual mobility by virtue of hard work and provide selective mobility to key groups and individuals.[11]
6. *Socialization*—instill the value of work in the cultural content of families and formal education; in fact, wed educational content and purposes to labor markets and work–career possibilities in such fashion that successful participation in education becomes a potential basis of individual economic mobility.[12]
7. *Fringe benefits*—provide expanded rewards (i.e., fringe benefits) to certain organized groups of workers only when necessary.[13]
8. *Public social welfare benefits*—set government benefits close to, but basically below, the least economically rewarding jobs in the free-enterprise system so as to reinforce the primacy of a job in the free-enterprise system and help to set up a dynamic whereby wages in the free-enterprise system may be kept low, which in turn keeps welfare benefits relatively low. Such dynamics, in a pluralist society, can promote dissensus within the lower social class pool of potential workers, especially if significant social differences, for example, race, age, and sex, are already present in such a stratum.[14]

Viewed collectively, this early on adopted set of processes has produced two major social consequences. First, it has helped to ensure that the interests of those controlling the economic institution would be served. Second, it has worked against the development of a strong, consciously shared class perspective on the part of the working class. In fact, the internal dissent that has emerged within the labor force has often been accompanied by a tendency of the working class to identify with both the position and the interests of the group above it, rather than with fellow workers, actual and potential, in inferior role positions.

Admittedly, over the years many factors have eroded some of the elements suggested in the set of processes described here. These include a growing realization of the need for some portion of work force to have discretionary income to spend so as to maximize the cycle of production and profits.[15] They also include the rise of unions to prevent gross manipulation of workers, by having workers themselves control the labor supply in certain job sectors, thereby ensuring for themselves some sizable degree of economic rewards and freedom in the marketplace.[16] Also, it has been recognized that some areas of the economy, especially given the nature of items produced, have tremendous cost pass-on possibilities to consumers and that therefore such industries, usually given the presence of unions and/or a limited supply of very skilled workers, can pay their workers wages well beyond survival levels.[17]

Finally, it has become increasingly clear that our type of society and economic order may not continue to need a large pool of cheap labor. It might be argued that this fact may encourage the increased use of social welfare to meet social control functions. Wilhelm has gone one step further and suggested that blacks, as a group, may face new assaults on them because they are no longer needed as a source of cheap labor.[18]

Nonetheless, it appears that many of the processes suggested here remain with us today and are especially applicable to certain populations—those with limited skills and/or those with existing positions of disadvantage by virtue of class or other key attributes, for example, sex or race.

It is with respect to these minorities that the dynamic among the work ethic, the economy, and social welfare continues to be most active and most directly connected to developments associated with the maturation of the current economic order. More specifically, these minority groups have traditionally been adversely affected by society's tendency to see and help those in need through the prism of work and work objectives. Operationally, this has meant over a three-hundred-year period a consistency in the classification of those in need and the kinds of services extended to them.

The original classification of the needy, which occurred in the 17th century, is to be found in the English Elizabethan Poor Laws.[19] Essentially the same classification occurs in our society's major piece of social welfare policy, the Social Security Act of 1936 and its subsequent amendments (which we will examine in detail in Chapter 10).

In both policy products, there is a threefold set of implied categories of need. Each category is tied to the ethic of work.[20] Simply put, the categories involve the following:

1. *Those not able to work.* Normally this has meant that there is a good reason to exempt this group from the mandate to work and to take care of themselves. In a sense this is an exempted group that is valued because it consists of people who presumably would work (or actually have worked in the past) but for forces beyond their individual control that do not allow them to work. Such a category would include the old, the blind, the physically disabled, and so on. If people such as these have need, they are "worthy," and we can help them without jeopardizing the value–interest thrust associated with work.[21]

2. *Those currently/temporarily unable to work.* Normally this category includes those who have worked but who, though misfortune (e.g., the closing of a place of employment, sickness, or work-related injury) cannot now be gainfully employed. In light of their past work efforts and their current situation, which is beyond their control, they are entitled to a social response from the rest of us. They, too, are a population that not only represents need, but for whom a welfare response does not violate the continued commitment to the work ethic. In fact, aid is an investment to help them return to the marketplace at a subsequent time.[22]

3. *Those with no physical impairment relative to work, but yet in need.* This category of needy people presents problems to a society organized around a work and production ethic. To provide aid

or benefits to this population, given the ramifications of the work ethic, it has been argued, is to encourage nonparticipation in the labor market, to reduce individuals' motivation to work, and possibly to produce a nonfunctional dependency relationship with the rest of a working society. Yet these people still have needs relative to their survival and sustenance. Historically, this category has produced programs of aid tied to workhouses, to deterrence, and to the current notion that aid for this category should be set at the lowest level of all welfare responses. In fact, in current times it has produced welfare responses whereby work, or work training, is a condition for the distribution of benefits, for example the Work Incentive Program (WIN) and periodic attempts by local communities to have welfare recipients do public jobs and other activities that free enterprise entrepreneurs will not do because of limited levels of profit and reimbursement.[23] In short, welfare help for this category is usually both minimal for, and lower than, other categories of need and carries with it a not so subtle message—to get more money, get to work. Obviously, such a message has the inherent possibility of defining and stigmatizing certain populations in the society. It also serves as a public reminder to the rest of the working population—keep on working.

Surrounding this work-engendered classification scheme for welfare there has been produced, over time, a series of principles that emanate from the value interest of work. Briefly, they include the following:

1. *Requirements for welfare assistance.* In the beginning—in fact, up to the second half of the twentieth century—these requirements largely revolved around the concept of residency. One had to live in a given place for a period of time before he or she could even apply for aid. In recent years, the concept has come to mean demonstrating need by proving within rather complex bureaucratic procedures that one is in dire straits. The very processes of application, it has been suggested, are a punishment and a deterrence to application.

2. *Encouraging the use of family resources.* Again, this principle suggests that a drain on the society is to be avoided if possible. It also implies that families can probably be more effective than government in regulating assistance, more guarded in the

amounts of money given for specific (limited) periods of time, and so on. It may very well have been based on the assumption that, for many, it is harder to ask for aid from someone they know personally than from the faceless corporate entity of government. This alone might suggest that it is better not to ask—period.

3. *Limited payments—"less eligibility."* If and when public aid is forthcoming, it is better that all categories of those in need, especially the able-bodied poor, receive a benefit lower than the wages normally given at the lowest level of the business sector.

Although work has been a significant item in shaping the conceptions of need and the range of responses in all developed societies in the western world, it has been most notable in the United States for several reasons. First, as a nation, we had no feudal tradition or experience; the nation was born in the context of the rise of a new economic order. Second, our country, because of its physical enormity relative to the size of the population, developed not only a work ethic but the corollary ethics of independence, self-survival, isolation and separation, and individual mastery of the environment. Although these were significant in helping us develop "character" and later technology, they were not supportive in developing a strong sense of social responsibility to and for others. Finally, our country from its formative years has reflected just not a strong tie to Protestant thought and all its concomitant processes but a pronounced tie to a peculiar variant of such thought—Puritanism. This relatively rigid, stoic, individualistic view of man, often in negative terms, has tended to exacerbate the predisposition to punish those who are not self-sufficient.

Summary

In this chapter we have shown that the value interest of work was, and is, part of a matrix of economic and social development. As a value, it has greatly influenced major institutional components of the society—most notably the economy and religion. As it has developed, it helped restructure the parameters of government relative to the economy. Of most importance to us as people concerned with the welfare of society's members, it has helped society to fuse welfare with work in terms of problem definition and modes of responses to people in need (policy and program benefits). Of no little importance, the value, as it has evolved over the years, appears to be highly significant and functional to those who receive the most benefits from our mode of economic organization. Correspondingly, those who appear to participate the least in our economy, and receive few direct rewards from it, have to confront a social welfare system that seems to reflect a concern with reinforcing the work ethic more than a concern with meeting the human needs of populations at risk.

Notes

1. Much of the discussion of the relationship between religious thought, economy, and social welfare is influenced by the following works: R. H. Tawney, *Religion and the Rise of Capitalism* (New York: Mentor Books, 1954), esp. pp. 98-106; Max Weber, *The Protestant Ethic and the Spirit of Capitalism*, trans. by Talcott Parsons (New York: Scribner, 1958); Samuel Mencher, *Poor Law to Poverty Program* (Pittsburgh: University of Pittsburgh, 1967), pp. 3-156.

2. The classic distinction between traditional Catholic notions of relief and early Protestant, that is, Calvin-influenced, thought is to be found in Reinhold Niebuhr, *The Contribution of Religion to Social Work* (New York: Columbia University Press, 1932), pp. 14-16.

3. Mencher, *op. cit.*, pp. 5-70.

4. See *ibid.*, pp. 6-10, for a discussion of worker's preference for social and economic relationships within the economic institution.

5. Weber, *op. cit.*

6. See Mencher, *op. cit.*, pp. 14-15, 98-100, for a discussion of many of these principles being adopted early in trade- and production-oriented societies.

7. Frances Fox Piven and Richard A. Cloward, in *Regulating the Poor* (New York: Pantheon, 1971), stress this point and many of the following ones in their analysis of social welfare policies and programs. See also Joe R. Feagin, *Subordinating the Poor: Welfare and*

American Beliefs (Englewood Cliffs, N.J.: Prentice-Hall, 1975), pp. 48–55.

8. Admittedly this issue of population is associated with many political and ethical issues. Nonetheless, it is not surprising that contraction of the birth rate patterns is least likely to be found in the lower social class.

9. Even the adoption of the Humphrey–Hawkins Bill in 1977 does not specify a societal commitment and strategy of implementation relative to guaranteed employment.

10. See David Gordon, *Theories of Poverty and Underemployment* (Lexington, Mass.: D. C. Heath, 1972), for an interesting discussion of twin concepts of unemployment and underemployment.

11. Robin Williams, Jr., *American Society* (New York: Knopf, 1970), pp. 454–461.

12. Leonard Broom and Phillip Selznick, *Sociology* (New York: Harper & Row, 1977), pp. 364–367.

13. Gordon, *op. cit.*, pp. 43–53.

14. Piven and Cloward, *op. cit.*, and Gordon, *op. cit.*, pp. 43–53.

15. Jeffrey Galper, *The Politics of Social Services* (Englewood Cliffs, N.J.: Prentice-Hall, 1975), p. 24.

16. Gordon, *op. cit.*, pp. 43–53.

17. *Ibid.*

18. Sidney M. Willhelm, *Who Needs the Negro?* (Garden City, N.Y.: Doubleday, 1971).

19. Walter I. Trattner, *From Poor Law to Welfare State: A History of Social Welfare in America*, 2d ed. (New York: Free Press, 1979), pp. 9–16.

20. Blanche D. Coll, "Perspectives in Public Welfare: The English Heritage," See *Welfare in Review*, 4 (March 1966), 1–12, for discussion of material related to several issues discussed in the rest of this chapter.

21. *Ibid.*

22. *Ibid.*

23. *Ibid.*

Chapter 7

Individualist and Collectivist Perspectives

OBVIOUSLY OUR SOCIETY HAS EVOLVED with several value–interest products, not just a work ethic. In this chapter we focus upon the ethic of individualism and the institutionalized adjustment to its excesses—modified collectivism. Both individualism and collectivism should be seen as dynamically interacting with our social conception of work in influencing policy–program responses in social welfare. In this chapter, we focus upon the roots of individualism and the role that American labor and social work have played in developing a form of collectivism that, strangely enough, can coexist with continued commitment to individualism.

The Roots of Individualism

Inherent in our society's notion of the responsibility to work, especially within the nature of the wage relationship, is the value of crude individualism. As capitalism developed against the backdrop of industrialization, a philosophical point of view was produced in the eighteenth and nineteenth centuries that greatly justified the clearly defined notion of the individual within society. That philosophical point of view, which was influential in Europe but has been and continues to be vitally significant within the United States, is sometimes referred to as *laissez-faire* (literally, to leave alone). Its major principle is that every person should be allowed his or her liberty within all institutional sectors of a society. Simply put, every person should be unencumbered by the rest of society in terms of how he or she conducts behavior within such areas as religion, government, and economy. Most especially, however, it argued for a conception of life, society, and human beings wherein the collective society has few, if any, responsibilities to any given person. Economy was the institutional sector in society that usually was most stressed in terms of individual freedom with a corresponding absence of society's responsibility.

Relative to the economy, the *laissez-faire* perspective espoused the following general principles:

1. Society is an abstraction; only isolated individuals exist.
2. Each individual has a range of self-interests, especially of an economic nature.
3. Reality is the pursuit of individual self-interests.
4. The state, as an instrument of the society, is secondary in time and importance to the pursuit of individual self-interests.
5. The role that the state government institution should have, given the foregoing, is essentially in the adjudication of conflicting self-interests.
6. Each person, in acting out self-interests, should compete with others, especially in the marketplace, so as to maximize his or her position and interests.
7. Because competition is a necessary, call it a natural process, no body of society including government should intervene into the marketplace and abort natural competition.
8. The type of society produced—in fact, what is socially good—is the product of antecedent, unfettered pursuit of self-interests.[1]

Obviously the philosophy and the specifics of *laissez-faire* were tied to certain assumptions. One apparent assumption was that man was basically nonsocial and driven by self-interests. A second assumption was that the business-model view of life, as initially espoused by Adam Smith, accurately captured all of man's nature—actual and potential. Needless to say, such assumptions had, and still have, profound implications for governmental responses in the areas of social welfare.

In America the impetus of an individualistic ethic was greatly reinforced in the late nineteenth and twentieth centuries by the influence of Social Darwinism. Hofstadter has suggested that it is the byplay between individualism and Social Darwinism that has helped make American social thought so distinctive.[2] Going one step further, it can be said that the overlay of Social Darwinism upon individualism has contributed heavily to the peculiar nature of American social welfare and to the relatively narrow and dependent social welfare institution.

Social Darwinism should be seen not as different from *laissez-faire* but rather as a thought schema that made individual competition the very basis upon which societies could evolve and make progress. Like *laissez-faire*, it stressed the individual as the key unit in life and perceived competition within the human species as a natural phenomenon. However it went beyond this premise and heavily stressed the functional role of competition and survival in society. Specifically, it suggested that through competition the best human forms will be produced and that social progress can be a linear, upward product. In tieing competition to the development of the human species and progress, it implied that the best competitors within the society should receive the largest amounts of material rewards. These material rewards, disproportionately shared, could serve as motivational devices to ensure the process of competition and progress.[3] Examined together, Social Darwinism and *laissez-faire* thought produced a conception of individualism that heavily reflected the following ingredients.

1. *The importance of competition.* Individualism was not just a static concept but one to be acted out in life, especially in economic life, as humans were largely conceived in economic terms. This principle of competition was expected to be acted out by all, that is, corporations (corporate people), employers, and workers.

2. *The justification of inequality within our society.* Not only was inequality predictable and natural, but the stratification of people within society was a social good, an instrumental means designed to ensure that the best (i.e., most successfully competitive) members of the species came forward to help society achieve progress. In a sense, poverty was not necessarily an evil but rather a predictable, tolerable, and even encouraged social condition that existed to ensure positions of advantage for those successful in competition.

3. *Affirmation of the principle of noninterference.* If government (i.e., a collective unit) were to interfere in the natural process of competition between and among individual actors within the economy, several evils would be produced. First, the individual—the most important unit of life—would have his or her freedom abridged. Second, the natural process of evolution would be slowed considerably. Third, if directed at helping "poor competitors," such interference might actually produce an investment in the maintenance of weak human forms—individuals and families. If competition was natural, interference with competition was unnatural.

Obviously these facets of individualism have profound implications for how people relate to, and care for, each other. Several of the implications are worth specifying because of the way in which they seem to influence our social thought concerning social welfare even today.

The first area of welfare thought influenced by this perspective has to do with the definition of the problem of need and the cause of individual need. If individualism is important to a society, it is likely that the major value will suggest that the reason that any person is in need stems from some failure on the part of the person. Cause and effect tend to come together, and "extra-person" factors, such as environment and circumstances, will be seen as extraneous to the real problem of individual shortcomings.[4]

Individual shortcoming has been interpreted in different ways at different times. It may be a "bad seed" or a mental deficiency, or a defect of character such as weak morality or laziness. In more recent times, new liberal explanations have suggested inadequacies in life-style, ego functioning, or mismanagement of existing resources and skills. Throughout the range of explanations cited, the focus upon the individual as central to his or her own problem has remained relatively constant. In part, this focus stems from the effects of individualism within the society.

A second area within welfare thought that has been influenced by individualism has to do with perception of the nature of social assistance. If individualism is important for all people, then the very notion of social assistance is basically a contradiction. In fact, social assistance to any individual may very well stimulate dependency relationships and reduce the individual freedom of both givers and receivers. Put another way, social assistance (i.e., welfare) can introduce noneconomic relationships into a society and can frustrate the imperative of both the successful and unsuccessful in pursuing economic independence.[5]

A third area of welfare thought affected by this perspective involves the role of the family. It has been argued by many, including Daniel Moynihan, that welfare breaks down the responsibility of family members to each other and, in fact, may break down families. Dispensing aid to individuals not only may be disastrous for the majority of society who transfers payments to those in need, but may concurrently ensure weak family forms for select populations within the society.[6]

A fourth area worth mentioning is that social welfare thought, including many welfare proposals, does not see that positions of economic advantage are intimately and negatively tied to those having positions of economic disadvantage. Rather, positions of gross advantage are often seen as socially good, and the problem of disadvantage, however it is conceived and studied, is often seen through a myopic lens.[7] Needless to say, such an approach is definitely functional to the interests of those who are in positions of great economic advantage.

In a very real sense the thrust of welfare suggested by an individualistic perspective, in ideal form, is to have no welfare. Yet people in various categories have need. Thus this philosophy grudgingly has suggested that to keep the value of individualism vital, temporary aid under local and preferably private (nongovernment) auspices should prevail. Along these lines, payments for welfare would be voluntary rather than tied to obligatory taxation and thus would be compatible with the notion of charity rather than of individual rights and social responsibility. Further, by having a locally controlled service response, there would be greater assurance that the social welfare program was more akin to the expectations of the local donor(s) and that the service would not jeopardize the position of economic advantage held by the donor(s) in the local community. In no small way individualism as a belief in the society helps support certain key individuals and groups in their attempt to exercise personal and exclusive control over their assets.

It would certainly be a mistake to conclude that the logic of individualism has not gone unchallenged or that it has not been modified. Clearly there have been modifications, some stemming from critical reflection of the ethic itself, others from developments elsewhere in the society. Together they have produced a unique blend of collectivism laid on top of a deep, continuing societal subscription to a type of individualism.

Intellectual Criticism of Individualism

As the decades of the twentieth century have unfolded, criticisms have been voiced that have shaken but not toppled the individualistic ethic. One criticism is that, if competition is a good and if individual self-interests should be pursued, what ensures that real competition occurs? Pure competition suggests that there may be times when an individual or organization, in pursuit of self-interests, takes steps to prevent another from competing. Similarly, competition in a normative sense implies exchange and competition among relative equals.[8] The issue raised by these two examples is whether a noncompeting force is required to ensure appropriate levels and types of competition within society. The answer that has been given is "yes," and that is a major role of government, most specifically the judicial branch.

Another criticism that has been leveled is derived from George Bernard Shaw's critique of Marxist extension of Hegel.

Shaw claimed that there was a faith principle operating when Marxists said that the dialectic (thesis, antithesis, synthesis) inevitably produced a synthesis of the best facets of prior forms of organization. Shaw argued that it was just as logical and perhaps equally likely that future states of organization might replicate the worst of prior forms of organization. Similarly, many have suggested that unfettered competition does not necessarily produce the social good; rather, it may simultaneously produce selective individual good and chaos for the society.

Finally, some have remarked about the confusion between the views of competition as a process and as an end point. Schumpeter has suggested that competition is a viable human process even in socialist societies, but, if a society is not careful, played-out competition can and will produce noncompetition.[9] Simply stated, does any economic unit that is capable of achieving a position of advantage continue to want real competition after the position of advantage has been achieved through competition? In fact, might the ethic of competition have within it the seeds of noncompetition, that is, monopoly?

Together, criticisms such as these suggested two things: (1) economic competition is a social good but (2) a social good that has to be monitored. It is within this perspective that the role of government, relative to the economy, first became articulated. Such role delineation does not suggest a tone of leadership for government but rather one of complementing and supplementing the economic institution. This tone of course has had tremendous implications for welfare and the range of policies and programs that it might offer. Specifically, it suggested that the role of government was to assist the economy and private sector in meeting human need or to help provide specific types of help to people when it was quite clear that the free economy would not do so.

American Collectivism and Labor

The intellectual criticisms referred to in the preceding discussion may or may not have been instrumental in modifying the role of individualism. The role of organized labor in modifying individualism and promoting a unique form of collectivism is much less obscure. To understand the role of organized labor relative to welfare in the twentieth century, several background comments are in order. First, because of the influences associated with the work and individualist ethic, American workers have never developed a strong sense of class or group identity. Second, labor throughout most of American history has been relatively cautious, perhaps even fearful of government as an institution. Third, American workers, primarily because of the absence of a class image, never seriously pursued the development of their own distinctive political party. This characteristic is quite unlike the development of many western industrialized countries. Thus, the United States has never witnessed a full-blown process whereby workers develop group image, articulate focused interests, and express them through a labor-oriented party, which in turn attempts to produce policy in government, which shapes and controls the rest of the society, including the economy. Schematically it would resemble the following:

I → We → Party → Government → Policies related to labor
interests and needs

As a result of how American labor has defined itself and related to government, the traditional solution of labor to the problem of how to have its interests and needs met is through organized activity and negotiation within the economy itself. As far back as the Knights of Labor and Samuel Gompers, American labor has consciously chosen not to be identified with a single political party. Rather it has involved direct bargaining with management using negotiating and cooperating strategies.[10]

In addition to this narrow conception of political behavior, the labor movement has often reflected patterns of social separation within the work force. Initially, it was usually the skilled workers who were organized in unions. Then the unskilled in certain industries became unionized and became affiliated with the CIO, while skilled workers gravitated to the AFL. Differences in skill and union base were often associated with differences in ethnicity and race. Even with the merger of the AFL–CIO, many have suggested that organized labor still reflects more of a commitment to nonminority members of our society. In a sense, organized labor in this country is not monolithic but riddled with occupational and skill differences that in turn are exacerbated by race, sex, and ethnic differences. This condition is further complicated by the fact that nearly 80 percent of the work force is nonunionized.

Nevertheless, organized labor has been quite cognizant of the predictable risks that people face in our society. As a result, it has been relatively successful in promoting two types of collectivism to protect sizable portions of the work force. These efforts include (1) the movement for *expanded fringe benefits* within the economic institution and (2) the movement for more *comprehensive social insurance programs* involving a partnership among employers in the free-market system, government, and labor.

Fringe benefits, as a concept, may refer to vacations, sick leave, health and hospitalization benefits, and the like. Basically these benefits are distributed within the marketplace, often as a result of union activity and/or tradition in certain sectors of the economy. They are distributed to groups, are relatively uniform within given industries and are most likely to be present in industries and occupational settings in which there are cost pass-on possibilities open to management. For example, a given auto maker can pass on the cost of a more comprehensive health plan for workers merely by raising the price of cars. Because the union that covers auto workers (same for steel and many others) is company- and industrywide, all auto manufacturers will be in the same position of increased labor costs. Similarly, all buyers of new cars face the same problem of relatively uniform prices. This is not the same in all businesses, especially businesses that are relatively small and operate in truly competitive markets or are at current positions of competitive disadvantage. An example of the latter might be a small, independently owned business in the retail food sector of the economy. Thus the fringe benefit possibilities vary tremendously within the economy by virtue of the nature of the business and the industry.

Logically, fringe benefits, as group (collective) coverage of individual workers, are a negation of pure individualism. Yet the term "fringe benefit," as well as the institutional location from which it is distributed (the economy), disguises the fact that it is collectivism, a type of social caring for people against the risks that all individuals face in our society.

The creation and expansion of fringe benefits have been a significant breakthrough for American labor in attempting to protect its members, but the strategy of having processes internal to the economic institution that collectively protect and help workers has serious limitations. First, as indicated previously, only a small portion of the work force is unionized, and the highest fringe benefits are often associated with the presence of certain unions. Second, the rate of unionization is essentially stalled and even shrinking. The prospects that more workers will become unionized, hence acquiring greater access to comprehensive benefits, is just not great. This is compounded by the fact that current areas of growth in the job structures of our country are associated with service occupations and white-collar positions—both areas that have been notorious for their resistence to organized labor. These factors are quite significant because many strong unions not only negotiate substantial fringe benefits but also offer their members fairly comprehensive union-sponsored benefits.

Many within labor today receive excellent fringe and group benefits and experience a positive position of collective/group support. For such workers, the growth of government-supported welfare programs is not perceived as necessary or functional to their interests. In fact, individual workers within organized labor are likely to perceive government collective benefits as dysfunctional to their economic interests because of the reality of taxation. Taxation, they perceive, would transfer potential discretionary dollars from one sector of the population to another. Put another way, why should a worker (relatively well covered by group benefits) be forced to pay for collective benefits to be distributed to others by government?[11]

The second type of collective protection associated with American labor is *social insurance* benefits. Social insurance as a concept rests on the assumption that many, if not all of us, run certain risks by being born into our society and that many of these risks are of such magnitude that individuals cannot be expected to be able to handle them personally. In our free-enterprise system, it is also assumed that the private economy cannot or will not be able to distribute sufficient benefits to those people who experience the full impact of these risks. Thus, social insurance is a social product that provides group coverage to certain populations for specified situations—advancing years, being disabled or blind, being a widow(er), becoming unemployed, and so on.

The precipitating event leading to the notion of social insurance in our society was the Great Depression of the 1930s. Under the orchestration of Roosevelt and his new urban coalition of ethnics, several principles central to social insurance were incorporated into American social welfare policy. Those principles spoke to narrowing perspectives of personal responsibility and a broadening of collective, social responsibility, through government, for specified risk situations.

In retrospect the tone of social insurance that was developed in our country was not uncontaminated by what the Depression was—a massive unemployment problem affecting a potentially powerful political group, the working ethnics. In a very real sense, social insurance was born as a political strategy to meet the interests of people who normally worked or would have worked. Through such a strategy potential social disruption of urban populations was minimized. It was further minimized when the economy returned to normalcy with the onset of war.

Yet even in social insurance we see a deep commitment in social welfare policy to the primacy of the economic institution and a reliance upon work and individualistic ethics.[12] Payments for social insurance were basically grounded in the context of the job and the wage. Individual employers and employees made individual payments to the federal government that distributed them to individuals and families if and when risks were subsequently encountered. Government's role was largely one of collecting, holding, and allocating funds. Social insurance does not suggest much use of general tax dollars for income security. The government-based, collective response through social insurance is in fact a supplement to the economy in many ways. For those workers who currently have good fringe benefits, social insurance is an additional means of coverage. For those workers who do not have adequate fringe benefits from the private economy, social insurance provides floor assistance that the economy could not. In so doing, government is supplementing the limitations of the private economy relative to across-the-board coverage of society members.

Perhaps of equal interest since social insurance is largely tied to contributions (or payments), individual recipients perceive benefits as something to which they are entitled. Further, one can experience the reality of socially sanctioned group support of members of society without abandoning the ethic of individualism.

The result of fringe and group benefits, plus social insurance coverage of certain categories of people, is that many within labor reflect the negative thinking of the dominant society concerning welfare and welfare populations. That is, many within labor see the poor along the dimensions of individual inability or personal failure. In some cases this reflects a hereditary tone. In all cases it seems to reflect a clear extension of the individualistic ethic.

When labor views government as a possible instrument of help, it sees government aid ideally coming in the promotion of collective bargaining and creating public works and other employment opportunities. It tends not to see government promoting basic structural changes of the private economy in such areas as ownership and distribution of profits.

By way of concluding the discussion of labor and collectivism, it might be prudent to paraphrase what many have called the "liberal response" to meet the needs of society's members. The solution incorporates a supporting role for government as it attempts to work with the private economy on social welfare concerns.[13] The skeletal elements of the liberal response are

1. To have the Social Security Act serve as a basic floor and supplement for a sizable part of the society.
2. To have collective bargaining within the economic institution serve as a main vehicle for benefit creation and distribution.
3. To attempt to limit the amount of money to be collected from general tax revenue sources for welfare and to rely instead on social insurance contributions for social insurance beneifts.
4. To have government attempt to stimulate and slow down the economy when necessary so that the private economy may function to serve the greatest number in the society.

5. To use public works programs and purchases by government as temporary devices to stimulate the economy by reducing unemployment and maintaining circulation of money within the private economy.
6. To have government stress training and education programs, when necessary, as investments in subsequent individual independence.

If one examines the variety of policies and programs developed over the last forty-odd years, whether by Democratic or Republican administrations, one sees the biplay of many of these points as they reflect society's fusion of individual and collective responses.

Collectivism and Professional Social Work Responses

In the previous section we discussed how organized labor has helped to produce a particular range of collective responses within the economy (fringe benefits) and within government (publically sponsored social insurance programs). In so doing, we have suggested that government has a particular role of supplementing the economy. We also suggested that the collective responses of the economy seem to work well for some populations but not for others because of structural variations within the economy mixing with ethnicity, race, and sex factors. The net effect is that some populations receive collective supports from the economy, whereas others have to depend upon the government.

If we now move to look at collectivism relative to American social work, we see similar distinctions between the public and private. In this case however, public still refers to government, but private relates to social work rather than the economy.

Prior to the Great Depression, social work services, as we have mentioned, were locally based, financed by donations, and almost always dispensed by private agencies. What these private agencies dispensed was usually some combination of relation-

ship, advice, and material aid. Admittedly, some approaches
social work were geared to political and environmental factor
whereas others stressed personal reform. In both cases, however, there was some basic agreement that social work was in the
business of providing material aid to people in need.

With the Depression came the recognition that private, local
agency responses to income deficiency were inadequate. Government, first local and later state and federal, was forced into
the business of providing for financial need. Yet agencies of a
private and local nature were in existence and had histories of
providing help. The resulting division-of-labor issue—what private agencies should do now that the public sector had moved
into the area of financial assistance—was heavily influenced by
the introduction of Freudian perspectives into America in the
1920s and 1930s.[14]

In fairly rapid fashion, the existing networks of private agencies with paid staffs perceived that their role was to provide
therapeutic services while the public sector's role was to provide
financial services. Over the ensuing years, several results were
produced from this marriage of convenience, and they affected
how professional social work oriented itself.

1. Reality came to be defined as the perception and use of the
   environment, not the environment itself.
2. The role of the unconscious was influential in affecting perception and use of environment.
3. Emotional factors and dynamics came to be stressed over
   material assistance in studying and treating problems.
4. Ideally, the populations served were to be treated in depth;
   this meant serving smaller numbers, as well as serving people
   who possessed characteristics congenial to the therapeutic
   approaches in use—for example, abstract thinking, reflection, verbal articulation, and the like.
5. There was less concern with social reform and less reliance
   upon social sciences that spoke to environmental phenomena
   via concepts of structure and culture.
6. There emerged a conception of social work identity and
   status needs to be met by acceptance of therapeutic roles in
   our society.[15]

Thus, social work as a profession designed to meet people's needs in social functioning increasingly came to the conclusion that the "real" services were offered in the private and local sector of the social welfare institution, while the more basic services tied to economic assistance should be dispensed by public sector workers who need not be as well trained as private sector social workers.

In moving toward a loose equation between the private sector and professional help and public sector and nonprofessional help, not only were the needs and interests of private agencies and workers met, but the structured division of public and private seemed to meet the needs and interests of select interest groups in local communities. Specifically, if professional services were to be found largely in the local private sector, such services would be, at least in part, funded by local contributions. This relationship between local distribution of services and fund raising for such service has produced what has often been referred to as the United Way movement. The movement has been criticized as oriented to the status quo, designed to preserve the existing relations between those in need and those not in need.[16] In fact Lubove has suggested that the United Way and Community Chest structure, because of its dependency upon private contributions, helps those in positions of advantage to control the range and parameters of services provided, introduces a linkage between social welfare in the private sector and corporate giving (and perspective), and institutionalizes a higher degree of concern with efficiency in services along business model criteria (i.e., fiscal auditing, avoidance of duplication, and promoting coordination) rather than with identifying gaps in services, making fundamental changes in service delivery, and overcoming possible biases in populations served and not served.

Summary

This chapter has explored the roots and role of individualism within our society. Special attention was given to the derived concepts of competition and inequality, the compensatory processes of group and fringe benefits, and the role of social work in developing a sense of modified collectivism in America. Such processes, while meaningful and functional for many members of the society, have distinct disadvantages in terms of where, how, and to whom benefits may be distributed.

If we consider the material in this chapter and in the preceding chapter on work, we can begin to see how these value–interest orientations can influence society's selective use and emphasis of the social science material discussed in Chapters 4 and 5. Social science variants that stress an individual level of analysis and person functioning relative to work are probably going to be emphasized. Further, problems are probably going to be expressed and understood within society in a narrow, nonstructured frame of reference. Logically, then, many social welfare policies and programs are going to focus on the maintenance of the dominant social system, the continued dominance of the private economy, and a supporting role for government and social welfare. In short, the value interests of work, individualism, and collectivism are best met when the specifics of order theory (sociology), orthodox economic theory, and traditional psychological approaches are the main prisms through which society views social problems and proposed solutions.

Notes

1. Several classical works discuss the major components of *laissez-faire* thought. Among them are Adam Smith, *The Wealth of Nations* (New York: Modern Library, 1973); Herbert W. Schneider, ed., *Adam Smith's Moral and Political Philosophy* (New York: Hafner, 1948); J. M. Clark et al., *Adam Smith, 1776–1926* (Chicago: University of Chicago Press, 1928).

2. Richard Hofstadter, *Social Darwinism in American Thought* (Boston: Beacon Press, 1955).

3. *Ibid.*

4. Robert H. Bremner, *From the Depths* (New York: New York University Press, 1956), esp. pp. 16–17.

5. The famous memo in 1969 from Daniel P. Moynihan to Richard Nixon commenting upon blacks, their families, welfare, and "benign neglect" is to be found in *The Wall Street Journal* 175, March 13, 1970, p. 26. See, also, Daniel P. Moynihan, "The Crises in Welfare," *The Public Interest*, 13 (Winter 1968), 3–29.

6. See Moynihan, *ibid.*, in which he fuses family structure and economic independence goals.

7. Jeffrey H. Galper, *The Politics of Social Services* (Englewood Cliffs, N.J.: Prentice-Hall, 1975). Much of the book is a critique of "liberal" welfare strategies that do not adequately address the structural problems in society because of their limited concern with relating positions of advantage to positions of disadvantage.

8. See Samuel Mencher, *Poor Law to Poverty Program* (Pittsburgh: University of Pittsburgh, 1967), pp. 175–183, for an excellent discussion of liberal thinking and the government mandate to promote competition.

9. Joseph Schumpeter, *Capitalism, Socialism, and Democracy* (New York: Harper & Row, 1942).

10. See Mencher, *op. cit.*, pp. 266–277, for an excellent discussion of the view and role of American labor; also, see Edward C. Kirkland, *A History of American Economic Life* (New York: Appleton-Century-Crofts, 1951), for an excellent summary of the early American labor movement and its perspective, esp. pp. 501–505.

11. These remarks are suggested by David J. Kallen and Dorothy Miller, "Public Attitudes toward Welfare," *Social Work*, 16 (July 1971), 83–90.

12. For a detailed discussion of the characteristics of social insurance, see Claire Wilcox, *Toward Social Welfare* (Homewood, Ill.: Irwin, 1969), esp. pp. 83–88.

13. Many writers and critics have reflected upon the role of the welfare state in contemporary society and its functions. See Dorothy Buckton James, "The Limits of Liberal Reform," *Science and Society*, 2 (Spring 1972), 311–312; Clauss Offe, "Advanced Capitalism and the Welfare State," *Politics and Society*, 2 (Summer 1972), 479–488.

14. See Roy Lubove, *The Professional Altruist* (Cambridge, Mass.: Harvard University Press, 1968), for an excellent and critical discussion of the dynamics involved in the changes in American social work, esp. pp. 85–156.

15. *Ibid.*, pp. 118–156.

16. Stanley Winocur, "A Political View of the United Way," *Social Work,* 20 (May 1975), 223-230; Dwight Adams, "Fund Executives and Social Change," *Social Work,* 17 (January 1972), 68-77; Leonard Simmons, "Agency Financing and Social Change," *Social Work,* 14 (January 1972), 62-68.

Chapter 8

Lower Levels of Choice for Social Welfare

IN THE PRECEDING CHAPTERS we have focused upon the interplay of dominant values and interests in the society that affect the social welfare institution. We have suggested that analysis of social welfare policy and program responses must be grounded in a sound appreciation of what we have been and are as a society. In this chapter we discuss a series of lower-level, often interrelated, choices made within the social welfare institution that structure actual caring responses. Obviously many, if not all, of the lower-level choices are affected by constraints derived from our value–interest packages. Basically the choice areas discussed will relate to groups to be covered, benefits,* modes of service delivery, and sources of support. Collectively they help constitute the social welfare institution in action.

Populations Covered

Once a social problem is recognized within a society, a major decision has to be made regarding *who (what people/groups) will be*

---

*The term *benefits* in this chapter will be employed in quite a broad sense, covering money, programs, and services within social welfare.

served and *to whom will society respond?* There is no automatic answer. In fact a broad variety of possibilities exist. The society may say that everyone is entitled to a response, including people who as of yet show no signs of a given problem or situation. Or society may chose to serve only those with the actual problem.

Another possibility is that society may choose to serve specific groups—for example, the blind, the aged, and so on. Further, the society can choose to serve all or only some portions within these "worthy" or "special" categories or groups.[1] Related to the choice of the categories and groups to whom it will respond, society may well choose to have social welfare provide compensatory rewards. Thus it may empower social welfare to provide special benefits to veterans, discriminated populations, and people with catastrophic illnesses, to name a few. Society's use of special categories and/or compensatory coverage of populations is most likely to occur when such categories are compatible with, or even valued by, dominant cultural thought.

A third option exists: social welfare benefits may be applied to a given type of person/group if some "objective," or professional decision (diagnosis), is made concerning the need for service. An example might be mental health services. The requirement of a special type of diagnosis before a person or group receives coverage is related to clients' demonstrating a clear need as regards a structured set of criteria. The most common example of this type of coverage is to be found in public welfare's use of income eligibility criteria (means test).

All these options for social welfare are affected by a very basic consideration: Should social welfare resources be disproportionately given to those in need? As Kahn suggests the more social welfare policy focuses upon universal coverage, less the social welfare concern with redistribution in the society.[2] The reason is that in our kind of society, which relies upon a free market economy, there are usually limited resources for social welfare. To allocate such resources universally may ensure maintenance of inequality among peoples and groups in the society. On the other hand, if the resources available for social welfare are scarce, focusing welfare benefits on populations in or close to positions of disadvantage may produce greater focus upon redistribution.

Thrust of Policy: Fairness, Adequacy, Equality

Fairness, as a concept and value, speaks to due process and access to opportunity structures. The concept, which basically has to do with protecting individuals and types of individuals within a society, is laden with legal overtones. How fairness is operationalized is essentially a political perspective. Is fairness tied only to people's or group's current experiences with how institutions and organizations function? If so, is it social welfare's role to ensure that current sources of discrimination are minimized or stopped? Or is fairness to be operationalized as longitudinal in nature, so that social welfare's role is to ensure the current protection of people and groups from discrimination while overtly recognizing the working of past discrimination in present situations?[3] It is clear that these distinctions and choices underlie affirmative action and the recent Bakke case. This choice area obviously is affected by how much selective compensatory strategies are operating for which populations. Fairness in and of itself does not necessarily relate to equality.

Adequacy concerns some floor level of coverage for some population.[4] It has limited direct implication for redistribution and in many cases is tied to the use of a "means test" whereby attempts are made to ensure that not too much aid is given to individuals and types of individuals. (But note, in operationalizing adequacy, the role of individual evaluation of each case.) If burden conceptions of welfare dominate, then this choice of the thrust of policy is likely to operate for select populations.

Equality as a policy thrust suggests a concern with distribution patterns and is focused toward reduction of prevailing skewing patterns within society.[5] This thrust obviously suggests a strong government institution relative to the distribution of economic rewards and benefits.

Level of Prevention in Policy

In addition to considering to whom social welfare will respond, the social welfare institution can reflect different approaches to the level of prevention selected. Three basic options are available in social welfare.[6] One level, usually referred to as *primary prevention*, suggests that conditions affecting the quality of life in our culture and society are germane to many social problems and, therefore, that something "ought to be done" about our way of life if the problem is to cease. Obviously, if social welfare policy reflects this perspective, the social welfare institution would be speaking to social changes in the very culture and society's institutions. Social welfare would have to have great legitimacy and power to be able to intervene to change how the major institutions of our society function. From material discussed earlier in the book, it should be clear that this option is not routinely pursued in our society. In fact the weakness of the social welfare institution in pursuing this approach is in no small fashion tied to the manner in which social problems are often perceived and defined in our society—that is, usually as the sum of personal problems, via person level constructs (e.g., personality, motivation, skills, etc.).

The second level that policy may address concerns how types of organizations relate to certain people and groups. When there is recognition within the social welfare institution that people may experience the effects of the dysfunctions of certain organizations (schools, places of employment, hospitals, etc.) and when the social welfare institution indicates that effort should be expended to changing how these organizations operate, we refer to this as concern with secondary prevention. Again, this level of policy presupposes the selection and use of certain social science constructs and the detection of correlations between certain social groupings and certain organizational connections.

The third level of prevention utilizes certain types of resources relative to populations that currently have the effects of some social problem. We normally refer to this level as tertiary prevention or direct service provision. Such a response is more likely to occur if problems are defined in personal terms, and where one of the dominant values in the society is individualism. Setting policy to this level has costs. One cost is the usually limited availability of resources for those with demonstrated problem effects. A second is that policy that operates only on this level may even ensure the maintenance of the problem effect in the society over time.

We are not suggesting that the choice areas just cited are either/or but, rather, that social problems must be addressed by policy at all three levels, or at least at the secondary and tertiary levels. The issue here is degree of emphasis. In fact a case might be made that, if the social nature of problems is understood and if only limited resources are available, then social welfare intervention might be more efficient (even in the narrowest economic sense) if it reflected greater concern with secondary levels of prevention. That our society, which prides itself on using business criteria in approaching life, does not stress more prevention seems to suggest that social welfare policy may have a latent function in perpetuating social problems rather than alleviating them.[7] That is, society does not want social welfare to wipe out or prevent certain problems because the solution may be more expensive than the costs of servicing people, thus in effect maintaining the problems.

Goal Mix

Inherent in this discussion, and elsewhere in the book, is the notion of multiple interests operating within a society.[8] Goals of social welfare and public policy in general reflect the reality that different groups want different statements of "ought to be." Sometimes these goal statements are incompatible with each other, perhaps directly conflicting with each other. For example, the government right now reflects the incompatibility of goals in the area of smoking. Despite its social welfare goal of trying to educate people about the dangers of smoking so as to prevent them from taking it up or continuing it, the government also gives price supports and subsidies to the people who grow tobacco. The very political power of the latter group produces a situation in which multiple goals are operating. Given the reality of multiple and incompatible goals, a considerable amount of social welfare resources is almost automatically earmarked for prolonged tertiary-level service responses. Similarly, preoccupation with employment rates (an economic and social welfare policy concern) is vitiated to a degree by the government's concern with trying to minimize inflation by tolerating relatively high rates of unemployment and underemployment. Thus, social welfare is encouraged to provide more unemployment benefits and training programs as a way of allowing the higher-ranked goal of controlled inflation to operate. The existence of incompatible goals, then, does not suggest that goals are equal; rather, it often suggests that the social welfare goal is toned down to a service (tertiary-level) response because of the presence of a higher-ranked goal (usually tied to more powerful constituencies). Thus there often is a relationship between incompatible goals and the production of tertiary service responses in social welfare.

Types of Benefits

Within social welfare, there is a variety of types of benefits that can be distributed to people and groups. Such variety leads to choices concerning distribution of money, benefits in kind, or services, and promotion of group power and greater accessibility to relevant organizations.[9] Money can be distributed broadly, to all children or to all families in an allowance fashion, or to people below certain levels of income. The broader the population covered by cash payments, the greater the financial cost for the society, and the greater the emphasis in policy upon the quality of life in the society, now and in the future. Broad coverage may actually be a long-term investment in the social and economic well-being of the society and its members. These potential positives are offset to some degree by the cost of such broad benefit distribution. Cost, in turn, suggests differences in rate and type of taxation. These in turn suggest role adjustments between the public sector and the private economy.

Money can also be distributed in a very narrow fashion, only to those in actual or demonstrated need. If this approach is pursued, efficiency in the short run is stressed. Further, if resources are limited, this policy ensures that benefits are going to the "right" population. But it also reaffirms the utility of means test criteria and the effect of possible stigma upon the recipient groups. An extension of money is "benefit in kind," such as food stamps, housing supports, and health services. In these instances, society, through social welfare, earmarks benefits for selected problem areas that the society defines. Discretionary consumer choices are minimized, so that welfare benefits are used exclusively within designated sectors of life and the society. Such benefits can be distributed, like cash, in a narrow or broad fashion. All the previously mentioned advantages and disadvantages of the actual parameters of distribution are applicable.

Benefits also may be distributed in a less economically oriented manner, by being geared to such service areas as counseling, training, and socialization. In this type of benefit, the service is an intervening strategy to allow the person ultimately to get out of or prevent some type of situation. Again, the parameters of who receives the service may be relatively broad or narrow.

Another dimension of benefit may relate to a focus upon increasing the political power of, or opportunity structures for, certain groups. Thus a benefit might be the distribution of money, programs, staff, or technical expertise to help certain groups become organized. It has been argued that such benefits mean a greater probability that relevant organizations will become responsive to such organized groups. In a similar fashion benefits may focus upon the limited opportunity structures afforded certain groups in our society. Thus policies of affirmative action and equal opportunity were designed to help whole groups of people, that is, minorities associated with certain racial and sex characteristics. In opting for benefits along these lines, there is probably greater recognition of secondary-level prevention (rather than pure tertiary-level responses) and also of the need for compensatory policy and benefit responses.

Structures of Benefits and Services

In addition to these choice areas concerning policy and benefits, there is a choice to be made relative to the way actual programs are put together. This area of choice involves responsibility for the benefits being legitimated: Who may actually provide the benefits to people?[10] In many countries acceptance of responsibility for benefits to people or categories of people is tantamount to assuming responsibility for the actual provision of such benefits. Conceptually at least a society might choose to have responsibility for ensuring that people have a right to benefits divorced from the actual provision of such benefits. In fact in our country, medical care for the elderly population is largely provided by and through private, independent physicians, but the government assumes that it has a responsibility to assist such a population in securing health care. On the other hand, our country also has a long tradition of the government's assuming responsibility and making provision for educational services. In general, however, many benefit areas operate on a division of labor whereby government assumes some responsibility for select categories of people whose benefits are actually met by private, voluntary agencies that often receive some level of reimbursement from the government through such devices as purchase-of-services agreements. Many of the services and programs offered under Title XX of the Social Security Act fall under this arrangement—government assumes responsibility for certain populations and types of problems and then contracts with local agencies that receive government payment for delivering a program to specified people.

Intimately associated with choices in the area of responsibility for, and provision of, benefits is the choice of the locus of control of benefits. One possibility is for the national government to assume responsibility for and actually provide the benefit to people through direct dealings with the recipients and/or through local offices of the national government. On the other hand, the national government may assume responsibility for a type of benefit, leaving to local bodies the manner of delivery. In the latter case, local bodies may indicate that local government will do it, or arrange with private sector agencies to do it. Finally, government at all levels may choose not to assume responsibility, but private agencies may wish to offer a program for a type of problem or population and rely on fees and voluntary contributions in financing the programs.

As with many of the choices discussed in this book, specific choices on benefit responsibility provision have distinctive side effects. Where government assumes responsibility and provision, especially at the national level, there is the possibility that government will arrive at a type of benefit that fits all people in a uniform way without necessarily ensuring that it affects many people in a relevant fashion.

On the other hand, when responsibility for and provision of benefits are structurally distinct, especially if public responsibility is national and provision is local and voluntary, there is some reason to assume that such a system of benefits is going to be terribly difficult to manage and shape. The reason is that voluntary agencies often have constraints deriving from their own organizational policies and constituencies as well as the traditions in local areas. The use of infused public funds may be contaminated by all such factors. If this occurs there is good reason to infer possible waste of public dollars relative to professed public responsibility for certain populations and problems. Such waste, however, may be quite functional or tolerable if various interests and beliefs are reinforced, including the needs of voluntary agencies to have predictable sources of revenue, the cultural belief in having services local and private, and the role of local ethos in shaping and operationalizing the broad thrust of a national policy for some population or group.

Distribution of Benefits—Direct or Indirect

The preceding discussion almost suggests that agencies, public and/or private, operationally define what will be offered to people within society. Admittedly public policy, whether at national, state, or local levels, does set up guidelines, often very clear and rigid guidelines. However such guidelines do not necessarily assume that the benefit will be given to a person through an agency. In fact in some instances benefits have been given directly to a population that then seeks out an individual or organization who will meet its needs. The clearest example of this is health services for the elderly. However, in many other cases the benefit is given to a client group through an agency.

This form of benefit distribution is important because of implications for supply–demand mechanisms, competition, and promoting ongoing changes in agencies.[11] All things being equal, if benefits are distributed to people through professionals and organizations, there is reason to assume that such groups can disproportionately control the operationalizing of the benefit. This may be done in such a fashion that the recipient population has no alternative but to deal with a given type of agency and agency program.

On the other hand, if benefits are distributed directly to recipients, recipients could then seek out programs and services where consumer-defined criteria are most apparent, for example, hours, type of staff, location, and the like. Assuming that benefits could be distributed directly to recipients and that no serious control of the supply process by professions (as in Medicare) and organizations exists, it is conceivable that some agencies would either have to change their current program or face the possibility of declining client use of programs and services.

Choice concerning the route of benefit distribution is of course affected by many factors, not the least of which are professional groups and organizations, but also the degree of trust that society confers upon the recipient population. Suffice it to say that the more focused the means-test-oriented services are, the less likelihood that clients will be viewed as consumers who can exercise informed judgments about ways to have their needs met. The corollary is that the more universal and valued certain categories of recipients are, the more individual freedom and discretion society and the social welfare institution might afford them through benefit distribution processes.

Purposeful Coordination—Duplication of Services

In dispensing benefits directly to recipients, there is the possibility that some service providers will compete with each other.[12] This would hold true, of course, only if supplies of service providers are not artificially kept scarce. In fact, competition by service providers could be a social choice legitimated within social welfare. It could occur by introducing a widespread system of vouchers for benefits or by purposeful duplication by voluntary agencies who offer benefits to specified populations for a variety of reasons. For example, religious and racial or ethnic organizations may wish to maintain group identities and values, as well as act out a commitment that they know how to relate to their own people.

The polar opposite of this could be a planned avoidance of competition by preventing the duplication of services. This is apt to occur if service funders and providers stress the goals of coordination and maximization of fiscal efficiency in existing services and benefits.

Competition, if chosen, suggests more efficiency in services in the long run, more individual choice among service providers, and probably some fiscal inefficiency in the short run. Planned coordination strategies among services providers are apt to produce greater financial efficiency in the short run, less choice by recipients and perhaps greater social distance between providers and recipients over the long run. Coordination-oriented strategies have also been criticized as being extensions of professional and organizational interests in such a fashion that the process of identifying gaps in services and benefits is neither stressed nor structurally ensured.[13]

Holistic Services—Specialized Services

The choices in this area cover a variety of factors. At one level is the issue of service benefit itself: Should services be broad and comprehensive for all, or should they be focused in nature and delivery? A second level is the way in which the service system should be arranged: Should it be characterized by a large amount of specialists in specialized settings, or should practitioners, services, and programs be more holistic in their approach to recipients? Specialized services in social welfare are clearly the norm. Where specialized services are the norm, devices have to be initiated to link multiple specialized services to meet what are often multiple needs of clients. In social welfare the processes that are designed to produce integrated systems of service to people are planning, allocation, and the referral process. With respect to planning and allocating the question is, Should such processes be controlled by professionals or by market mechanisms related to consumer choice? (See the preceding discussion on distribution and purposeful duplication.)

With respect to referrals, severe criticisms have been leveled at the excessive use of referrals in social welfare, and two of the major ones are worth citing. As Kirk has suggested referrals almost predictably ensure that large portions of the recipient population will be denied service because they do not survive the very referral process itself.[14] Lance has characterized this as the "referral-fatigue" syndrome.[15] A second criticism comes from Blau, who suggests that specialization is appropriate if large amounts of high-level expertise and experience have to be efficiently marshalled and exploited.[16] The question before the social welfare institution is simply: Do we have such levels of knowledge and expertise? Perhaps. If we do not, continued reliance upon referrals may help ensure the absence of service rather than the provision of service. Although in a sense this is wasteful, in another sense it is cleverly cost efficient in gross terms.

On the other hand holistic and integrated service networks, which could focus on serving many people in many ways or relatively few people in many ways, run counter to the value of keeping costs down. They may also run somewhat in opposition to the means by which different helping professionals and organizations sometimes strive to meet their needs of identity and autonomy.

Role Relations Between Providers and Consumers

Much of the discussion related to areas of choice at least implicitly speaks to how professionals and clients should act. The predominant characterization of the service arena views clients as individuals receiving a professional service or program from a professional within an organizational or private practice context. In this characterization, the client is seen as a separate entity (or within a family setting) who is relatively passive (i.e., he or she gets something) and client status tends to preclude all other role possibilities. At considerable variance with this view is the position that a recipient may or may not be passive in his/her role status as client, but the recipient certainly can be active in the role status of being a consumer of service.[17] Such a view sees consumers as providing collective information about services, their utility, and relevance, and possibly in some eyes as a potentially organized group that can promote change in service delivery patterns. Within the social welfare institution those who stress the political nature of social services often advocate broadened, aggressive roles for clients, whereas those who view clients through a psychological and clinical lens often continue to stress the narrow notion of treatment for the client.

Collection and Allocation of Resources for Welfare

In one sense a society has relatively few possibilities concerning the raising of revenue for social welfare benefits and their allocation. Revenue can be collected from (1) general tax revenue, (2) earmarked taxes, (3) voluntary contributions and donations, (4) fees of some sort, and (5) some combination of the above.[18]

To rely heavily upon resources generated from general tax funds presupposes a strong commitment on the part of society and a position of strength on the part of the government in dealing with individuals and corporations. For every dollar raised in this manner, there is one less discretionary dollar left to individuals who may not perceive themselves as receiving benefits. Even if this approach to raising revenue is pursued within the society, there is no guarantee that the purpose of social welfare policy will be developmentally focused or that coverage will be extensive. In fact in our society's reliance upon public sector financing is often associated with burden and social control perspectives, and benefit coverage is relatively selective.

Earmarked taxes, such as use of sales taxes as well as Social Security among others for specific groups or problems, is another societal possibility for funding social welfare responses. The raising of revenue through these devices is usually an ad hoc response to the actual or potential collective power (political) of some constituency. In recent years our society has witnessed expansion in the relative numbers of older Americans in our society, and the combination of their numbers, their political organizing, and their position of increasing esteem has produced in many states a collection and funneling of tax dollars for benefits for the elderly. In many such states disguised selective taxes in the form of lotteries have been introduced. Social Security contributions by employers and employees are a special type of earmarked tax dollar for social welfare. But even in this case the funds are earmarked for specific categories of recipients, under special conditions.

Unlike reliance upon general tax revenues, which theoretically takes contributions from everyone, while distributing benefits to the many or to the few, earmarked taxes are doubly regressive. They tax only certain people (e.g., purchasers of cigarettes, liquor, etc., and they tax in a regressive rather than progressive fashion. Under these conditions it is usually difficult to have mass benefits widely distributed, when revenue is raised in a limited way from only a limited portion of the society. Thus, because of political realities and economic constraints, benefits funded in this fashion will often be focused and restrictive to special or exempt categories.

Voluntary contributions also suggest the possibility of specified coverage of specified populations. Benefits that are compatible with the interests and expectations of donor groups will undoubtedly take precedence over policies and programs that might jeopardize the positions of advantage of donor groups. Thus voluntarily supported benefits may have a built-in bias not to change organizational and institutional life within a community, but rather to stress "exempt" populations (children, the elderly) via tertiary level (direct service) strategies. While some have criticized the apparent relation between voluntary contributions and status quo benefit provision, others have suggested that the class and racial characteristics of donors often prevent service providers from questioning the role of such social factors in causing and reinforcing many social problems. Finally, because reliance upon voluntary contributions is likely to occur within the context of a local community agency, the existing community ethos may be taken as a given or as a constraint in designing programs.

Funding for social welfare that relies upon payment for services by clients or by third-party arrangements (e.g., insurance contracts) may suggest social class factors in service. Simply, services will tend to respond to those who can afford them, and often those who can afford them will want services of a clinical nature rather than those that stress environmental supports. Thus it is no accident that private therapy is often assumed to be a middle-class service.

The last possibility of funding of benefits is a combined strategy using two or more of the above methods. Basically public tax dollars, either general or earmarked, are put with contributed and/or fee connected revenue patterns. Often such a strategy is employed in voluntary local agencies or in quasi-public local agencies, for example, community mental health centers. In addition to the difficulty of convincing some clients that these are public agencies to which they are entitled to go, there is the increased possibility that some clients will be handled and processed in different ways from other clients. Fees have often been associated with relating services and programs to properly motivated people and preventing inefficient, capricious use of scarce resources for frivolous reasons. On the other hand, excessive concern with these objectives may disguise the fact that many clients may not come forward for needed services simply because of possible biases and stigma associated with the presentation, context, and process of service distribution.

Just as resources may be collected in a variety of ways, so resources, especially those in the public sector, may be distributed in a variety of ways. On the most liberal end of the continuum government may turn over lump sums of money to local bodies to do with as they wish—whether in welfare areas or elsewhere. Basically, the Nixon strategy of a "new federalism" through revenue-sharing strategies dispensed public money in this fashion with few strings or specific purposes defined. Hence social welfare benefits were not priority items for many communities, and social welfare was not stressed. Even where this was not the case, social welfare responses often were affected by community attitudes and prevailing racial and class perspectives concerning the parameters of services.

Funders may also dispense a certain amount of money by block grants for certain populations and/or types of benefits. Thus the government may allocate to states and counties money for area offices on aging, to help the expansion of services to the elderly. Some discretion is afforded to local service providers concerning the specifics of programming and services.

Finally, funding may be distributed to a unit of service, usually specified, being provided. An agency or program would usually enter into a contract with a public funder for certain amounts of money, provided that certain amounts of service units are given in a specified manner to a specified population. In this situation, additional provision of service by the agency may not necessitate reimbursement by the funder. This pattern of funding has the most control built into it in the sense that every dollar can be accounted for. However, preoccupation with accounting definitions of efficiency may produce biases in the types of clients selected by agencies for service, which ones are referred (and maybe lost), and how long clients may stay in the position of receiving services. Suffice it to say that emphasis upon purchase of service arrangements may be most likely during times of social concern with reducing public expenditures and thwarting inappropriate use of tax dollars.

Evaluation

Choices within social welfare concerning evaluation basically involve the purposes of evaluation, type of evaluation, and key audiences.[19] Two polar extremes and points between are suggested: (1) evaluation that is tied to a planning model and (2) evaluation that is a disjointed monitoring process. Relative to purpose, one type of evaluation could be geared to whether benefits achieve the objectives that they were designed to meet. Purpose in this sense presupposes clarity in the objectives to be pursued and an ongoing interest in ascertaining whether strategies are useful or not. This purpose of evaluation is obviously the one most associated with the planning process and is deemed useful as a technology that can refine the systemic problem–policy–program process over time. Within this broad purpose, benefits/programs can be categorized as pilot, model, prototype, and institutionalized. Such categorization is ideally influenced by the nature of objectives pursued. Objectives may range from collecting information all the way to measuring specific, desired outcomes. If the former is pursued, case studies and collection of survey information is applicable; if the latter, effect studies using some type of experimental design become applicable. In this approach to evaluation key audiences can include policy makers, program implementators, and even recipients.

Once elements that are more political in nature become apparent in the policy–program process, disjointed evaluation procedures may be produced. For example, greater stress may be given to attempts to show that financial excesses are not present. Thus evaluation may become more geared to whether certain benefits are being distributed, not whether they are effective or not. Accounting and auditing criteria might take precedence over level or performance and impact. In benefit areas where evaluation is tied to a narrow concept of financing, it is conceivable that objectives may be vague or specific only in the sense of minimizing financial wastage. It is clear that the evaluation that is heavily influenced by this type of purpose does not systemically offer very much to ongoing performance adjustments in the program–benefit area, as such benefits may be institutionalized very quickly if they are shown to be functional to certain audiences and are not riddled with excessive amounts of financial waste. What adjustments occur, whether in the direction of conserving or liberalizing, are more apt to come from political phenomena and pressure outside the evaluation process.

One should not conclude from this discussion that politics is present only in the latter type of evaluation. Politics is present at the stage of goal setting and formulating objectives for all policy products. All we are saying is that disjointed evaluation of a certain type (accounting oriented) is most apt to occur when there is little commitment to specificity in objectives that will be examined in terms of impact upon recipients.

Functions, Methods, Roles

In social welfare programs choices can be made relative to functions, methods, and roles.[20] Functions stem from objectives and relate to discrete outcomes. Obviously, if objectives are very vague, immediate problems and options present themselves. Methods have to do with the way different resources may be put together to achieve certain functions. Roles are often defined as the activities associated with one's professional training. One unimaginative way of looking at the three is to fuse them together. Thus, if a function of a program is to provide more therapeutic services to children, it is possible to conceive that therapy means the method of psychiatry being dispensed by psychiatrists. Obviously this example is extreme, but not that extreme. More important is to note the possibility that professionals may have a vested interest in working from their "turf" base in operationalizing methods relative to function.

When a high degree of fusion exists among functions, methods, and roles, typically less creative use of actual and potential resources in programming may occur and the cost of programs, because they are tied to professional roles, may be considerably higher. Needless to say, certain professions that have been institutionalized and legitimated within our society probably will have a vested interest in not making greater distinctions among the three discussed items as they occur in actual programs. This of course becomes compounded when benefits are distributed through professionals and organizational settings rather than to clients or recipients directly.

124

TABLE 8.1.

IDEAL TYPE I: PRIMACY SOCIAL WELFARE	IDEAL TYPE II: DEPENDENT SOCIAL WELFARE
Universal or broad coverage, with perhaps emphasis upon populations at risk	Narrow, selective coverage
Primary and secondary levels of policy being important	Focus people who have problems
More appreciation of equality	Tertiary-level benefits
Reliance upon the public sector for responsibility for people	More appreciation of adequacy
	Continued reliance upon the private and local care-giving organizations
Use of public and general tax dollars	Use of fees and donations, as well as special tax dollars
Goals equal to other goals within the society	Goals dependent upon other goals in society; tertiary response heightened
Benefits/programs comprehensive—cash, in kind, service, collective power	Benefits/programs—cash and "in kind," usually means-test-based, service, often tied to professional judgment or diagnosis
Benefits to individual and to individual through organization	Benefits often through an organization
Concern for gaps in service, unmet needs	Stress upon coordination—avoidance of duplication
Evaluation more geared to impact of program upon clients and client satisfaction	Evaluation often tied to auditing and use of financial resources; effort oriented
Greater equality between consumers and providers; expanded roles for clients	Client more dependent upon service providers; limited role options for clients

Summary

In this chapter we have examined several interrelated choices that can and do occur within welfare in action. Some of the choice areas are so tied together that exercising a particular option in one choice area heavily determines choices in other areas. If we relate the choice areas we have discussed to the concepts of a primacy social welfare institution and a dependent social welfare institution, we see the ideal types of policy and program illustrated in Table 8-1.

In the context of these ideal types, certain choice areas seem to be potential targets for planned reform by social workers. That is, social workers could have a significant impact upon how options are decided and operationalized in the areas of benefit distribution; coordination–gap–identification strategies; role relations between consumers and providers; imaginative use of resources in the orchestration of function, method, and roles; design and use of evaluation processes; and creation of holistic or at least better integrated services. Focused, planned activity related to normative expectations of social workers within these areas may very well be the appropriate agenda for social work geared to realistic social change strategies.

Notes

1. An interesting article that focuses upon the effects of broad versus focused population coverage is George Hoshino, "Britain's Debate on Universal or Selective Social Services: Lessons for America," *Social Service Review*, 43 (September 1969), 249; also Richard Titmuss, *Commitment to Welfare* (New York: Pantheon, 1968), pp. 113–123.

2. Alfred J. Kahn, *Social Policy and Social Services* (New York: Random House, 1973), pp. 93–94. See also S. M. Miller and Pamela Roby, *The Future of Inequality* (New York: Basic Books, 1970).

3. Neil Gilbert and Harry Specht, *Dimensions of Social Welfare Policy* (Englewood Cliffs, N.J.: Prentice-Hall, 1974), pp. 40–41.

4. Richard Titmuss, "Equity, Adequacy, and Innovation in Social Security," *International Social Security Review*, 2 (1970), 250-267.

5. Gilbert and Specht, *op. cit.*, p. 40; Richard Titmuss, "The Role of Redistribution in Social Policy," *Social Security Bulletin*, 23 (June 1965), 1-7.

6. For an excellent discussion of levels of prevention, see Alfred J. Kahn, *Planning Community Services for Children in Trouble* (New York: Columbia University Press, 1963), chap. 2.

7. Kai T. Erikson, "Notes on the Sociology of Deviance," in Earl Rubington and Martin S. Weinberg, *Deviance* (New York: Macmillan, 1973), pp. 26-30.

8. Martin Rein, *Social Policy: Issues of Choice and Change* (New York: Random House, 1970), pp. 126-128, 249-270.

9. For excellent discussion of benefit options, see Gilbert and Specht, *op. cit.*, pp. 81-106; see Alva Myrdal, *Nation and Family* (Cambridge, Mass.: M.I.T. Press, 1968), pp. 141-151, for benefits in kind; Milton Friedman, "The Role of Government in a Free Society," in Edmund Phelps, ed., *Private Wants and Public Needs* (New York: Norton, 1962), pp. 104-117; Alice Rivlin *Systematic Thinking for Social Action* (Washington, D.C.: Brookings Institution, 1971); Shirley Buttrick "On Choice and Services," *Social Service Review,*44 (December 1970), 427-433, for a spectrum of thought concerning benefit types and individual consumer choice.

10. Gilbert and Specht, *op. cit.*, esp. pp. 107-126.

11. Thomas M. Meenaghan and Michael Mascari, "Consumer Choice, Consumer Control in Service Delivery," *Social Work*, 10 (October 1971), 50-57; Anthony Pascal, "New Departures in Social Services," in *Social Welfare Forum* (New York: Columbia University, 1969), pp. 75-85.

12. Nelson Reid, "Reforming the Service Monopoly," *Social Work*, 17 (November 1972), 44-54; Gilbert and Specht, *op. cit.*, p. 125; Martin Landau, "Redundancy, Rationality, and the Problem of Duplication and Overlap," *Public Administration Review*, 29 (July 1969), 346-358.

13. Reid, *op. cit.*, pp. 44-54.

14. Stuart A. Kirk and James R. Greenby, "Denying or Delivering Services?," *Social Work*, 19 (July 1974), 439-447.

15. James E. Lantz, "Referral-Fatigue Therapy," *Social Work*, 21 (May 1976), 239-241.

16. Reid, *op. cit.*, pp. 51-54.

17. Thomas M. Meenaghan, "Role Changes for the Parents of the Mentally Retarded," *Journal of Mental Retardation*, 12 (June 1974), 48–49.

18. Martin Mogulof, "Future Funding of Social Services," *Social Work*, 19 (September 1974), 607–613; K. Wedel, "Contracting for Public Assistance Social Services," *Public Welfare*, 32 (1974), 57–64.

19. See Edward Suchman, *Evaluative Research* (New York: Russell Sage Foundation, 1967); Carole H. Weiss, *Evaluation Research* (Englewood Cliffs, N.J.: Prentice-Hall, 1972); Robert O. Washington, *Program Evaluation in the Human Services* (Milwaukee: Center for Advanced Studies in Human Services, University of Wisconsin), Monograph no. 1, n.d.

20. Ray Bard, Michael L. Lauderdale, and James Peterson, *Planning for Change* (Washington, D.C.: Education, Training, and Research Sciences, 1971), pp. 29–30.

Chapter 9

A Framework for Studying Social Welfare Products

IN THE PRECEDING CHAPTERS, we have examined the role of social choice in affecting social welfare responses. Choices occur at two levels. In Chapter 8, we discussed choices at a lower level concerning specific issues in social welfare responses. At the higher level they concern what type of caring responses a society will have, the manner in which care is institutionalized, the appropriate purposes of social welfare policy, and the manner in which social problems are recognized and defined. In discussing choices at this level the possible role of interests affecting cultural values was raised. Both interest and culture in turn appear to affect the selective use of social science constructs.

In this brief chapter, we synthesize the items of choice relative to both levels. Development of an integrated scheme of analysis will serve as a bridge to our discussion of selected social welfare products in the four subsequent chapters.

Analyzing Social Welfare Products

In light of the material presented in this book, we would like to integrate the topics related to social welfare choices in such a way that the discrete items may be fused within an analytical process. Ideally, this process could then serve as the basis for personal and professional prescriptive alternatives.

In moving into the process of developing an integrated scheme for social welfare analysis, we are assuming that the policy–benefit levels are the loci of initial description and study. Sequentially, this could lead to an exploration of implicit and/or explicit problem definition(s) associated with the welfare product. Analysis of problem definition formulations in turn could occur in terms of degree of inclusiveness of the problem statement and the use and influence of dominant social science constructs. Finally, inferences could be made concerning possible relations among dominant cultural items and interest perspective in triggering problem–policy–benefit responses.

Schematically, the general process we are suggesting can be presented as in Figure 9-1.

Expanding on the above diagram, we would suggest that description and analysis of policy and benefits might proceed in the following manner:

WHAT IS THE SOCIAL WELFARE PRODUCT?

This first step would require the analyst to *describe the social welfare product* and to *seek its source*. Possible sources could include legislative, administrative or executive, and judicial decisions. Attention should be given to *those who are covered, with what benefits,* and *for what purposes.* In searching out the policy, *identification of key actors* and *groups* in the development of the product should occur as should specification of *precipitating events* and *situations* that may have contributed to the development of the social welfare product.

Once these background factors are ascertained, *funding and allocation* characteristics should be explored. Essentially you are asking, How are resources collected to meet the manifest purposes of the social welfare product? Generally you are looking at the degree to which taxes are used, what types of taxes are levied, and what level of government (federal, state, or local) collects the taxes. There would also be an examination of

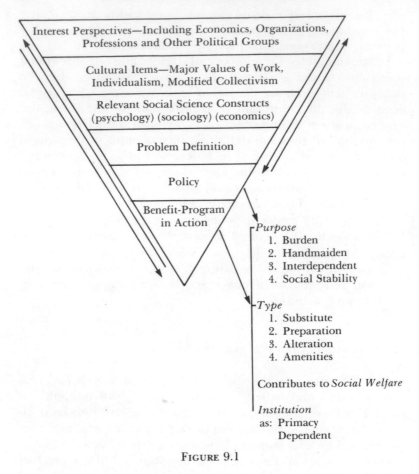

FIGURE 9.1

whether fees, donations, and other revenue-collecting devices are utilized. In describing how resources are collected, attention is given to specifying how resources are allocated for implementation. Possibilities would include grants, which may or may not be earmarked, service contracts, and payments (cash and in-kind) to individuals.

In the examination of the product, attempts should be made to identify the *type and level of prevention* that appears to be stressed. Does the product seem to speak to conditions in the society, to the way in which organizations function, or to individual effects of problems. In a related fashion, the social welfare product ought to be assessed in terms of its *general thrust:* Does it speak to equality and redistribution, or does it seem to relate to fairness of treatment to people, or does it speak to bringing people up to some level of adequacy according to some minimum set of standards?

Finally, the analyst would like to understand how the policy in question may or may not *relate to other policies in the society.* These policies could include those within social welfare as well as public policy in general.

IMPLEMENTATION: LOOKING AT BENEFIT MEETING PEOPLE

Once the basic social welfare product is understood, the second major activity for the analyst is the assessment of how the benefits are implemented. In light of the type of benefit, you would identify the *structure of the benefit.* This would involve asking who provides the benefit: is it the government and which level(s) of government. You would also identify the role, if any, afforded to local private organizations. Special attention should be given to delineating the elements of centralization and decentralization in the relationship between the federal government and local areas.

Very related to the issue of structure is the issue of the *method of benefit distribution—How do people actually get the benefit?* This issue seeks to explore the degree to which there is reliance upon organizations and professionals in dispensing benefits. In this regard you would also examine the *degree of autonomy and freedom afforded clients when they receive the benefit*—Is there consumer choice in using the benefit and how much?

You would also like to know to *what degree the benefit(s) under analysis works in concert with or presupposes the existence of other benefits.* Finally, the analyst would like to ascertain *the degree to which the benefit works*—the degree to which the purposes behind the benefit are met. This would require the analyst to identify and critique the evaluation activities associated with the benefit being distributed over time.

UNDERSTANDING THE PROBLEM PERCEPTION BEHIND
THE SOCIAL WELFARE PRODUCT

This stage of analysis would ask the analyst to examine which *social science constructs seem to be implicit and/or explicit in the policy and benefit product.* Essentially, there should be an attempt to understand the *level of analysis that is stressed*—individual group, organizations, institutions—as well as the *specific social science concepts that are stressed.* They could include personality characteristics, skills, training, norms, values, socially induced stress, opportunity structures, conditions of relationship in the marketplace, ownership, and distribution patterns. If this occurs, *inference concerning prevailing causal explanations* behind problem–policy–benefit responses might be possible.

ASSESSING THE POSSIBLE ROLE OF CULTURAL AND
INTEREST ITEMS

The role of the three major cultural–interest items—work, individualism, and modified collectivism—is examined relative to the problem–policy–benefit. Generally this stage looks at the degree to which individual responsibility is stressed, the relation between help and work, the categories of people who are helped, the ongoing role for the private economy, and the relationship between government and the private economy. This section would also include exploration of how the cultural items may relate to the interests of economic, political, and professional groups.

Summary

In this chapter we have attempted to put into a format several of the major topics discussed in previous chapters. The format assumes that a significant amount of description of social welfare products must precede critical analysis. In moving from description to analysis, the analyst considers the possible options related to lower-level choices in social welfare (Chapter 8), the possible purposes of social welfare products (Chapter 2), and the actual utilization of social science constructs shaping the problem–policy–benefit program response (Chapters 3–5). Such considerations can help delineate the respective roles of culture and interests in shaping the structure and application of welfare responses (Chapters 1, 6, and 7). The next four chapters will utilize this format in four case studies.

Chapter 10

The Social Security Act: Social Insurance and Public Assistance

THE SOCIAL SECURITY ACT is the cornerstone on which the American notion of the welfare state is built and largely operationalized. This act is a major attempt to achieve a condition of income security for millions of Americans. It should not be construed that it is the only product of the welfare state that speaks or could speak to income security. Certainly, tax exemptions to certain groups, for example, the blind and government activity in manpower training and public employment (see Chapter 11), are additional approaches that speak to income security.[1] In this chapter we will focus on the cash benefits as well as medical in-kind benefits emanating from the Social Security Act.

Background

Given the values and interests discussed in earlier chapters, the role of the federal government in social welfare through the first part of the twentieth century was quite minimal and restricted to certain populations and problems. The dominant culture–interest arrangement heavily structured social welfare in the direction of private–local charity. This did not mean that government did nothing in the area of welfare, but it does suggest that what occurred was often not at the federal level, nor was it comprehensive at any level of government.[2] Certainly, it did not suggest a major role for the federal government in promoting income security.

At the state level some states in the early twentieth century had pensions for widows and dependent children and the aged.[3] Some states had policies and programs for workman's compensation and disability. Many local communities had limited public assistance systems. The point here, however, was that there was no system of welfare covering relatively broad categories of need.

At the federal level the absence of a public system of broad benefits and services was even more apparent. The federal government limited its constitutional requirement to "promote the general welfare" to relatively few people. It offered services, though of a questionable nature, to Indians through the Bureau of Indian Affairs from the late eighteenth century. The federal government also entered welfare areas with a monitoring concern for immigrants and federal prisoners. Although this involvement was of a questionable welfare nature, one population the federal government did serve more positively was the serviceman and veteran, largely through its public health system. These were groups for whom government felt an obligation, and as such they fell into a special category.[4]

A second category to which the federal government spoke involved another special or exempt category—children. Starting as early as 1909, there were White House conferences on children. Specific recommendations from these conferences covered such areas as state licensing of foster homes and state pensions for widows and mothers with children. But even relative to children the federal government clearly recognized that this group's needs should be met within a state and local area service arena involving state government and voluntary local child welfare agencies.[5]

The federal government became more involved and more aggressive with the onset of the nation's financial difficulties in the late 1920s. It should not be assumed that the federal government willingly moved into a position of responsibility. On the contrary, it did so grudgingly and only after it was clearly demonstrated that local agencies, both public and private, and state government could not address the problems created by the Great Depression.[6]

Upon taking office in 1932 Franklin D. Roosevelt introduced several key acts that delineated the evolving role of the federal government in the area of income security: (1) the Federal Emergency Relief Administration (FERA); (2) the Work Relief Project, which had several components, the most famous being the Works Progress Administration (WPA) and the Work Programs for Unemployed Youth; (3) the Wagner Act; and (4) the Social Security Act.

The first act, FERA, introduced the concept of federal responsibility in the period of economic crisis and was clearly predicated on the premise that individuals could not control their unemployment and derived economic need. The Work Relief Project emanated from the federal government's decision to create public jobs and job activities as a means of promoting economic security. The Wagner Act was the forerunner of labor's being able to organize and negotiate salaries and benefits within the private economy. These pieces of legislation formed the basis of the government's and the economy's respective development of a role in granting income security in America.

What Is the Social Security Act?

As the Depression continued through the 1930s, the Roosevelt administration began to recognize the need for a permanent program of security.[7] Previous legislation and policy were clearly temporary. It was felt that a program of security involving the federal government and the free-enterprise system was needed to meet certain predictable and probable risks of life in our society. Most especially, the risks were those of death, advanced age, and unemployment. In 1935 a bill was introduced that came to be known as the Social Security Act. This act was the culmination of the evolving role of government in society.

The initial act, though modified over the years, was comprised of three major units: a social insurance section, a section covering public categorical assistance, and a section relating to maternal and child health. These components of insurance, assistance, and services still characterize the structure of the act.

SOCIAL INSURANCE

This component is clearly tied to the notion that certain untoward situations are predictable and patterned in our society and that steps have to be taken to minimize the adverse effects of such situations.[8] One specific step is literally to force certain employees and employers to have some of their income taxed to meet and handle some of the effects. The Social Security Act in the 1930s specified that old age and survivorship (this term first meant widows and dependent children) were conditions with which most people had to be helped. In addition to initial coverage for old age and survivorship (actually in 1939), an unemployment insurance system was instituted. This provided for time-limited payments to workers who had worked specified amounts of time in designated occupational settings.

Although a disability insurance benefit was instituted in 1956, a major addition to the insurance component occurred in 1965. In that year Health Insurance for the Aged (Title XVIII) was incorporated into law. Marmor has written of the various attempts from Truman through the 1960s to establish a national health insurance system.[9] All such attempts failed, and by the 1960s it was decided to fuse the benefit of health care especially to the category of the aged. This incremental strategy of the Democratic Party clearly spoke to the interests of a growing segment of the society. As a result, under the social insurance section of Social Security medical benefits to the elderly were to be provided under two sections. Part A provides benefits in hospitals, extended care facilities, and certain types of home services. Part B provides additional services which are of an in-patient and out-patient nature. In both parts, deductibles and co-payments are present.

CATEGORICAL PUBLIC ASSISTANCE (WELFARE)

The original Social Security Act also had provisions for those who were currently in positions of financial need.[10] However the federal government did not initially assume responsibility for all of those who might be in such need. Rather it limited aid to specified categories, that is, to those who had special status as viewed through the value interest of work. Again those in financial need who were elderly, had dependent children, or were blind were the first ones included within the Social Security Act. All the categories were special in the sense that they probably either had worked (the aged) or were too young or were incapable of working and thus exempt from work.

The federal government did not offer any financial need to those needy people who did not fit any of the initial categories just cited. Assistance to these types of people was left exclusively to state and/or local authorities.

Over the years several key changes have occurred relative to the assistance program. In 1950 the federal government indicated that people who were disabled were entitled to categorical public assistance (Title XIV). In 1961, Aid to Dependent Children (ADC) was changed to Aid to Families with Dependent Children (AFDC). Subsequently this component of categorical public assistance was broadened from aiding families in which one parent was incapacitated, dead, or absent from the home to include aid to dependent children of unemployed parents (AFDC-UP).

In 1962 the federal government provided a disproportionate amount of dollars to states to train caseworkers and to provide social services to those in need as a functional route for their escape from financial need. The federal government agreed to put up 75 percent of the cost, with states carrying the remaining portion.

In 1965 the law that authorized health care of the elderly via the support of the federal government also had a provision of medical care for the needy of all ages (Medicaid, Title XIX, 1965). Needy refers to those who are eligible for public assis-

tance, as well as to those who are too poor to purchase needed medical service.

In 1967, the government amended the AFDC program.[11] The amendments sought to encourage the movement of some welfare recipients back into the labor force and for them to assume positions of economic independence. Day care centers were authorized so that work and job-training experiences might become more usable options. Refusal to pursue offers of training or work could result in termination of public assistance. Also, incentives to individuals in the guise of having certain portions of earned income exempt from eligibility determination were introduced. This incentive program, stressing work and/or job training, was referred to as the Work Incentive Program (WIN) by many legislators and public officials. Others, especially critics and some recipients referred to it as WIP.

In addition to emphasizing work and job training, the 1967 amendments heavily stressed the role of social services. So important were the social services considered that these amendments indicated that local welfare departments could purchase such services from private agencies when such services were part of a plan for dealing with a person or family.

Two fairly progressive features were present in the amendments concerning social services. First, the types of services covered by the amendments were relatively broad, including counseling, testing, and job-training supports. Second, the definition of population to be covered in purchase of service included not only the current welfare recipient, but also potential and former recipients. This broad definition of population in part related to early intervention and prevention that will be discussed later in the chapter.

In January 1974 the federal government replaced the programs of old age assistance, aid to the blind, and aid to the disabled with the concept of a national floor of income support—in a sense a guaranteed level of income, for three populations (SSI). It also recognized that millions of people in America do not have adequate income from private pensions, Social Security benefits, and other sources. Finally, it introduced on a nationwide basis a flat cash payment approach rather than individual budgets that were used in some states and communities. Aid was to be given with discretionary decision making left to the recipient.

SERVICES GRANTS TO STATES FOR SERVICES: TITLE XX, 1975

In many respects the period of 1935–1962 was characterized by an emphasis upon provision of money to select populations and categories. From 1962 to the present there was a great expansion of public dollars for income security and increasing emphasis upon the use of social services. Title XX in a sense is a culmination of the institutionalizing of social services within a public welfare context. Basically Title XX is a federal law that revises previous service provisions to establish a consolidated program of federal financial assistance to encourage the provision of services by states.[12]

Through Title XX the federal government directs that services within local areas must be focused upon the following five broad goals:

1. Achieving or maintaining economic self-support to prevent, reduce, or eliminate dependency.
2. Achieving or maintaining self-sufficiency, including reduction or prevention of dependency.
3. Preventing or remedying neglect, abuse, or exploitation of children and adults unable to protect their own interests, or preserving, rehabilitating, or reuniting families.
4. Preventing or reducing inappropriate institutional care by providing for community-based care, home-based care, or other forms of less intensive care.
5. Securing referral or admission for institutional care when other forms of care are not appropriate or providing services to individuals in institutions.[13]

KEY FACTORS AND SITUATIONS—SOCIAL POLITICAL CONTEXT

Having described the content of the Social Security Act in terms of social insurance, categorical assistance, and social services, it would be useful to specify key actors and events that have helped forge the evolving nature of the act.

First perhaps was the role of Franklin D. Roosevelt in the context of a Depression. As president, he introduced several new dimensions to the federal government. He set a new tone of a more aggressive national government in the society; he legitimated in a variety of ways the notion of federal (collective) responsibility for some of the predictable patterned risks of industrial society; and he operationalized this notion of public responsibility very much in the context of the emerging political power of the old (northern European), urban ethnics and the continued existence of an essentially industrialist–capitalist economic order. In large part, the Depression came to be perceived as a massive unemployment problem, affecting work-motivated ethnics in a way that was beyond their control and their individual solution. What Roosevelt developed in policy response under the term "New Deal" was predicated on limited structural change of the economy and a greater role for government to serve as a support to the predictable problems associated with an industrial, free-enterprise system.[14]

In his first term, Roosevelt leaned toward a solution to the economic crisis that emphasized a planned economy and the role of American business and corporate leaders. This approach did not work. On the one hand, business became increasingly dissatisfied with Roosevelt and government. On the other hand, groups and key leaders in the society were pushing for more leftist-oriented strategies. People like Long and Townsend with their guaranteed income proposals offered serious and attractive solutions that could have undermined Roosevelt's sources of support, that is, the urban coalition of ethnics within the Democratic Party. The upshot of business dissatisfaction and the presence of leftist solutions led Roosevelt to move in the mid-1930s toward an increasing leftist position, but one that also led him away from governmental planning and more toward the direction of having government provide support for the free-market system. Thus Roosevelt introduced the notion of government as a necessary support system for the risks associated with an industrialized free-market system.

The next major period of reform was the period of the mid-

1960s. The Kennedy–Johnson years were largely characterized by social awareness and the need for more liberal social reforms. Given the social climate of these years, plus the increasing perception of poverty due to the writings of such people as Harrington and Kyserling and the aggressive posture of Wilbur Cohen, major additions to the Social Security Act occurred.[15] There were the social service amendments of 1962 and 1967, for example, and the introduction of Medicare and Medicaid in 1965.

Various attempts to establish a national health insurance system from the Truman administration through the 1960s had failed. By the 1960s a coalition of liberals involving legislators, labor, and professional groups such as the National Association of Social Workers (NASW) decided to promote the benefit of health care to the category of the aged. This incremental strategy, basically within the Democratic Party, clearly related to the group interests of a growing segment of the society—the elderly. As a result, the social insurance component of Social Security was modified to include medical support with a strong focus upon the aged. The same coalition was instrumental in securing passage of Medicaid—a program of medical assistance to low-income and medically indigent populations. This component, however, was influenced by the characteristics of significant state involvement and statewide participation in definitions of need and benefits.

Some of the groups that were significant in the development of health benefits were also involved in the development of SSI of 1974. However these groups were active within a different social and political context—namely, the Nixon period. Although conservative, Nixon had embraced the notion of more federalization of welfare and had accepted Moynihan's proposal of judicious welfare reform and a federal guaranteed income. Thus, liberal and conservative coalitions, in concert with the political realities of an apparent need to do something to promote and maintain the economic security of the elderly, joined forces to have the federal government provide floor levels of support for the aged as well as the blind and disabled.[16]

Strangely enough it was also the Nixon and Ford administrations that contributed the movement that led to the Grant to

States for Services—Title XX—in 1975.[17] To understand the development of Title XX at least three factors should be kept in mind: (1) the growing movement of adding social services to financial aid for many people, (2) the purchase of service arrangements developed in the 1960s, and (3) the crucial role of a sitting conservative president in the midst of blossoming public welfare expenditures.

The Nixon administration as early as 1969 declared that public welfare was in a state of chaos. First, expenditures for social services were accelerating rapidly. Second, the services already in existence were not only disorganized but were marred by considerable overlap and lack of integration. Third, the accountability structures relative to social service expenditures were weak and in some cases nonexistent. Thus part of the background to Title XX is a concern for welfare reform that had a large concern with fiscal management. In addition to a commitment to developing better fiscal controls within welfare, the Republican administration also had a commitment to a "new federalism" wherein states had major roles in defining needs and spending money. Given the interplay of fiscal concerns and a major role for states, a beginning strategy was developed by the federal government. In very abbreviated form this strategy indicated that emphasis should be upon goals ideally leading to self care and self support. Goal Oriented Social Services (GOSS) was introduced in 1971, along with a social service auditing system. Essentially, caseworkers had to show barriers that clients faced relative to goals and how the social service plan would address them. In 1972 states were required to "submit a program budget for social services backed by a separate accounting system . . . so that . . . basic program information concerning types of services rendered, costs of particular services compared to number of types of recipients" could be developed.[18] In short, the elements of goal setting, planning on case and state levels, and accountability structures were coming into existence.

In 1973 the federal administration pushed for equating social services with self-support services. In addition to this the administration recommended that the eligibility for "former" clients and "potential" clients of social services in public welfare be reduced to three months and six months, respectively. These recommendations produced many negative reactions, which in turn led to coalitions that worked for compromises.[19] These included NASW, labor, social service organizations, and the national governors' conference. The compromises subsequently produced Title XX, which was signed into law on January 1, 1975.

FUNDING AND ALLOCATION

The Social Security Act and its amendments utilize a variety of ways by which to collect and allocate resources for its major components of insurance, public welfare, and social services. The old age, survivors, disability, and health insurance component has basically relied upon special matched contribution of employers and employees that are collected in the work setting. The unemployment insurance program is financed by taxes from employers. The Medicare component is funded by contributions from employers and employees, general tax revenue, as well as deductibles.

The public welfare component, including Medicaid, relies for its funding upon general tax dollars. States define whom they will serve and with what levels of support, and the federal government allocates the locally defined standard of support via earmarked allocation.[20] Support comes from revenue collected from general taxes, not from revenue associated with contributions from employers and employees.

Social services are similarly tied to general tax sources, with the federal government generally supplying 75 percent of what each state spends on services directed by states to the five federally defined goals of Title XX. Purchase of service arrangements are permissible and thus allow local organizations to provide the services.

Finally, the federal government relies on general tax revenue to raise money for the SSI benefits. This money is distributed by the federal government to qualified individuals in the appropriate categories.

PREVENTION AND INTERVENTION

Because the Social Security program speaks in many ways to many different segments of the population, different types of prevention may be detected. Prevention in the true sense of the term is certainly indentifiable in the insurance component of the act and in certain portions of Title XX. The insurance component presupposes that need will occur if certain situations beyond individual control present themselves, for example, advanced age, premature death of major wage earner, and unemployment. Thus the system attempts to plan for these possibilities through the working years of individuals. Certainly, Title XX speaks to social services that in part are designed to maintain peple's ability to be self-supporting and to prevent income dependency. Similarly, Title XX attempts to prevent inappropriate institutional care and abuse of certain groups. In fact it funds services that are expressly designed to prevent serious need from occurring. Title XX also stresses more tertiary-level prevention via services to people who are already in serious need of support and help.

SSI and AFDC provide income benefits to people who are currently in positions of financial need. Although both basically relate to tertiary-level responses, both also incorporate some elements of more basic prevention. SSI benefits are based upon the societal recognition of the fact that millions of people in America do not have the ability to have adequate income from such sources as private pensions, Social Security benefits, or other sources. Thus, although the given recipient has to be in need before the benefit is distributed, the SSI package is designed to help meet the predictable financial needs of types of people. Even AFDC reflects some appreciation of prevention by giving payments for children so as to encourage the development of children in such a way that current needs are met and the likelihood of future need is prevented or reduced.

GENERAL THRUST

Basically the Social Security Act stresses the concept of adequacy or floor levels of income being achieved for many individuals within certain categories. What redistribution occurs essentially is only as a by-product of attempts designed to secure a minimum standard of security. In a certain sense the thrust of the Social Security Act is to supplement the benefits derived from the free-enterprise system or, in some cases, to provide

TABLE 10-1.   **Distribution Patterns of Income**

| | PERCENTAGE OF HOUSEHOLDS BELOW STANDARD | | | |
INCOME STANDARD	1955	1965	1970	1975
$ 3,000	12.6%	7.4%	5.3%	4.5%
5,000	22.9	15.6	12.0	12.0
7,000	35.7	24.7	19.5	20.3
10,000	58.3	39.8	32.5	33.1
12,000	13.1	50.8	42.1	42.0
15,000	84.3	66.8	56.9	55.4
25,000	97.2	91.8	87.4	85.7
Median income	$8,841.00	$11,876.00	$13,676.00	$13,719.00
Fuchs point	4,440.00	5,933.00	6,838.00	6,859.00
Percentage below Fuchs point	19.0%	20.0%	19.2%	20.3%

Source: Adapted from U.S. Department of Commerce, Bureau of the Census, *Current Population Reports: Consumer Income,* Series P-60 (Washington, D.C.: U.S. Government Printing Office, 1976).

income support for those people who clearly are not adequately served or protected by the economic system. Thus during the last quarter century, the period of massive expansion of government involvement in social welfare, the number of Americans who have had their absolute income levels raised has grown tremendously. However, change in relative distribution of income has not been marked. The former point speaks to absolute poverty conceptions, that is, poverty as below a fixed dollar standard, whereas the latter speaks to relative poverty, that is, poverty as any thing under one-half of the median income in the United States (referred to as the Fuchs point). Absolute poverty in turn relates to adequacy perspectives, whereas relative poverty has implications for equality perspectives.

Table 10-1 presents a summary of income distribution for the period that reflected the growth of government activity in the area of income supports.

Implementation—Benefits to People

Social Security is a complex structure that distributes different benefits to different segments of society. The social insurance component is essentially public and national. It distributes cash benefits directly to covered populations. After application for benefits is approved, basically through a local Social Security office, subsequent cash benefits are mailed directly to recipients. The medical insurance component is a little more complex in the sense that, once the prescribed age requirement is met, the federal government issues a card to the recipient who in turn can use that card for securing appropriate health services in local areas. Medical care vendors then bill the government for reimbursement.

Unemployment benefits are related to a federal–state structure that is supervised by the U.S. Department of Labor. Once proof of employment disruption and the required length of prior employment is shown, benefits are distributed directly to recipients. Recipients are required to be looking for new employment during the period of time-limited benefits.

SSI benefits also emanate from the federal government to recipients. SSI benefits may work in concert with state and local public welfare cash benefits in cases where local standards of income requirements exceed federal SSI payments.

The public welfare component of AFDC is public but presupposes a major role for state–local government. States and local areas define the eligibility requirements and what level of cash benefit is appropriate relative to need, and the federal government earmarks funds to the lower government level. Thus local political and financial realities affect the structuring and distribution of benefits. Medicaid is structured in the same manner— that is, the states basically determine the amount of payment for services.

Relative to Title XX, states have the right to define and plan the specifics of which services they will offer relative to the five federally defined goals. In operationalizing the specific services, the states must offer at least one service geared to each of the goals, provide at least three services to the SSI population, and use at least 50 percent of the federal money for services to AFDC, SSI, or Medicaid populations. When a state participates in Title XX, the federal government will generally fund 75 percent of what each state spends on services directed to the five goals, administration costs, and training.

In this federal–state partnership there are specific federally

defined eligibility requirements for people who can receive Title
XX services. Essentially eligibility is restricted to those people
who are receiving financial assistance from AFDC or SSI or to
those people who do not receive payments from the former
programs but whose income does not exceed 115 percent of
their state's median income adjusted for family size. Thus services are earmarked to the poor, to the working poor, and to
some of the middle class. Two specific types of services must be
provided to people of all incomes. They are information and
referral services and protective services for children and adults
that are related to the third goal of assisting adults, children, and
families.[21]

In viewing these different types of benefits and the way in
which they are structured, there are varying degrees of how
organizations participate in benefit distribution. Insurance cash
benefits suggest a government role only in ascertaining eligibility
and in making subsequent cash payments. Similarly, medical
insurance requires initial proof by prospective recipient of category requirement, and the federal government issues payments
to appropriate medical personnel and organizations when the
benefit is actually utilized. In SSI and public welfare assistance,
government takes a stronger role relative to determining income
eligibility via a form of "means" tests. Lastly, Title XX suggests a
complex division of labor inasmuch as they are all federal goals
and guidelines, but states must develop their own plans, and
local organizations, public and private, play key roles in determining eligibility of clients as well as in delivering services
through purchase of service agreements.

CLIENT CHOICE AND AUTONOMY

Corresponding to these variations in structure, clients have
different levels of autonomy and choice with benefits. With cash
benefits from the federal insurance program, no means test is
required, and recipients have total freedom to spend and use
benefits as they see fit. Similarly, medical insurance benefits can
be used by clients in many medical facilities with a variety of
medical personnel and services.

SSI benefits require prior demonstration by clients that they are in financial need. Once they start receiving benefits, such cash allotments can be used by clients as they see fit. Public welfare for AFDC people again requires client demonstration of financial need, but it does not in all states and local areas necessarily allow clients to spend the distributed benefits as they see fit. Budgeted amounts for certain items still occurs in certain areas. Other local units rely on flat grants that theoretically will allow recipients to use funds as they see fit. Medicaid again requires demonstration of need to state and local units, but the somewhat restricted number of medical facilities and personnel who will serve Medicaid recipients greatly reduce the choice options of such recipients.

Title XX gives a major role to local public and private organizations in determining eligibility for funding reimbursement. Clients that seek services can theoretically go to agencies of their own choice, but often the state plan for services restricts the number of funded service providers so as to minimize costly overlap. Thus, the greatest amount of autonomy afforded recipients is to be found in the insurance component that distributes cash benefits.

INTERRELATION OF BENEFITS

Because Social Security is a complex system comprised of many different benefits, it is not surprising to note that many recipients may derive different combinations of benefits. For example, an elderly person may be receiving an old age pension, SSI, and Medicare coverage. Similarly, a mother in a family of AFDC may be part of a household that also receives Medicare as well as some service from an agency funded by Title XX. Thus the benefits should not be seen as mutually exclusive; rather, they operate in many cases in conjunction with each other. In addition to recipients' receiving two or more benefits within the Social Security package, many recipients receive other benefits designed to promote income security. Basically, these benefits are the in-kind benefits within the areas of housing and food. All recipients of SSI and AFDC automatically are entitled to food stamps. Many low-income people in turn qualify for housing assistance.

EVALUATION

Over the years, but most especially in recent years, several studies have looked at many of the benefits associated with social insurance and public assistance. The studies have often stressed coverage of populations as well as trends in dollar use for income security. Many of the studies have been undertaken by the Institute for Research on Poverty at the University of Wisconsin.

One finding is remarkably clear. The Income security benefits have grown dramatically during the last two decades (see Table 10–2).

The data in the above Table 10–2 also suggests that over the last quarter of a century the social insurance program has grown over the entire period but that public assistance growth has largely occurred in the 1965–1975 period. Heffernan has analyzed these developments and his calculation are shown in Table 10–3.[22]

These figures also suggest that long-term expansion of benefits is most likely to occur in the insurance portion of income security approaches.

TABLE 10-2. **Insurance and Assistance Programs for 1950–1977 Period Relative to Gross National Product and Wage Income (billions)**

YEAR	GNP	WAGE INCOME	SOCIAL INSURANCE	ASSISTANCE
1950	$ 286.2	$147.0	$ 7.0	$ 2.3
1955	399.3	211.7	13.1	2.5
1960	506.0	271.9	23.9	3.3
1965	688.1	362.0	34.2	4.1
1970	982.4	546.5	65.4	9.5
1975	1,528.8	805.7	143.7	20.9
1977*	1,869.0	986.5	169.3	21.9

*1977 year is estimate.
Source: *Social Security Bulletin*, October 1977, Table M-39, p. 65.

TABLE 10-3. **Recent Growth Rates in Insurance and Assistance Programs in Comparison with Gross National Product**

PERIOD	GNP	SOCIAL INSURANCE	PUBLIC AID
1950–65	140%	389%	78%
1965–75	122	320	410
1975–79	23	18	5

If we now return to the figures cited in our discussion of the thrust of the Social Security Act, we can entertain the notion that such expansion of coverage can certainly be instrumental in raising the floor level of income for millions of Americans but may not have much impact on relative income distribution patterns within the total society (refer to Table 10-1).[23]

Looking at the data from another perspective, we can also conclude that the period of massive expansion of social insurance and public assistance benefits have helped reduce the total number of Americans below official poverty levels. Specifically the 14.7 percent rate in 1966 was reduced to 12.3 percent by 1975. Even more dramatic 1966's 28.5 percent rate of poverty for those sixty-five and over was reduced to 15.3 percent by 1975.[24] This undoubtedly has been reduced even further by the continuing presence of SSI benefits. As Lampman has stated in 1977, "with the advent of SSI, the poverty rate among the aged should approach zero, even while the national average rate stands near 12 percent."[25]

Less positively affected during this period were low-income populations in the South and those of minority status, that is, black households and family units headed by women.

Critiquing the Problem Perception

Rather directly related to the components of the Social Security Act are some differences in how individuals and types of individuals are handled. Basically individual recipients are all seen within some group or category. But the groups and categories vary in terms of how much they are positively valued. There appears to be a direct relation between how valued the category is and how the benefit is operationalized.

With respect to the insurance component, the level of valuation is essentially to past work performance. In effect the individual in this category is seen as someone who is entitled to compensation for past efforts. The very notion of previous contribution reinforces the level of valuation present both in recipient and broader society.

Even SSI assistance benefits that are distributed to individuals are not randomly distributed to all in need. Rather, the federal government assumes responsibility for a level of income security to people who are in groups who frequently cannot provide for themselves through their own work efforts.

On the other hand, AFDC recipients tend to be seen as individuals within a category that should be encouraged to seek greater amounts of personal responsibility for their economic well-being. Admittedly, economic assistance occurs, but the major role afforded states and local areas in setting income standards and the actual amounts of economic assistance provided seems to indicate that people within this category are not valued as highly as others having income problems.

In addition to this, AFDC is distributed within a context of services to recipients. As positive as these may be, these served arrangements strongly suggest that individuals and families should change in some way to advance their economic position. This seems validated by the nature of training and job placement efforts frequently associated with AFDC benefits. It would appear that training and work emphasis, as operationalized, is laden with perceptions that individual characteristics in terms of life-style, skills, motivation are central to the issue of income deficiency. Little or no emphasis seems to be given to the possible role of structural features in the society and economy relative to expansion of opportunities or to minimization of such things as possible race and sex discrimination elements in job structures and income determination processes.

In terms of prevailing causal explanations, it appears that different types of explanations are to be found in the insurance and public assistance components. In the insurance component and to some corresponding degree, even in SSI, individuals are not seen as being at fault; individuals are not seen as the cause of their income shortage or need for support. Rather it appears that the society, for insurance and SSI populations, tends to accept the position that our industrialized economy cannot routinely meet the income needs of certain segments of the society. In a sense the society itself has a responsibility because the society itself, by its nature, helps to produce the problem. Put another way our social system has a strain built within it—we value the people within certain categories, and yet they predictably can have income problems for which they seem not to be responsible. This strain is handled by income supports through the Social Security Act.

On the other hand, the AFDC population presents a somewhat different case. We tend to value the children to a real degree, but we often do not understand why the parents of children in income-deficient families cannot do more for their families. Thus the goals of greater motivation and gainful employment are often pursued. Not so implicitly we tend to see the cause of the income condition as within the parameters of the parents and sometimes within the parameters of the lifestyle and culture of those parents. No great appreciation of fault or responsibility is seen within the broader social system. Yet the children are in need; they need things that money will buy. This produces a different type of strain for the society—How can we help the children yet not produce still greater amounts of social and income dependency by the parents? In part, the solution to this strain is to provide assistance and, where possible, opportunities for work and job training.

A more positive atmosphere concerning causation seems to be emerging in part with Title XX. Admittedly, the services have a strong focus on low-income families, they also tend to reflect a strong emphasis on prevention and securing appropriate care for people. In addition to this, many of the services funded by Title XX seem to reflect more of a concern with broader individual development than just work motivation and skill accretion. In a real sense Title XX seems to suggest that individuals and families have human needs and that these should be met. Concern with whether individuals are at fault or not is not strongly stressed.

Before closing this section it might be useful to at least identify major social science constructs not present in the Social Security Act. These would include blocked economic opportunities, wage and income distribution patterns within the private economy, degrees of access to job markets, and the nature of private ownership of property.

Cultural-Interest Perspectives

Within the Social Security Act it is possible to detect selected aspects of work, individualism and collectivism. The influence of work is clearly seen within the insurance component wherein contributions and benefits are largely tied to current and past work efforts. Similarly, such benefits are often distributed when continued ability to work is not possible for reasons beyond the recipient's control. A work orientation is also present in the AFDC component in which training for work, as well as work, are closely associated with benefit distribution.

Individualism is apparent within the Social Security Act. In a positive sense, individuals, especially in the insurance component, receive benefits in such a fashion that they are able to make decisions concerning how they will act in their own best interests. Less positive aspects of individualism are to be found in the AFDC component of assistance. Use of means tests and possible use of job-training approaches suggest, in part, that individual characteristics may be intimately involved in producing the income deficiency. Similarly, there appears to be some level of concern in the AFDC program with minimizing individual dependency and expanding individual capabilities to be self-sufficient.

Collectivism is present and to some degree presupposed in the Social Security Act. It is clear that the entire act reflects the notion of government's responsibility to certain people who have income difficulties. It suggests, through insurance, that collective steps have to be taken for predictable situations that many individual cannot handle totally by themselves. The value of collectivism within the private economic sector is to some degree presupposed in terms of insurance benefits complementing fringe benefits derived directly from the private sector employer. Yet the act also shows in varying ways a collective responsibility for valued categories of people—the aged, blind, disabled, and dependent children—in terms of assuring them some floor standards of income (SSI) when they do not have adequate protection from the private economy.

Finally, public sector collectivism is increasingly found in the Title XX provisions that provide services to a relatively broad segment of the society concerning broad needs.

Group interests were and are met by the functioning of the Social Security Act. First, the interests of political actors who recognized and advocated that certain people are not personally responsible for some of their needs should be kept in mind. These actors had needs for sources of political support, and thus Social Security was and is used as a device to orchestrate votes from selected categories of voters, that is, old ethnics, the aged. Not surprisingly, the groups that have benefited the most, with little or no welfare stigma, are those constituencies that are perceived as having bloc voting power.

Second, the interests of the helping professions are met in part by the creation and implementation of service strategies. The 1962, 1967, and even Title XX changes, while relating to individual and family needs, also help support agencies and define and legitimize roles for many individual-oriented professionals and approaches. Thus expansion of social services may very well help people in need, but it also facilitates private organizations and professionals in laying claim to public dollars.

Third, the economic needs of state and local taxing bodies were also met in part by the federalization of income benefits within SSI.

Fourth, Social Security helps meet the varied needs of those who have a commitment to maintaining the private economic system. At its outset the Social Security Act helped to diffuse labor's criticisms of the society and has helped to contribute to greater degrees of social cohesion within the existing social order. Social Security also helps the private economy by providing income and supports for those who cannot be self-sufficient within the private economy of an industrialized country. Implicitly at least Social Security deflects possible criticism away from serious structural changes of the private economy. Finally, the difference between insurance and assistance, between valued and not so valued categories of people within the Social Security Act, may help separate large masses of people from each other—even though they may share in income-related problems. Such a separation, whether designed or not, may be instrumental in minimizing large-scale social discontent with the working of the economy in our society.

Recommendations for Change

Prescriptively the Social Security system could be strengthened if several discrete objectives were pursued:[26]

1. Increasing the reliance upon the federal government for public assistance—specifically transferring AFDC to the federal level and making the federal government assume total responsibility for income benefits.
2. Expanding the range of categories for whom the federal government has responsibility. Initially this could mean medical benefits for all, independent of age and means tests. Special attention could be given to all children and families via family (or children's) allowances.
3. Raising the level of benefits currently operating because cash payments are often inadequate to live on.
4. Relying even more on general tax revenue sources at the federal level to finance existing and proposed programs and benefits. This would be important because it would promote a stronger role relationship on the part of the government to the economy and could facilitate serious consideration of proposals involving broader coverage and higher benefits.
5. Making Social Security insurance less related to work contributions.

6. Making Social Security less dependent on the role of fringe benefits and services being provided by the free-enterprise system. Continued reliance on such benefits largely renders Social Security to the role of supplementing the private free economy.

Summary

In this chapter we have described and analyzed the major social policy product in the United States, the Social Security Act. Basically the act addresses itself to the goal of income security in an industrial society, and as such it offers a variety of benefits to different groups. As indicated, it can and does work in concert with other benefits in the society related to adequate income levels—especially in-kind benefits.

It would appear that the original act and its many amendments over the years reflect a strong continuing commitment to the role of work in our society, a strong commitment to certain valued categories of people, and a role for government in assisting those who are not adequately protected by the private economy, as well as in supplementing for many others the economic and social benefits that they actually receive from the private economy.

Notes

1. A variety of income security approaches exist, and they include (1) the creative use of tax structure—deferrals, deductions, exemptions, and preferential taxes, (2) use of government spending for public works and manpower training, (3) minimum wages and fair employment, and (4) the approaches discussed in this chapter.

2. Several excellent works focus upon the historical development of social welfare responses. Among them are Walter I. Trattner, *From Poor Law to Welfare State: A History of Social Welfare in America*, 2d ed. (New York: Free Press, 1979); Samuel Mencher, *Poor Law to Poverty*

158   SOCIAL POLICY AND SOCIAL WELFARE

Program: Economic Security Policy in Britain and the United States
(Pittsburgh: University of Pittsburgh, 1967), esp. pp. 267–345.

3. *Encyclopedia of Social Work* (New York: National Association of Social Workers, 1971), p. 1584.

4. Mencher, *op. cit.*, pp. 279–309.

5. *Ibid.*, p. 304.

6. Walter Friedlander, *Introduction to Social Welfare* (Englewood Cliffs, N.J.: Prentice-Hall, 1961).

7. Several varying works discuss the context in which the Social Security Act evolved. See Edwin E. Witte *The Development of the Social Security Act* (Madison: University of Wisconsin, 1963).

8. Wilbur J. Cohen "The First Twenty Years of the Social Security Act," in *Social Work Year Book* (New York: National Association of Social Workers, 1960), pp. 49–62.

9. Theodore Marmor, *The Politics of Medicare* (Chicago: Aldine, 1973).

10. An excellent critical review of public welfare, including general assistance, that is beyond the scope of this chapter is found in Joan Huber, "Mechanisms of Income Distribution," in Joan Huber and Peter Chalfant, eds., *The Sociology of American Poverty* (Cambridge, Mass.: Schenkman, 1974), pp. 103–123.

11. A thorough discussion of 1967 amendments is to be found in Charles E. Hawkins, "The Welfare and Child Health Provisions of the Social Security Amendments of 1967," *Welfare in Review*, 6 (May–June 1968), 1–34.

12. See Paul E. Mott, *Meeting Human Needs: The Social and Political History of Title XX* (Columbus, Ohio: National Conference on Social Welfare, 1976), for a thorough discussion of background and nature of Title XX.

13. *Ibid.*, p. 87.

14. Witte, *op. cit.*

15. See Michael Harrington, *The Other America* (New York: Macmillan, 1962).

16. See W. Joseph Heffernan, *Introduction to Social Welfare Policy* (Itasca, Ill.: Peacock, 1979), pp. 235–268, for an informative discussion of the process of welfare reform in the 1968–1978 period.

17. Mott *op. cit.*, especially pp. 27–43.

18. *Ibid.*, p. 19.

19. *Ibid.*, pp. 30–45.

20. Relative to federal allocation for AFDC two types of formulas are available to states for reimbursement. In general the complex funding involves the federal government's committing a fixed portion of dollars as well as a variable portion calculated by formula. Relative to structuring at the state and local level, almost half the states (22) delegate major responsibilities to counties, and the remaining states (28) have programs basically administered at the state level.

21. Mott, *op. cit.*, p. 87.

22. Heffernan, *op. cit.*, p. 126.

23. There has been considerable debate concerning how much reduction of income inequality has occurred in the last several years. However, several major works tend to support the conclusion that minimal, if any, income inequality reduction has occurred. See Robert J. Lampman, "Changing Patterns of Income, 1960-1974," *Institute for Research on Poverty*, Reprint Series 235, 1977, p. 114; Robert Haveman, "Poverty, Income Distribution, and Social Policy: The Last Decade and Next," *Institute for Research on Poverty*, Reprint Series 252, 1977, p. 22; Lester C. Thurow, *Generating Inequality* (New York: Basic Books, 1975).

24. U.S. Department of Commerce, Bureau of the Census, *Current Population Reports*, Series P-60 (Washington, D.C.: U.S. Government Printing Office, 1976).

25. Robert J. Lampman, "Comments on Taxes, Equity, and Income Distribution," *Institute for Research on Poverty*, Reprint Series 247, 1977, p. 36.

26. Where the notion of reform and modification of existing income support systems has been accepted, there tends to be differences in strategy and purposes. One strategy is related to tax reform, see George Break and Joseph Pechman, *Federal Tax Reform: The Impossible Dream* (Washington, D.C.: Brookings Institution, 1975). A second is to proceed from the existing combination of cash and in-kind transfer programs, with a reliance on extending coverage, raising benefits, setting national standards for states, and adding new benefits, for example, comprehensive national health, child care, and housing subsidies; see Gilbert Steiner, "Reform Follows Reality: The Growth of Welfare," *Public Interest*, 34 (Winter 1974), 47-65. We have chosen to highlight aspects of both approaches.

Chapter 11

Manpower Policy and Legislation

ALTHOUGH THE TRAINING, development, and use of human resources for meeting the skill requirements of the economy have long been a matter of public interest, only since the 1960s have federally supported manpower programs emerged as a major tool of economic and social policy.[1] The decade of the 1960s was one of growth and change in many areas of social policy development. The dramatic proliferation of manpower programs was significant evidence of the commitment of the federal government to social equity and equal opportunity. Before 1961, only limited governmental funds were allocated to improve the functioning of the labor market and to provide remedial services for those who experienced difficulties in competing for sustained gainful employment.[2]

Since the 1960s, the scope of manpower policy development has been modified, and this has had a profound effect on economic, educational, and military policies not to mention its impact on programs in community and urban development. In fact, today, there is a manpower dimension to almost every aspect of economic, social, and political policy development.[3] Despite the pervasiveness of manpower concerns in public policy since the 1960s, the federal government has been criticized consistently for the absence of a single, coherent, and cohesive strategy for developing and using human capital as a major resource in the labor market.

Many experts contend that the ad hoc, piecemeal approach to human resources development is clear evidence of the absence of a viable manpower policy and the government's inability to carve out a clear-cut manpower policy, despite feverish efforts to deal with unemployment, underemployment, and the shortcomings of a free-market economy. Proponents of this point of view question whether we can ever have a manpower policy in the sense that it will serve the needs of most of the people who make up the labor force. Garth L. Mangum observed, "I do not suppose we ever really make policies in a democracy. We attack particular problems that seem to have reached crisis proportions. Then, we look back later and perhaps—if we are lucky— see some kind of coherence."[4] Experts who support this point of view argue that the lack of national coherence leads to uncertainty as to what the appropriate mission of the federal government should be in the matter of manpower planning. As a result, government officials are given the responsibility of administering manpower programs and services built on bits and pieces of legislations that never seem to coalesce and make possible an orderly, dependable, long-range approach to addressing manpower problems. "Without a clear concept of what the basic objectives and mission are, we end up with a crazy-quilt pattern of overlapping and competing programs."[5]

There are also observers who insist that, although manpower programs and services lack national balance or well-defined and consistent objectives, we do, in fact, have a manpower policy. These supporters suggest, however, that manpower policy comes in pieces; and pieces do not fit easily into neat patterns. This is so, these experts argue, because manpower policy necessarily must be directed at the full range of human problems. Therefore, no single, consistent, or cohesive strategy can emerge for developing a set of fiscal and monetary policies on the one hand, and social policies, on the other, that can promote a vigorous and sustained demand expansion without causing undue inflation. Moreover, according to this point of view, because demand expansion is necessary for overcoming cyclical joblessness, no single strategy can be devised for dealing with the growing problem of structural unemployment—the kind of unemployment that even in the best of times affects the undereducated, the unskilled, and those who are considered too young or too old or who are subject to discrimination.

Background

We support this proposition and argue that the controversy about whether or not we have a manpower policy is based not on the absence of a broad and generally accepted manpower goal, full employment, and the guarantee that every adult American will have a useful and remunerative job but, rather, on methods of implementation, the amount of effort and resources that should be expended to achieve the desired goals, as well as the most effective policy instruments for achieving it.

The ideological base of present-day manpower policy is rooted in the Protestant ethic. During our formative years as a nation, the morality of the Protestant ethic was interpreted to construe individual initiative as virtue, wealth as a confirmation of grace, and work as the road to salvation. Work, for example, has always been as good a clue as any to the course of a person's life, his social well-being, and social identity and is the key role around which all other roles are organized. The work situation, the nature of the work performed, and the norms derived from occupational reference groups greatly influence nonoccupational patterns of one's behavior.[7] We propose that, because society holds that a job is one's most important status symbol and, in turn, that it influences many aspects of one's life, a basic premise of federal manpower policy is that government, as society's functionary, has a responsibility to guarantee job opportunities and protect the public interest for those who wish to work and to ensure full employment for the nation.

We contend, also, that manpower policy fundamentally is concerned with the development and use of human labor as an economic resource and as a source of individual and family income. To the extent that it attempts to identify problems of human resources development and utilization with the intention and decision mechanisms to do something about them and to the extent that programs and services have been developed to address these problems, *we have a manpower policy.*

Today's manpower policy is the product of an evolution in public policy that began with the Morrill Act of 1862 and is reflected in a patchwork of legislative programs that have been enacted since then. Implicit in these legislative programs is a commitment to (1) full employment as a right and guarantee for all who are willing and available, (2) corporate growth in the form of guaranteed market expansion and assured return on capital and guaranteed inputs in the form of supply of money, (3) research and development, (4) development of raw materials and energy, and (5) the supply of competent labor.

An early effort to consolidate these intentions was the passage of the Employment Act of 1946. However, the job guarantee was displaced by triple-layered guarantees to ensure corporate growth, that is, assured expansion of market demand, assured returns on capital, and guaranteed supply of inputs including trained or educated labor.

Bertram Gross and Jeffrey Straussman contend that, whereas these growthmanship policies successfully averted mass depression, they also created restrictive definitions of "full" employment that, in turn, obscured the growing supply of labor able and willing to work for pay but outside the officially defined labor force. "The expansion of labor supply has branded millions of people 'surplus' and has, in effect, contributed to many of the social ills whose symptoms are labeled the urban crisis."[8]

What Is the Comprehensive Employment and Training Act (CETA)?

The predominant piece of legislation governing the implementation of manpower policy today is CETA of 1973 and its 1974 and 1978 amendments. The enactment of CETA introduced new concepts to manpower programming by establishing a flexible decentralized system of federal, state, and local manpower activities. Prior to CETA, there were more than twenty existing categorical manpower programs that had been administered by a wide range of separate and often competing bureaucracies through which the federal government entered into contracts with different service deliverers (such as boards of education, community action agencies, community organizations, etc.) to perform such services as classroom training, on-the-job training, and work experience. Individuals moved into and out of the jurisdiction of these separate agencies with no one attending to personal difficulties, or negotiating these systems, or accepting responsibility for the workings of the system as a whole. Under CETA, the federal government assigns this responsibility to state and local governments (prime sponsors) who are then relatively free to decide who will be their subcontractors and what services they will provide. Most of the services provided under CETA are services that were available under earlier pieces of legislation. What is new about CETA is that it streamlines the delivery of services by (1) consolidating programs under one legislative umbrella, (2) reducing the restrictive funding requirements for programs that formerly had specific labels and combining the funds into one grant, and (3) decentralizing planning, design, and administration of local programs from the federal government to state and local governments.

CETA, as amended through 1978, included seven major sections or titles. Title I permits "prime sponsors" to establish programs of comprehensive manpower services, including recruitment, orientation, counseling, testing, placement, classroom instruction, institutional and on-the-job training, allowances for persons in training, supportive services, and transitional public employment jobs. The greater part of Title I funds (80 percent) is distributed among prime sponsors according to a formula based on each area's manpower allotment in the previous fiscal year and on the number of unemployed persons and the number of adults from low-income families in each area.

Of the remaining Title I funds, 9 percent is available for vocational education and other manpower services on a statewide basis and 5 percent may be used to encourage consortia. The remainder is for the discretionary use of the secretary of the U.S. Department of Labor, but the monies must be used to fund a limited number of rural Concentrated Employment Programs (CEPs) as prime sponsors and ensures that all prime sponsors receive at least 90 percent of their previous year's allotment. Title I replaced the Manpower Development and Training Act of 1962 (MDTA) and the manpower provisions of the Economic Opportunity Act of 1964 (EOA). These two laws created such national programs as the Neighborhood Youth Corps (NYC), Job Corps, Operation Mainstream, New Careers, Special Impact programs, and MDTA classroom and on-the-job training.

The shift of responsibility for manpower programs to local governments requires them to submit a detailed plan for spending the money to the secretary of labor for his approval. The plan would have to meet certain standards. It would have to assure "that to the maximum extent feasible manpower service will be provided to those most in need of them . . . and that the need for continued funding of programs of demonstrated effectiveness is taken into account in service to such groups and persons."[9]

Title II provides for transitional public employment programs in areas that have a 6.5 percent or higher unemployment rate. The act specified that at least $250 million of any funds appropriated for CETA for fiscal year 1974 had to be used to operate public employment programs and at least $350 million of the 1975 appropriation had to be used for these programs.

Eighty percent of Title II funds were distributed among eligible areas on the basis of unemployment figures. The remainder was distributed at the discretion of the secretary of labor.

Title II replaced the expired Emergency Employment Act, which was passed in 1971. This legislation was a direct effort to create jobs at a time when unemployment was on the upswing. Although the legislation suggested target groups, the Emergency Employment Act program never really served those groups (with the exception of the veterans). A weakness of the EEA was that it provided jobs for the unemployed, but not for the seriously disadvantaged. Although the transition to unsubsidized employment was relatively high, it was the beginning of revenue sharing and the dependence on the federal government to provide money and employment in times of tight local budgets and rising unemployment.

The 1978 amendments to CETA specified new targeting provisions under Title II D. For example, eligibility was restricted to those individuals who are unemployed for fifteen or more weeks or who are public assistance recipients. In addition, the individual's family income cannot exceed 70 percent of the Bureau of Labor Statistics' lower living standard—adjusted regionally.

Title III specifically provides for federally supervised manpower programs for Indians and migrants. Supplementary manpower services under federal supervision are also authorized for other special target groups: youth offenders, older workers, persons with limited English-speaking ability, and others with particular labor market disabilities.

Additionally, this title authorizes federally supervised research, experimental and demonstration programs, evaluation of all programs under the act, and the development of a comprehensive system of labor market information.

The intent of Title III is to provide for a continuing direct federal role for certain activities that Congress feared might not be adequately supported by local prime sponsors. Title IV continues the job corps program under direct federal funding and supervision. Title V establishes a National Commission for Manpower Policy that is responsible for examining national manpower issues and advising the secretary of labor on ways and means for dealing with manpower questions. Title XI contains general "housekeeping" provisions, such as conditions governing work and training, prohibitions against discrimination and political activities, criminal provisions, and required reports.

In 1974, CETA was amended because rapidly rising unemployment rates convinced Congress of the need for an additional public service employment title. PSE became the new Title XI and the general provisions title was renamed Title VII. Under new PSE requirements, eligible individuals must be public assistance recipients or have been unemployed ten out of the last twelve weeks. The individual's family income cannot exceed 100 percent of the BLS lower living standard. In addition, the length of an eligible person's participation in either Title II–D or Title VI programs is limited to eighteen months. However, the secretary of labor may extend the limit to twelve additional months in areas where unemployment rates exceed 7 percent.

In late 1978, CETA was amended authorizing continuation through fiscal years 1982. The current CETA spells out, for the first time since manpower legislation was introduced seventeen years ago, a clear objective for itself: Increase the earned income of persons who go through the program, thereby making it clear who may participate in most CETA activities—they must be the economically disadvantaged.

The underlying intent of all the changes that were made in the reauthorized law is to increase the efficiency of the dollars to be spent in finding employment for the poor. The original CETA of 1973, basically an instrument to handle structural unemployment, was designed as a more balanced economic tool to counter both structural and cyclical unemployment.

KEY ACTORS—SITUATION

A stagnant economy and a growing unemployment problem in the 1950s helped create new imperatives for manpower programs in the 1960s. The exodus of middle-class whites and blacks to the suburbs and the inflow of poorly educated rural blacks to central cities resulted in massive losses of jobs and a qualitative deterioration of the labor force. Federal intervention in manpower development was, therefore, concentrated upon the social component of manpower policy—particularly on the development of manpower programs aimed at the disadvantaged. It is against this backdrop that a series of key actors—Douglas, Kennedy, and Johnson—pushed for legislation that ultimately produced the Manpower Development Training Act and its amendments in the 1960s. In part these pieces of legislation serve as the basis for CETA in the 1970s.

Ruttenberg describes three major sociopolitical forces that influenced federal intervention during the 1960s.[10] First was the continuing existence of poverty in America. Second was the emergence of the civil rights movement and the growing awareness of the increasing economic gap between the income and social well-being of blacks and whites in this country. Third was the urban crisis that erupted into riots and civil disorders, which led to a federal–city alliance that sought to address the problems of unemployment, alienation, and social ills spawned by idleness and identity crises.

Senator Paul Douglas (D., Ill.) was particularly concerned with the problems of various sections of the country as well as sectors of the populations that had not shared in the general pattern of economic growth. Douglas proposed a multipronged attack on these areas' problems and offered a bill requiring the secretary of labor to develop training facilities in these areas and to authorize the extension of unemployment benefits for those undergoing training. Versions of the bill were passed by Congress in 1958 and 1960 but were vetoed each time by President Eisenhower. Finally in 1961 Congress passed and President Kennedy signed the Area Redevelopment Act (ARA). This legislation was designed to stimulate economic growth by providing incentives to companies and communities. It also authorized $4.5 million for vocational training of unemployed and underemployed persons living in redevelopment areas. During the first year and a half, 15,360 trainees were placed in programs and given training stipends for sixteen weeks. This program and those that were to follow emphasized "rehabilitation, not relief."

The ARA was not a success. Its total expenditures of $322 million made no noticeable dent on unemployment in the depressed areas in which it was spent. But the act was significant for manpower development because it was the first to apply the G.I. bill principle of federal payment of training allowances to groups other than veterans. This principle was later applied to the Manpower Development Training Act of 1962 (MDTA). The initial objectives of this legislation were to retrain mature, experienced family heads who had been displaced by technological and economic change, while providing them with income to make training possible. The law allocated funds to two different training programs. One was the institutional or classroom training program that offered instruction in skills for occupations for which there were reasonable expectations of employment. Training allowances, at levels equal to the state's average unemployment compensation benefit, were provided to heads of families of at least three years of labor market experience. Youths of nineteen to twenty-one years of age were eligible for a smaller allowance.

MDTA also provided on-the-job training. This program subsidized employers for training costs incurred in hiring and training new employees. This program was attractive for several reasons. First, it was considerably less expensive than classroom training. Second, the client had a job when the training ended and knew that he had a job during the training period. This was an extra incentive. There was no need to duplicate industry's expensive equipment in a classroom setting. Despite the great optimism attached to this program, it never reached its goal. It was more difficult to manage than had been expected, and employers contended that the temporary subsidy was not adequate to cover the loss of production. Later, the Department of Labor expanded the program by negotiating contracts with a few major national employers. This action was publicly criticized because many observers felt that employers would have hired and trained the employed without federal support because, by then, the economy was strong and labor markets were tight.

As the 1960s progressed, MDTA was amended several times. Essentially these amendments expanded the notion of job training and the length of training periods. The 1966 and 1968 amendments in particular were designed to extend MDTA to a larger number of disadvantaged people, to reduce barriers to employment and education, and to alleviate skill shortages as well as eliminate hard-core unemployment.

Throughout the 1960s, the Kennedy–Johnson administrations attempted to have government promote prospective employees gainful entry and rerentry into the labor market. Johnson in particular called upon American industry to establish a National Alliance of Businessmen (NAB) to press the attack on the employment problem of the cities. One result of this was the JOBS program whereby private enterprise employers contracted with the federal government to hire and train disadvantaged persons. The government, in turn, reimbursed the employers for training and service costs.

With the Nixon administration and its "new federalism," the manpower programs underwent serious scrutiny during the early 1970s. Questions regarding the programs' efficiency and efficacy prompted the government to reexamine its manpower policy. The prevailing policy theme during the 1960s had been "opportunity." The goal of eliminating poverty through the opportunity to work and direct employment programs was not achieved. This failure led to a policy of helping people out of poverty by providing them with money through some new form of income maintenance. Public employment programs were then conceived as the new strategy for income maintenance. The government concluded that, without an income maintenance strategy to supplement the opportunity strategy, the goal of eliminating poverty could not be reached. Policy analysts also called for the development of community manpower systems in which local leaders determined programs shaped and designed in relationship to the local economy.

Although CETA was several years being created and passed into law, the basic push behind it was not on the whole a concern for an improved manpower policy. Rather, it was, the attempt to implement the political theory of "new federalism—involving local decision making and local control. There were individuals in the Congress who insisted that manpower programs should be for those who were disadvantaged both economically and socially. But the administrative thrust was political and insisted on the local elected official being the decision maker. "Decentralization" and "decategorization" were the themes.

FUNDING AND ALLOCATION

The federal government finances CETA programs through its use of general tax revenues. The money that is to be used for manpower purposes requires state and local governments to submit to the federal government a plan concerning possible use of dollars. Once the plans are approved, the local government units (prime sponsors) are relatively free to decide with whom they may subcontract and which services will be provided.

Intimately involved in this funding pattern, which involves the local control of federal grant dollars, is the key role of federal procedures and guidelines. The 1978 amendments especially stress strict guidelines. So detailed is this piece of legislation that it reads almost like a set of regulations. Specifically the issues of eligibility relying upon formulas, duration of program participation, and local supplementation of wages are handled in a detailed fashion, as are mandates to promote increased monitoring to avoid fraud and abuse.

PREVENTION AND INTERVENTION

Because CETA has developed in the context of Manpower Development Training Acts of the 1960s, with its stress of opportunity expansion and the "new federalism" of the 1970s, the act reflects two basic orientations. Increasingly it has reflected a public works approach related to promoting adequate income supports. As such, its distribution of cash and related services definitely connote a tertiary-level orientation.

However, the background to CETA and continuing aspects of CETA seem to reflect an awareness that certain people, especially certain groups of people, have predictable problems in the area of work in our economy. Therefore, the act continues to reflect a commitment to help people modify their current situations so that they might better deal with or minimize the rather predictable patterned effects of the job market.

Manpower policy as reflected in ARA, MDTA, and CETA has also attempted to address both primary and secondary levels of intervention.

For example, the Nab-Jobs experiment with labor and industry was an attempt at institutional change and social rearrangement in the labor market. This theme is continued but at a lower profile in CETA through the administration of on-the-job training programs at the local level.

GENERAL THRUST

Along with the last two decades' change in social thinking, there has been a corresponding shift in the general thrust of manpower legislation. Whereas the 1960s stressed equality of opportunity to produce a fairer state of competition in the marketplace, the 1970s and CETA seem to reflect more concern with ensuring adequate income support levels to workers and economic stability. Admittedly, many workers because of the training and work experiences afforded by CETA will have better chances to negotiate the labor market, but it appears that adequacy orientations have become increasingly present in CETA.

If you reflect upon the previous remarks concerning prevention, especially the expansion of income support purposes in CETA, you see that there is a possible relation among level of prevention, general thrust, and the sociopolitical climate of the 1970s.

Implementation—Benefits to People

STRUCTURE AND DISTRIBUTION OF BENEFITS

The benefits distributed through CETA basically involve the federal funding of work experiences that have cash (wage and/or benefits tied to them, as well as support and preparatory program) to facilitate prospective workers' successful movement into the economy. Resources for benefits—cash and programs—are distributed by grants to "prime sponsors" at the state and local levels who then are charged with the actual implementation. For prime sponsors to receive funding, there must be an area-based plan approved by the federal government. Once there is approval, the actual amount of funding is determined by various federally defined formulas, which include the amount of local unemployment, the number of adults from low-income areas, and so on.

Some provisions of CETA, specifically the continuation of Jobs Corps, the National Commission for Manpower Policy, and the guidelines and the procedures related to standards, remain under the structure of the federal government. Similarly federal supervision is retained for programs earmarked for such target groups as Indians and is related to a fear that local areas and sponsors might not have enough interest in serving these populations.

Local government units may subcontract pieces of their program to local bodies that in turn can offer employment, training, and support services.

To ensure some level of citizen and industrial input to CETA, the federal guidelines require states to have two bodies. One body is the Manpower Advisory Council, which involves citizens and recipients; the other is the Private Industry Council, which basically is comprised of management and labor representatives who can offer advice concerning job markets and opportunities.

CLIENT CHOICE

The role of choice in CETA is really limited to two major areas. Local governments can choose to request federal funding through CETA, or they can choose not to do so. Obviously local units with high unemployment rates, as well as those with large amounts of CETA-designated target group members, are structurally induced to participate in CETA. In a sense, part of the client or recipient designated by CETA is the local area, and the intent is to provide federal help to local areas under the concept of new federalism.

Within this context, individuals are free to apply for work or training or services offered locally. Obviously, if individuals reside in areas not participating or minimally participating in CETA, the individuals' rights to benefits are severely limited.

Individual recipients are judged either to meet or not meet federal guidelines and procedures. If accepted, then they are funneled into benefits (work, training, services) that are defined and controlled by governmental units and possible contract organizations.

INTERRELATION OF BENEFITS

Because of the increasing income support orientation within CETA and its increasing focus upon low-income populations, many of CETA's benefits and programs are interrelated with public assistance programs. For example, some WIN recipients may be assigned to CETA for jobs and training. CETA also interfaces with Title IX of the Older Americans Act. Specifically, unemployed low-income people over fifty-five may be referred to CETA.

EVALUATION

Although there has been a proliferation of manpower programming since the 1960s, these efforts have reflected our government's traditional style of incrementalism in social policy making with relatively few programs and services systemically integrated or linked to monetary and fiscal policies.[10] Manpower programming of the 1960s reflected, in general, an ad hoc, piecemeal approach to limited income redistribution with little planning, supporting Gil's notion that planning follows events.[11] Programs were criticized as being poorly conceived with unclear goals, designed with poorly selected output measures, and with reporting systems that yielded little information on the effects of programs or even on progress toward short-term objectives.

Manpower programming during this past decade (1970s) has concentrated on the "social" component of manpower policy—particularly on the development of manpower programs aimed at the disadvantaged. Although many of these programs and services offered needed income to participants, they have added little to their long-term employability, a fact that suggests that substantial training and job development components are essential to any manpower strategy.

There is considerable bias among analysts with respect to the degree to which manpower programs benefit the economy. A prevailing consensus among most of them is that manpower programs are unlikely to produce benefits that exceed the costs in terms of long-run economic growth, structural balance, and economic stability. From their vantage point, if governmental intervention in manpower programs is to be justified, it will have to be justified on the basis of its consequences on income distribution patterns. This benefit, to continue this line of thinking, is based on the premise that efforts at affecting income distributional consequences are socially preferred to transfer payments, for example, unemployment insurance and/or public assistance. As Weisbrod states, "Manpower programs are not likely to have significant demand effects on employment and prices because the alternative to public spending on manpower programs is, presumably, increased spending on other public programs, or decreased taxes and increased private spending. Thus, it seems reasonable to assume that aggregate demand for labor is essentially independent of the presence of manpower programs."[12]

Weisbrod also argues that questions about the impact of manpower programs should begin from the presumption that they are not economically efficient in the sense that benefits, as measured by earnings, exceed the real cost of the program. What the policy analyst must remember, as Weisbrod admits, is that, although manpower programs are generally assessed as inefficient, this does not imply that such programs are undesirable.[13] As a policy instrument, manpower programs have multiple goals. They are aimed not only at slowing inflation or reducing unemployment, but also at augmenting the flow of resources into human capital investments and shifting the distribution of income to the disadvantaged.

Manpower programs have proliferated with the expectation that benefits would exceed costs. However, careful studies of individual programs and their performances suggested that this expectation has not yet been realized. Manpower policy has vacillated through the years between being social policy and economic policy, with the emphasis dictated primarily by economic conditions. Manpower planners have been criticized as using manpower programs as income maintenance programs when economic conditions are severe, but these are the first programs to be cut when economic conditions improve. Through the years, the country has not made a clear-cut decision regarding the goals of manpower policy. Is it part of our overall social welfare policy, or is it more germane to economic policy? Even if the latter is the case, we have only sporadically expressed concern about the supply side of the economic ledger and have seldom tried to affect the demand side.

Critiquing the Problem Perception

UNITS OF ANALYSIS—SOCIAL SCIENCE CONSTRUCTS

As manpower benefits have proliferated over the last two decades, they seem to reflect a strong appreciation of individual, group, and institutional influences. It is clear that individuals are seen as being affected by unemployment and underemployment problems. It is the individual who is perceived as needing work and/or job training and/or skill upgrading. Similarly, with the recent developments in CETA, it is the individual who must be helped through the work experience so as to achieve a measure of adequate income.

However, CETA also reflects a strong appreciation of the "disadvantaged" as a target group to whom benefits must be distributed. Further, CETA continues to reflect a commitment to particular groups such as the migrants and Indians. In fact, CETA makes a special attempt to ensure that benefits will accrue to the latter group by housing much of the benefits for these groups in the federal structure.

As CETA has developed, there continues to be an appreciation that disadvantaged group members are not prepared by previous socialization experience to compete within the labor markets. Thus CETA continues the training and counseling services approach of MDTA to facilitate participation within the private economy.

In short, CETA seems to be cognizant of individuals that experience the effects of an economy notable to absorb them with their current skill levels and the role of group affiliation and conditioning upon individuals relative to the economy. .

CETA is also based on a perception of some problems in the economy itself. Such a perception is based on the fact that the economy itself cannot absorb all workers at all times. At time, cyclical phenomena tied to recession and periods of increasing unemployment make individual participation in the economy quite difficult. At other time, the evolution of the economy and its reliance on technically trained people structurally ensures employment problems for certain people. CETA attempts to respond to both of these conditions stemming from the economy by providing public-assisted jobs (cyclical) and by offering training and skill development opportunities (structural).

CAUSATION

In light of the foregoing, CETA seems to embody a multicausal perspective on employment problems. This would include individual skill deficiencies, conditioning influences that have negative impact on work attitudes and motivation, and basic discontinuities in the labor market itself.

Cultural-Interest Influences

The cultural value of work is a major influence on the development of CETA. Positive work experiences, as well as the ability to work, are seen as necessary for people and their own sense of worth. The basic thrust of CETA is to promote people's ability to work and to help ensure people's right to a job. Further, CETA recognizes that, in our technically developed economy, many people have to be helped to maximize their abilities to secure work and/or to develop better worker attitudes and skills to enter the economy. It is precisely within this context that the federal government assumes collective responsibility for development of individuals to secure work, training, and income. Even more specifically, the federal government, through its grants to local areas and to quite specific guidelines regarding eligibility, attempts to focus its responsibility to those who are having the most difficulty negotiating the economy.

CETA in its strong commitment to both work and collectivism basically relies upon the local area as the place where these two values of work and collectivism will be operationalized.

Perhaps the biggest interest that is achieved through CETA is the promotion of economic stability within local areas. Obviously areas that have high unemployment or other serious economic discontinuities within the job market are going to be subject to serious stress. Such stress can involve depressed economics and problems in the circulation of money and the production and distribution of goods. CETA helps to minimize these possible effects, thereby helping local economies to be stable and somewhat free of potential disruption. In this way the interests of local economic units and political units are reflected in the implementation of CETA.

Recommendations for Change

Some critics contend that a major roadblock to the effectiveness of manpower programs and services is the absence of broad-scale, comprehensive manpower planning. Part of the reason for this deficiency surely lies in the fact that there has been no amicable resolution between the *laissez-faire* philosophy that influences all federal planning behavior and our conception of the social welfare function of society. This dilemma is historically rooted in the American ethos that has very little tolerance for any governmental intervention that may conjure up the image of socialism or governmental regulation. Another impediment to federal manpower planning is the fact that the "politics" of federal planning and policy making often result in compromises in which goals and directions shift, alternatives are opted for, and new strategies for programming are adopted. There are continued changes in the structure of programs and in their level of funding almost on a yearly basis—a constant obstacle to structural changes. With short-term appropriations on a year-to-year basis and no assurance that substantive provisions will remain unchanged over extended periods, planning can be little more than a patchwork approach to reducing poverty and removing barriers to social opportunity.

Manpower programming seeks to achieve three goals: (1) to create employment opportunities for all who want them in jobs that balance free occupational choice and adequate income with society's relative preferences for alternative goods and services, (2) to provide education and training capable of fully developing each individual's production potential, and (3) the matching of people and jobs with a minimum of lost income and production. Obviously, many of us might very well argue that these goals are not complete because the workings of the current economy ultimately precludes it from ensuring that sufficient income is distributed to all.

However, if manpower programming is to achieve these goals, then there must be a continuing shift from the creation of new programs to the creation of better delivery systems (i.e., lateral coordination, joint-planning, etc.,) involving (1) continued reliance upon decentralization to the states and localities relative to implementation within a federal commitment to employment goals and employment opportunities; (2) continued decategorization and bloc grants to improve flexibility and encourage local planning, initiative, and accountability relative to federal employment and opportunity goals; and (3) greater coordination and agency linkages to minimize waste and inefficiency and political conflict, growing out of the fragmented, duplicative, and competing programming.

Finally, if manpower programming is to serve as a policy instrument for social fairness and social opportunity, then we must provide a proportionately larger investment in this area as a policy choice.

Summary

As manpower legislation has developed in recent years, there appears to be increasing recognition of the need to deal with the disadvantaged as a priority and to focus more on people who have employment problems stemming from structural and cyclical features of the economy. Benefits appear to revert to a specific population—those who are disadvantaged and who might or should have their income-producing opportunities raised. Benefits in recent years have increasingly become tied to work, and the distributed benefits through the 1970s involve federal responsibility (use of federal grants to states and local communities), state and local area definition of subcontractors for

180   SOCIAL POLICY AND SOCIAL WELFARE

employment, and specification of which services will be provided (i.e., federal responsibility, with local provision through local organizations, including the private sector). These trends seem to support the contention that legislation follows the prevailing climate of the society. In the 1970s that climate has spoken to a focused role of the federal government and an expanded reliance on local areas and initiative.

Notes

1. *The Nation's Manpower Programs,* National Manpower Policy Task Force, Washington, D.C., January 7, 1969.
2. Sar Levitan and Robert Taggart, III, *Social Experimentation and Manpower Policy: The Rhetoric and Reality* (Baltimore: Johns Hopkins Press, 1971), p. 1.
3. National Manpower Policy Task Force, *op. cit.,* p. 7.
4. Garth L. Mangum, "Perspectives on a Positive Manpower Policy," in George F. Rohrlich, ed., *Social Economics for the 1970s* (New York: The Dunellen Co., 1970), chap. 4.
5. E. Wight Bakke, *The Mission of Manpower Policy* (Kalamazoo, Mich.: W. E. Upjohn Institute for Employment Research, 1969), p. 6.
6. "The tasks of achieving sustained high employment and conquering inflation are not mutually exclusive. They can and must be attacked simultaneously. Therefore, any steps toward healthy demand expansion need to be accompanied by a range of measures to make the economy less inflation-prone. These should include steps to increase its competitiveness and efficiency, to eliminate restrictive practices in product and labor markets, and to enlarge capacity and supply availability." Research and Policy Committee of the Committee for Economic Development, *New Directions for a Public Private Partnership,* New York, January 1978. p. 12.
7. Deborah I. Offenbacher and Constance H. Poster, *Social Problems and Social Policy* (New York: Appleton-Century-Crofts, 1970).
8. Bertram Gross and Jeffrey Straussman, "Full-Employment Growthman ship and the Expansion of Labor Supply." *Annals, American Academy of Political and Social Sciences,* 418 (March 1975), 1.
9. C.E.T.A., 1978 amendments.

10. Stanley Ruttenberg assisted by Joselyn Gutchess, *Manpower Challenge of the 1970s: Institutions and Social Change* (Baltimore: The Johns Hopkins Press, 1970).

11. David Gil, *Unravelling Social Policy* (Cambridge, Mass.: Schenkman Publishing Co., 1973), p. xiii.

12. Burton A. Weisbrod, "Benefits of Manpower Programs: Theoretical and Methodological Issues," in G. G. Somers and W. D. Wood, eds., *Cost Benefit Analysis of Manpower Programs* (Kingston, Ont.: Queen's University, 1969), pp. 4–5.

13. *Ibid.*, p. 15.

Chapter 12

The Community Mental Health
Acts

THE HISTORY OF DEVELOPMENTS within the field of mental health
strongly suggests that mental health policy has been formulated
largely on the basis of prevailing ideological currents. In this
chapter we will focus upon the social welfare products related to
mental health that have been developed in the last quarter of a
century. Specifically they are the Community Mental Health
Centers Act of 1963 (PL–88–164) and the revisions and amendments of the 1963 act that are found in PL–94–63, which was
passed in 1975.

Background

During the early period of mental health policy development,
the prevailing ideology was hard work, individualism, *laissez-
faire*, and Social Darwinism.[1] Mental health services were associated with philanthropy and charity as well as with
generalized efforts to aid the poor and destitute and were provided by well-intentioned and well-to-do individuals and local
charitable organizations. Kingsley Davis characterized these
early efforts as charity performed by individuals whose ideas

and values were based upon "an American version of the Protestant Ethic."[2] Mental illness was viewed as an indication that the individual had fallen from grace and, therefore, was responsible for his own lot rather than as evidence of social, economic, and emotional stress or deprivation. Many Americans continued to believe that, because the nation at the time had unlimited natural resources and opportunities for success, poverty and mental illness were the results of individual moral failure—idleness, intemperance, immorality, and lack of religion.[3] This conception of mental illness created a policy context in which mental health services were provided as "moral treatment." This was based upon the assumption that the best way to alleviate mental disorder was through kindness and humane treatment.

As the concentration of the population in urban areas along with the influence of the reform movement in Europe began to generate public awareness of deviant behavior, American society began to realize that good intentions and charity were not enough to address the problems of pauperism and insanity. Professionally trained persons and systematically developed programs were required to care for and treat the mentally ill. As a result, increased public activity at the state level led to the rise of state hospitals. Between 1825 and 1865, the number of state mental hospitals grew from two to sixty-two, and by 1890 fourteen states were operating at least one institution for the mentally ill.[4]

During the period of increasing public (state) responsibility for the mentally ill, the federal government took the position that it did not have the power to assist the mentally ill. In the midnineteenth century, President Pierce contended that care of the needy, including the mentally ill, is a power reserved by state and local governments. He stated that "it cannot be questioned that if Congress has power to make provision for the indigent insane, it has the same power for the indigent who are not insane."[5] The essence of the Pierce position reflected the view that the "general welfare" clause in the constitution could not be interpreted to give such authority to the federal government. Therefore, for nearly a century, care of the mentally ill was left to state and local governments as well as to private charitable agencies.

It was to take the federal government nearly one hundred years before it reexamined its role in the area of mental health. What forced new federal concern was World War II. Over a million out of nearly five million men had been rejected from military duty because of mental or neurological disorders. Of those inducted and subsequently given medical discharges, about 40 percent, or close to 400,000 men, were dismissed for psychiatric disorders.[6] This condition elevated the concern for mental health to another level. The nation was no longer concerned about the quality of mental health in this country on merely moral or religious grounds. Mental health became a manpower issue, as the mental and emotional conditions of men affected their fitness as a manpower resource both for the labor market and for national defense. It was now apparent that mental illness constituted a major social problem in this country.

This recognition brought attention to the need for more knowledge about the causes of mental and neurological disorders, better trained psychiatrists and other workers, and better hospitals and methods of treatment.

In 1946 the National Mental Health Act was passed. This act created a Mental Hygiene Division within the U.S. Public Health Service and a center for information and research. The act provided for a comprehensive national mental health program by enabling states and private institutions to obtain federal funds for research, professional training, and community mental health programs. As its statement of mission from section 2 notes:

> The purpose of this act is the improvement of the mental health of the people of the United States through the conducting of researches, investigations, experiments and demonstrations relating to the cause, diagnosis and treatment of psychiatric disorders; assisting and fostering such research activities by public and private agencies and promoting the coordination of all such researches and activities and the useful application of their results; training personnel in matters relating to mental health; and developing, and assisting States in use of, the most effective methods of prevention, diagnosis, and treatment of psychiatric disorders.[7]

The act also provided for a National Advisory Mental Health Council that would recommend support for research that might make "valuable contributions to human knowledge with respect to cause, prevention, or methods of diagnosis and treatment of psychiatric disorders."[8] Subsequent legislation added a number of specific social problems with which the program should be concerned. In 1949 the Public Health Service Division of Mental Hygiene became the National Institute of Mental Health, (NIMH) and was formally established to administer the mental health programs using a traditional public health approach.

During the 1950s the successful politicization of the mental health movement led to the creation of the Mental Health Study Act of 1955, which produced the Joint Commission on Mental Health and Mental Illness. This group produced a report in 1959, *Action for Mental Health*, which ultimately became the basis for passage of the Community Mental Health Centers Act of 1963.

The Community Mental Health Acts, 1963

On February 5, 1963, President Kennedy, in a special message to Congress on mental illness and retardation, recommended a new national program for mental health as well as another program to combat mental retardation. This was the first time in the history of the country that a president had given support to mental health efforts, and it represented a major coup for proponents of mental health services. As a result of the president's aggressive leadership PL–88 164 was passed. This act authorized federal grants to construct public and other voluntary nonprofit community-based mental health centers. Federal matching funds of $150 million over a three-year period were provided for use by states in constructing comprehensive community mental health centers. This act also indicated that regulations should be issued that would speak to the kinds of services that were required for *adequate* local care.

In 1964 the regulations were promulgated, specifying that to qualify for federal construction funds a community mental health center would have to offer at least *five essential* mental health services:[9] (1) inpatient services, (2) outpatient services, (3) partial hospitalization, including day care, (4) emergency services providing twenty-four hours per day response within at least one of the three previously cited services, and (5) consultation and education services to local agencies and professionals. In some cases, these services could be subcontracted, in part, to local, often private, agencies.

Adequate services were defined as comprising the five essential elements plus diagnostic services, rehabilitative services (including vocational and educational services), precare and aftercare services in the community (foster home placement and halfway houses), training, and research and evaluations. This act was initially amended in 1965 to authorize federal staffing grants to implement services envisioned as being offered by centers.

In 1970 the CMHC Act was amended again to provide for longer periods of federal funding. It increased federal funds for centers in poor areas as well as support services to children, drug addicts, and alcoholics.

In 1975, PL–94–63 was passed, and it redefined the scope of community mental services.[10] The services that a comprehensive mental health center must provide are

—Inpatient, outpatient, day care, and other partial hospitalization and emergency services.

—Programs of specialized services for the mental health of children and the elderly including a full range of diagnostic, treatment, liaison, and follow-up services.

—Consultation and education services for individuals and entities involved with mental health services to develop effective mental health programs, promote coordination of services, increase awareness of mental health problems and services, and promote prevention and control of rape.

—Screening services of individuals for referral to a state mental health facility and provisions where appropriate, for treatment of such individuals

—Follow-up of residents discharged from a mental health facility.

—Transitional halfway house services for those discharged from a mental health facility or those who would otherwise require inpatient care in such facilities.

—Provision of services for prevention and treatment of alcoholism, drug addiction and abuse, and rehabilitation for drug and alcohol abusers.

—Services that are available and accessible twenty-four hours a day, seven days a week.

—An identifiable unit for consultation and education services

—Coordination of activities with other service providers (health, social services, and state hospitals) to ensure clients' access to all services that they may require.

In short the idea of community mental health centers as reflected in both acts gave new policy direction in mental health services by advocating a de-emphasis on long-term hospitalization and institutionalization. Instead, the notion that treatment facilities should be more accessible to a wider range of population within local areas was legitimated.

KEY ACTORS—SOCIOPOLITICAL SITUATIONS

The 1963 act can be best understood as the culmination of a long-standing mental health reformist orientation within the American society. Cameron, in his analysis of ideological context of mental health policy making, suggests that all the mental health reform approaches have stressed themes related to sentiments and values of the period.[11] In the process of achieving state hospitals in the nineteenth century, three themes were stressed: (1) scientific respectability, (2) religious righteousness, and (3) economy.

With regard to the first, Cameron argues that psychiatrists and other ideologues of the nineteenth century movement insisted that mental illness was curable in most cases. This affirmation was coupled with a religious appeal to humanism: since the mentally ill can be cured of their suffering, the argument went, it would be unrighteous and inhuman to allow them to be brutalized in poorhouses and prisons. But the most telling argument for policy makers was, notes Cameron, the appeal to economy. To continue placing the mentally ill in noncurative institutions, where they would probably remain for life, would mean increasingly heavy burdens on the public purse, whereas the construction of hospitals, where the mentally could be easily and rapidly cured, would result in great savings.

In recent reform approaches Cameron suggests that the community mental health ideology was based upon the same themes of scientific respectability, moral righteousness, and economy. Although the societal value orientations were the same, the sociopolitical context within which they operated created a different policy definition and, in turn, a different policy thrust. For example, to be scientifically respectable, the new mental health ideology required a shift in focus from treatment of the individual to intervention into community situations judged to be associated with mental illness—for example, poverty, racism, unemployment. This entailed moving patients out of hospitals and into the community and was coupled with a heavy emphasis on returning patients to their families.[12]

Cameron suggests that the notions of freedom from incarceration and the right of every citizen to treatment in his community provided the *moral imperative* for CMHCs. With respect to the third value orientation, *economy,* Cameron argues that CMHCs were more economical and efficient to operate than state hospitals. He also claims that emphasis on the primacy of the traditional family unit and the moral responsibility of the family to care for the patient provides both an ethical and economic justification for CMHCs. Thus the value orientations that comprise the community mental health ideology were consanguine with certain characteristics of the emerging social structure of the 1960s.

> That is, out of a wide range of possible conceptions that society could have "chosen," the ideological components of the community mental health movement reflected significant changes taking place in the larger social context. As in the case of mental health reform during the early nineteenth century, the community mental health ideology served to legitimize a fundamental redirection in policy.[13]

Further, Cameron sees the community mental health centers as a part of federal initiative to circumvent state and municipal governments who were unable or lacked commitment to respond to the growing urban unrest of the 1960s. Community mental health programs played an integral part in the federal strategy of the 1960s that spoke to social planning as well as to socialization and social control. According to Cameron, the community mental health movement must be viewed in the context of the larger effort of the federal government to deal with the growing disorder in the cities. The social reform legislation of the 1960s may be seen as directed at ameliorating the rapid growth of deviant behavior that emerged in the major cities. The social mechanisms for socialization and social order—the "pattern maintenance functions" in Parsons' (1951) words—were ineffective in large urban areas.[14]

The influence of the sociopolitical context of the 1960s was the culmination of a series of events and the activities of several key people and organizations that preceded it. We have already referred to the role of World War II and the urban disturbances of the 1960s. Reference has also been made to President Kennedy's strong personal role in mental health reform. All these were important, but several others are worth mentioning.

The mental health associations across the country, especially in the period between 1946 and 1954, helped politicize mental health problems and contribute to a climate for congressional reform. So successful was the politicalization of mental health that federal expenditures jumped from $9 million in 1949 to $68 million by 1959. Further the politicalization led Congress in 1955 to pass the Mental Health Study Act, which created the Joint Commission on Mental Health and Mental Illness, consisting of representatives of thirty-six agencies and organizations. This prestigious commission studied the status of mental health in the country, and its report in 1959–1960 was seized by President Kennedy as the basis for reform.[15]

While all of the above was going on, a revitalized post–World War II Veterans Administration had already taken a leading role in the mental health arena through it network of hospitals, psychiatric units, and outpatient clinics. This not only stimulated the growth of general psychiatry, clinical psychiatry, psychiatric social work and research and training in mental health, but clearly suggested that mental health services should be relatively proximate to the natural environment of clients.

Right after the passage of the 1963 act a significant impact upon the spirit of the community mental health movement was made by the works of the Gerald Caplan, who advocated intervention into the social and political environment affecting people's lives and a greater commitment to the concept of prevention.[16]

FUNDING AND ALLOCATION

Money is collected and distributed for community mental health in a variety of ways. Federal matching grants were made available to states in 1963 to institute community mental health centers. States and local communities have to contribute a certain amount of public money to receive the federal funds. Relative to staffing, states are categorized according to their positions of relative worth and, depending upon their categorization, are entitled to 75 percent or less decreasing federal funding over a number of years. This means that as the years pass states and local areas have to assume increased fiscal responsibility for the community mental health programs. To handle increasing local financial responsibility, community mental health centers and local governments have had to increasingly rely upon state and local general taxes, special funding levies, and client payments.

Client payments have always been present in community mental health services, but until quite recently they have not been stressed. However as the federal staffing grants approach termination, and as the federal government increasingly allocates smaller amounts of money, there has been an increased reliance upon collecting fees from clients served. Fees can be out-of-pocket expenses for clients, but increasingly they are tied to the private insurance plans of individual clients. In addition, for lower-income populations served, Title XX provides reimbursement to the community mental health centers.

Because of the increasing reliance upon private insurance plans to help pay for community mental health services, the community mental health centers and programs are increasingly relating to PSRO Standards and the Joint Commission on Accreditation of Hospital; private insurance companies' reliance upon the latter group for assessment of mental health programs before insurance claims are honored is notable.

With the changes in how resources are being collected, clearly it is easier to raise money for direct services to clients than it is for consultation and educations services. The latter services, because they don't rely upon client fees or insurance reimbursement, have to now attempt to generate funds from tax dollars.

Even with PL-94-63, which introduced operating grants to community mental health centers, the issues of funding remain significant. PL-94-63 authorized grants to meet a portion of the costs of operating a CMHC providing comprehensive services (or who will within a two-year period) according to an eight-year schedule, again relying upon a decreasing percentage basis (90 percent down to thirty percent in poverty areas; 80 percent down to 25 percent in nonpoverty areas). But the issue represented is the need for local areas to assume greater amounts of financial responsibility for the centers and/or to rely more and more upon client fees and insurance payments for direct services.

PREVENTION AND INTERVENTION

It is clear that PL-88-164 and PL-94-63 strongly embody a commitment to prevent mental illness and to promote mental health. One area of prevention is in the lowering of incidence rates. The acts clearly specify that staff should be concerned with social and medical considerations that are associated with potential mental disorders. Thus staff is to relate "through consultations with general practitioners, teachers, ministers, judges about specific cases and about general mental health principles," so that the community mental health center "can increase the knowledge and ability of those who deal with the public, so that they will be able to promote mental health by helping people meet life crises in constructive ways."[17]

In addition to this type of prevention, which relates to lowering incidence rates, the community mental health services are charged with the responsibility of preventing, where possible, long-term hospitalization. Many of the services within the community mental health context are designed to service clients in such a way that a preventive goal is also present.[18]

Lastly the acts, especially the recent revisions in PL-94-63 put a great emphasis upon promoting mental health by coordinating mental health services with the existing broad range of resources and services within the community. In this way, more comprehensive services are afforded people, service gaps are minimized, and duplication of services is reduced. Pursuit of broad services integration strategies is also related to promoting greater accessibility of services to clients.[19]

GENERAL THRUST

The general thrust of the community mental health acts is related to equality, fairness, and adequacy. Equality is present inasmuch as community mental health centers are charged with providing services to all people, regardless of income. Although income is taken into consideration in determining fees, limited income or high income do not affect whether one is entitled to or receives services. Fairness is present in the sense that certain groups, for example, children, the elderly, and substance abusers, are now handled by community-based professionals. Prior to the community mental health acts, mental health services for such populations, as well as services for low-income areas, were less than inadequate and not commonplace. Similarly, transitional services to people were often not available. For these populations and problems, the acts basically indicate that something has to be done to remedy previous service patterns. Adequacy is present in the context of the concept of a system of services being provided to help ensure that people are handled within their communities and that professional help is offered and available for crises in life situations.

If one had to indicate which of the three possible thrusts dominate, a case might be made that the value of equality is most present. Under the community mental health acts, it is presumed that people are all entitled to services and that people are entitled to responses that promote their health and adjustment in the social domains in which they operate daily.

Implementation—Benefits to People

BENEFITS AND STRUCTURE

People, as individuals and as residents within geographical areas, receive two types of benefits. Both benefits are of a service nature. First, there are the services that they can receive if they are already experiencing some mental disturbance. Second, there are the consultation programs of the key organizations and institutional representatives in their local areas (e.g., clergy and teachers) to prevent certain types of situations from developing or, if they do, to deal with problems in natural settings where large numbers of people interact. Thus benefits relate to service and preventive strategies.

The benefits are distributed within a *catchment* frame of reference.[20] That is, the services presuppose that people who live in proximity to each other may share certain problems and/or situations that can affect their mental health. Therefore services should be geared to this reality. The catchment concept speaks to this as well as to the notion that services should be close to the people, visible and accessible.

The community mental health center is basically a public or nonprofit corporation that applies to the federal government for funds. To receive the funds for construction, if necessary, and staffing and operations, it has to comply with the service requirements specified earlier. In this way, federal expectations interact with the unique and idiosyncratic features of different catchment areas, with differing combinations and types of people, problems, and situations. Put another way, there is a strong role for the national as well as the local government, as state and/or municipal government units enter the picture with supplemental funding, salary scales for workers, and planning for mental health services.

PL-94-63 requires the community mental health center to provide overall plans and budgets to meet mandated service requirements, paying special attention to how data will be collected for costing of programs, patterns of use of services, availability and accessibility of services, and acceptability and impact of services upon the mental health of residents. To help ensure that good planning links federal expectations to local areas, PL-94-63 includes the provision of one-year planning grants to enable public and nonprofit bodies to assess the need for services in the area, design a CMHC program based on needs assessment, secure necessary financial and professional assistance, and develop local community involvement. So as to not have community mental health centers within each state working in a disjointed fashion, PL-94-63 also requires each state to draw up state plans for mental health services. State planning is encouraged to develop effective planning for community alternatives for institutionalization (often in state hospitals), to develop a program for the CMHCs within the state, and to design minimum standards for the maintenance and operation of the centers.

CLIENT CHOICE

Clients are offered an opportunity to receive a broad range of services and are the indirect recipients of consultation, education, and prevention programs delivered within the catchment area. Although accessibility to local services has grown tremendously, services are controlled basically by the community mental health centers and agencies with whom the CMHC may subcontract certain service functions. In short, the benefits to people are clearly distributed through organizations and mental health personnel. As a result clients really have limited discretion as to whom they may go for services. Basically they may go to the CMHC, another agency that provides a related service, or, client's income and/or insurance permitting, to a professional in private practice. However, once they leave the orbit of the CMHC or its contract agency, the client is really receiving benefits that are not directly grounded in the community mental health acts.

PL-94-63 requires the CMHC to have a governing (or advisory) board composed, where practicable, of individuals residing in the area who are representative of the catchment's charactertistics in terms of age, sex, employment, and other demographic elements. This is a major change designed to promote relevance and accountability of centers to the catchment's inhabitants.

The 1978 presidential commission, apparently with some cognizance of the CMHCs' (and its staff's) control of benefits, did recommend that appropriateness of care for clients may require a broad range of people providing a broad range of services under the supervision of physicians, psychologists, social workers, or nurses. This recommendation, if implemented, may contribute to more client choice in securing services.

INTERRELATION OF BENEFITS

One very positive feature of the community mental health acts is their emphasis on a comprehensive system of benefits. As a result the mandated services really comprise a continuum of responses to possible client needs, and clients can be moved when necessary through services or receive several mental health services concurrently. PL-84-93 went even further by stating that services existing in the community should be orchestrated with mental health benefits because they have impact upon the functioning of individuals. Thus community mental health centers often reflect a strong commitment to the practice concept of case management, in which a case manager is responsible for ensuring that appropriate benefits and services are dispensed to clients.

A key way in which benefits to low-income populations occurs is through the CMHCs and contract agencies serving people who are entitled to Title XX services. In fact, PL-84-93 almost promotes dispensing services to Medicare, Medicaid, and public assistance populations by the manner in which funding and allocation care currently occurring in community mental health.

EVALUATION

Attempts to examine what has occured because of the Community Mental Health Acts, especially PL-88-164, have gone in different directions. At the annual meeting of the Kittay Scientific Foundation in 1976, its director, George Servan, representing one type of criticism, characterized the "golden age of mental health" (1973-1975) as an era "supported by scanty social evidence produced by fragmented social research."[21] He charged that community psychiatry and the CMHC movement were used by social activists, self-styled guradians for the rights of the mentally ill, as a springboard for personal political objectives. The correlation between mental illness and social class became the justification, according to Servan, for attempts to replace the medical model with a sociopolitical one, "which allegedly would have cured not only the social imperfections of society but also our mental illness." But it did not, insisted Servan and the move away from the medical model and what has been characterized as the massive indiscriminate discharge from the hospitals of mental patients produced a "revolving door" policy.

Other observers of the community mental health movement have been more charitable about its impact. For example, the proponents of the 1975 amendments of the CMHC Act called community mental health care the most effective and humane form of care for the majority of mentally ill individuals: (1) CMHCs have fostered coordination and cooperation between various agencies responsible for mental health care, which in turn has (2) resulted in a decrease in duplication, waste, and inefficiency of services and resources, and (3) have brought comprehensive care to all in need within a specific geographic area regardless of ability to pay.

It is very clear that community mental health centers and deinstitutionalization of mental patients have brought primary locus of care to the communities. In 1955 there were 550,000 mental patients in institutions. By 1975 there were only about 200,000. Also, it appears that the number of people served through community-based programs has risen sharply, and so have costs—from $1.7 billion in 1955 to over $17.0 billion in

1975.[22] Yet the goal of establishing two thousand CMHCs has not been met, and the provision of quality psychiatric services to middle- and low-income people is still not fully achieved.

In 1969 Mechanic, in speaking to the topic of crisis therapies often utilized in community mental health, commented that "the value of such therapies is difficult to determine since no careful comparative studies of such care in contrast to other forms of care are available. Moreover, the criteria to be used in judging such efforts are not established."[23]

We are not suggesting that the importance of evaluation is minimized within the community mental health field. On the contrary, PL-94-63 requires all CMHCs to spend at least 2 percent of their budgets on evaluation. Further, the National Institute of Mental Health, founded in 1948, and the umbrella under which the CMHCs have developed, has spent over $1 billion on research, much of which relates to epidemiology and incidence. Rather, it appears that community mental health is just approaching the stage when fairly definitive statements can be made concerning effort and outcome.[24] A good example of outcome research is reported by Bolin and Kivens, and their findings speak to clear achievements in community mental health programming. They report that "in the first full year of operation . . . the center achieved a forty-seven percent reduction in admissions to state hospitals . . . in the second year eight-seven percent of the outpatient clients attained their therapy goals in an average of 4.2 treatment sessions."[25]

We believe that the spirit of PL-84-93 and the prevailing theme of accountability in our times suggest continued effort in evaluating community mental health services. Already in motion, due to PL-84-93, are provisions for quality assurance programs, including utilization and peer review systems.

Problem Perception Critique

UNITS OF ANALYSIS—SOCIAL SCIENCE CONSTRUCTS

In examining PL-84-164 and Pl-94-63, it appears that the area of mental health is approached in a variety of ways. One unit of analysis is the individual—especially in terms of the mandate to provide necessary services to all individuals regardless of income. However, group influences are clearly present in these acts. First, the concept of catchment clearly suggests that individuals live within geographically and socially shared areas. Such areas can provide a learning environment for individuals, as well as have within them sources of environmentally based stress. The acts, especially PL–94–63, try to capture the possible influence of these contextual elements by creating governing boards, comprised of area residents, and by requiring CMHCs to overcome the geographic and cultural barriers to the receipt of services.

In addition to an appreciation of group influences upon individuals, the acts are also sensitive to the risks of certain groups who appear to be disproportionately vulnerable to sources of stress and situational crises. Such groups as children and the elderly as well as low-income populations are specifically designated as groups at "risk." In short, PL–94–63 appears to strongly recognize that individuals born into any of the above-mentioned groups are apt to be affected by the high correlation rates of their groups' characteristics with mental disorders and problems in social functioning. Thus the acts seek to help individuals, but they also take into account variations among groups.

There also appears to be a strong appreciation of the roles of organizations and their key representatives. The acts speak to training and educating key organizations and staff in how to promote people's health, minimize sources of organizational malfunctioning and stress, and help people cope with pressures in their daily life space so that acute disorders do not occur. The premise behind this approach appears clear: if key organizations and professionals in the natural environment can effectively relate to people, then the well-being of any given individual stands a better chance of being achieved. Again the concept of seeing the individual relative to social environment is present.

Given the preceding discussion it appears that the causation perspective in community mental health involves an appreciation of how individuals and groups of individuals interact with environmental circumstances. In light of this interaction, the specific concepts of socially induced stress, organizational malfunctioning, crises tied to life stages (e.g., divorce), and situational pressures are most prevalent. As Mechanic has stated, "the social stress perspective assumes that every person has his breaking point and that mental illness and psychiatric disability are products largely of the cumulation of stress in people's lives; this stress eventually overcomes their coping abilities."[26]

Acceptance of this causation principle is important for a variety of reasons, not the least of which is the logical imperative to engage in preventive activities and activities designed to promote mental health.

Cultural-Interest Perspectives

If we now look at the major themes of work, individualism, and collectivism, we see that the community mental health acts have a unique blending. The influence of a work ethic does not seem to be present in this social welfare product. The only way in which it may indirectly present itself is in terms of a work setting's being a possible source of stress and/or continued employment's being a goal and indicator of individual social competence. That work has a value in and of itself is not stressed in the services derived from these acts.

Individualism is present in the acts but in a basically progressive sense. First, it is understood that all individuals have the right to services that are geared to minimization of mental illness and the promotion of mental health. Further, it is clearly understood that such help for individuals must be available because individuals may have limited control over the environment that is impinging upon them. Thus individuals have a right to service and a right to develop their social competence as much as possible. Finally, individuals have rights to be maintained in their communities and not to be institutionalized if at all possible.

Increasingly individuals are being asked to assume, where possible, more responsibility for the cost of services provided them. The increasing reliance upon individual fees and reimbursement by the individual's private insurance company is a reflection of this.

Collectivism is probably the strongest theme present in the acts. The acts clearly indicate that we are responsible for each other's mental functioning in the type of society we have produced. The federal government by the passage of the acts, the enumeration of mandated services, and the availability of construction, staffing, and operating grants has acknowledged a responsibility in the mental health sector. However it is also important to note that given the spirit of the 1970s the federal government, through decreasing funding patterns, is attempting to have more responsibility assumed by state and local governments. As the federal government attempts to promote increased collective responsibility within a decentralized framework, there will be a greater reliance upon collectivism through private insurance companies.

In looking at the range of interests possibly met by the introduction and continuation of the community mental health acts, we detect the following. First, there are the interests of humanists. The area of mental health has a rich tradition of humanism, stemming all the way from the period of Dorothea Dix and Clifford Beers. In our current period much of this work has been extended by the Mental Health Associations and the Community Mental Health Centers Association.

Of a related, but somewhat of a less altruistic, nature are the interests of the major professional groups associated with community mental services; psychiatry, social work, and psychology have been rather successful in having their roles and professional identities blend into the range of services that normally prevail within community mental health centers. Employment opportunities for these professionals have greatly expanded, and it is in their best interests to have continuing programs in community mental health.

We are not suggesting that there is anything wrong about these groups' promoting the concept of community mental health. In fact a strong case might be made for the fact, that when humanism is fused with professional and organizational interests, then there is a greater chance of achieving and maintaining service modifications.

Finally, we would like to identify the emerging interests of the community mental health centers. As the federal share of funding decreases, that local mental health centers will be structurally induced to provide services to clients for which there is reimbursement. Thus centers may be increasingly led to a greater reliance on direct service strategies provided by professionals who are approved by insurance and accrediting groups. In this way funding patterns may have rather direct consequences for types of services, staffing, and range of innovation.

Recommendations for Change

In February 1977, President Carter established the President's Commission on Mental Health to review services throughout the country and to project needs and appropriate services for the coming twenty-five years. The commission completed its work in mid-1978 and delivered a report that offered a broad view of the future. In extending the spirit of the role of social and environment factors upon mental health, the commission stated that service responses must "include the damage to mental health associated with unrelenting poverty and unemployment and the institutionalized discrimination that occurs on the bases of race, sex, class, age and mental or physical handicaps" and must also include responses "which do not fit conventional categories of classification or service."[27]

The commission recommended the expenditure of an additional $500 million in new federal funding for mental health over the next five years. It called for new legislation, a Community Mental Health Services Act, that would phase the current Community Mental Health Center approach into a more flexible program. The commission's recommendations addressed the following areas:

1. *Community Support.* The commission urged the government to identify and support linkages between community mental health services and informal support systems such as families, friends, neighbors, clergy, schools, work place, justice systems, and alternative services such as "free clinics."

2. *Service Systems.* This section of the report recommended "going beyond" CMHCs to more flexible "new initiatives"

through new legislation to be funded at a rate of $75 million the first year and $100 million for two more years. The new service program would be directed toward special local needs and underserved populations such as the elderly, children, teenagers, racial minorities, and the chronically ill. For the care of the chronically mentally ill, the commission gave particular emphasis to the National Institute of Mental Health pilot projects in community support systems for former mental hospital patients now "deinstitutionalized." This is currently a small demonstration program. The commission recommended a $50 million national plan for closing large mental hospitals and strengthening community services for former patients. Service recommendations included consolidation of mental health services and social services on the local level and parity in mental health and physical health financing and planning.

3. *Insurance.* The commission recommended a system "where payment is based upon need for care, not diagnosis, and upon the appropriateness of care, not the discipline of the provider." Specifically, the report noted that both public and private providers should offer a range of coverage and reimbursement for the most appropriate and least restrictive care supervised, but not necessarily furnished, by physicians, psychologists, social workers, or nurses. A number of program and statutory changes were recommended for the Medicare and Medicaid programs to make them more reasonable in eligibility and benefit provisions and to discourage states from manipulating rates and favoring institutional care. HEW was encouraged to explore creating a new system or a modification of Supplemental Security Income that would offer a variety of services to the chronically ill and follow such patients from hospitals, through intermediate care, and into the community. The report also recommended more outpatient mental health insurance benefits.

4. *Personnel.* To increase mental health personnel, the report called for $85 million increase in training scholarships. Additionally, it suggested that funds be made available for training human service paraprofessionals and case managers, administrators, evaluators, and advocates.

5. *Basic Human Rights.* To ensure that each person has maximum rights and options, the report recommended the es-

tablishment of state advocacy systems (similar to those for the developmentally disabled) and the rewriting of commitment statutes to "precisely and unambiguously describe the types of conditions and behaviors that can lead to loss of personal liberty."

6. *Research.* The commission recommended more funding for trained researchers and investigation, especially in the areas of incidence of mental problems and utilization of services; needs and problems of underserved populations; delivery of services; and major mental illnesses, mental retardation, and basic psychological, sociological, biological, and developmental processes.

7. *Prevention.* The report placed heavy emphasis upon prevention—that is, providing treatment programs to keep people from becoming mental patients. Specifically the report recommended that NIMH create a Primary Prevention Center with a $10 million research budget plus demonstration and evaluation projects. There were suggestions that early childhood programs such as Head Start and Child Health Assessment Program be expanded and that areas such as parent education, genetic counseling, amniocentesis, food supplementation for pregnant women, and extended use of school buildings for recreation, remedial, and enrichment programs be studied.

8. *Public Understanding.* The report also recognized the need for higher-quality public information on mental illness, recommending that the media could more accurately portray emotionally troubled people, Movement in these areas, we feel, would strengthen and expand the achievements emanating from the community mental health acts discussed in this chapter.

Summary

In this chapter we have sketched the background and character of the community mental health acts that attempt to bring relevant services to people in their natural environments. The role of the concepts of environment and socially induced stress were and are significant in the development and implementation of the acts. Critical issues may have to be examined in the next few years as funding patterns evolve and as greater reliance upon local funding and insurance occurs. These issues stand in marked contrast to the broad view of services and government responsibility offered by the 1978 presidential commission.

Notes

1. Richard Hofstader, *Social Darwinism in American Thought* (Boston: Beacon, 1955), p. 5.
2. Davis Kingsley, "Mental Hygiene and the Class Structure," in Patrick Mullahey, ed., *A Study of Interpersonal Relations* (New York: Hermitage, 1949), pp. 364–385.
3. Walter I. Trattner, *From Poor Law to Welfare State*, 2d ed. (New York: Free Press, 1979), p. 59.
4. *Ibid.*, p. 58.
5. *Ibid.*, p. 59.
6. *Ibid.*, p. 172.
7. The National Mental Health Act (1946).
8. *Ibid.*, Sec. 201.
9. Raymond Glasscote; David Sanders; H. M. Forstenzer; and A. R. Foley, *The Community Mental Health Center* (Baltimore: Goramowe/Predemark Press, 1964), pp. 7–8.
10. Much of the following discussion on PL–94–63 is based upon the law itself and the memoranda of the National Association of Mental Health Centers concerning PL–94–63 (unpublished).
11. James M. Cameron, "Ideology and Policy Termination: Restructing California's Mental Health System," *Public Policy*, 26 (Fall 1978), 533–570.
12. *Ibid.*, p. 545.
13. *Ibid.*, p. 550.
14. *Ibid.*, p. 548.
15. Glasscote et al., *op. cit.*, p. 6.
16. Gerald Caplan, *Principles of Preventive Psychiatry* (New York: Basic Books, 1964); Gerald Caplan, "Community Psychiatry: Introduction and Overview," in S. E. Goldstone, ed., *Concepts of Community*

Psychiatry (Washington, D.C.: U.S. Government Printing Office, 1951), pp. 3–18.

17. Glasscote et al., *op. cit.,* p. 9.

18. *Ibid.,* pp. 9–10.

19. National Association of Mental Health Center, *op. cit.*

20. A catchment is a defined geographical area and population toward which a delivery system is responsible for provision of services.

21. "Scrutinizing Community Mental Health," *Science News,* April 10, 1976, 232–233.

22. "Emptying the Mental Wards: New Treatment Stirs a Controversy," *U.S. News and World Report,* 78, February 24, 1975, 71–73.

23. David Mechanic, *Mental Health and Social Policy* (Englewood Cliffs, N.J.: Prentice-Hall, 1969), p. 43.

24. Milton G. Thackeray; Rex A. Skidmore; and William Farley, *Introduction to Mental Health: Field and Practice* (Englewood Cliffs, N.J.: Prentice-Hall, 1979), pp. 253–257.

25. David C. Bolin, and Lawrence Kivens, "Evaluation in a Community Mental Health Center," *Evaluation,* 2 (June, 1974), 26.

26. Mechanic, *op. cit.,* p. 43.

27. Report of the President's Commission on Mental Health (Washington, D.C.: U.S. Government Printing Office, 1978), p. 9.

Chapter 13

The Older Americans Act and Other Policy Instruments Serving the Elderly

SOCIAL CONCERN FOR THE ELDERLY antedates biblical days; how-ever, provisions for their care were generally accepted to be the responsibility of the aged themselves or their family. Public re-sponsibility to the needs of the elderly began in this country during the nineteenth century by public-spirited citizens, the church, and charities who established almshouses for the poor, the paupers, the old, and the infirmed. Social policy initiatives on behalf of the elderly did not evolve until the twentieth cen-tury. This is so, in part, because the number of persons who grew to be old was not large enough to attract widespread atten-tion of the general public and the government. At the close of the American Revolution, there were only 50,000 persons among an estimated 2.5 million inhabitants who were aged sixty-five or older. The median age of white males was fifteen years, and, by the time of the Civil War, this average had in-creased by only four years.

During the early seventeenth century, the population of the colonies was about 2,500, with an average life expectancy at birth of thirty years. By 1830, one out of twenty-five persons was sixty years of age or older. Table 13–1 provides information about the

TABLE 13-1. **Average Life Expectancy at Birth and at Age 65 in the United States for Various Years, 1900-1970**

	1900	1939	1949	1955	1959	1970
At birth	47.3	63.7	68.0	69.6	69.9	70.9
At age 65	11.9	12.8	12.8	14.2	14.4	15.2

Source: U.S. Public Health Service, National Center for Health Statistics, *Vital Statistics of the United States, 1970. Vol. 2—Mortality* (Washington, D.C.: U.S. Government Printing Office, 1974), part A, Tables 5-1 and 5-5.

average life expectancy at birth and at age sixty-five for the period 1900-1970.

Cutler observed that the person who was already aged sixty-five in 1900 could expect to live another twelve years, approximately to age seventy-seven. In 1970, a person who was already aged sixty-five could expect to live another fifteen years, or until about age eighty. So, between 1900 and 1970, the increase in old age life expectancy was only about three years. This is quite different from the relative life expectancy at birth in 1900 and 1970. A baby born in 1900 could expect to live to be forty-seven, whereas in 1970 the newborn baby could expect to live to be about seventy-one years old, an increase of twenty-four years.[1]

These data indicate that the U.S. population is living longer. That more persons are surviving to the upper age brackets than ever before in our nation's history is largely responsible for the phenomenal rate of growth of the population over age sixty-five. Increases in life expectancy are primarily a reflection of decreased mortality rates at the younger age categories rather than increased longevity after age sixty-five. Reduction of maternal and infant mortality rates and the eradication and control of many diseases that proved fatal among younger age groups have made it possible for more people to survive to old age.[2]

Background

From a historical perspective, public concern about the conditions of the elderly began to emerge as a result of two interrelated demographic factors. First was the rise in the number of adults living beyond the period of parental responsibility. Second was the increasing freedom of the older adult from the need to continue to work beyond a certain age. These two conditions created new problems that the elderly, society, and the government were not prepared to deal with. They included maintaining income during the retirement years, preserving of health and the capacity for active participation in the mainstream of social life, making suitable housing and living arrangements, finding new activities and roles that afford meaning and satisfaction, and establishing new social relationship to replace those lost by departure of children from the home, retirement from work, and social isolation resulting from death of relatives and friends.

Early efforts to address the needs of the elderly began to develop as a part of the social reform and humanitarian movements during which, Mohl notes, "groups were formed for every imaginable purpose," including assistance to widows.[3] Federal response to the needs of the aged did not come until later, with the advent of the Depression and the passage of the Social Security Act. As a matter of fact, prior to 1935 the problems of elderly citizens were either given extremely low priority by the government or ignored completely. This was so, as already pointed out in part, because of the absence of a "public interest." That is, there were no political or cultural ethos, social values, or interest group perspectives for defining the common good with regard to the role of the government vis-à-vis the elderly.

Kerschner suggests that the Depression brought into painful focus the realities of life under which the elderly lived. "Hundreds of thousands of citizens over the age of 65 were either living in desolate poverty on their own or compelled to live as charity cases within the homes of their children."[4]

With the passage of the Social Security Act and its provisions for Old Age and Survivor's Insurance as well as disability benefits, federal government action for the first time significantly affected the incomes of the elderly. In addition to income, the provision of other essential services has become a concern of the federal government, and the elderly have been frequently singled out for special attention, as for example in the provisions for public housing for the elderly under the Housing Acts of 1937, 1956, 1959, and 1974. This trend had a far-reaching effect with the implementation of Medicare, a policy product that may be the beginning of a national health insurance system for the elderly.

As the nation moved toward midcentury, value perspectives about the aged began to change. Retirement was viewed as a reward for past contributions, and retirement began to gain respectability. By this time, there had been a marked increase in the elderly population in the United States and the need for public policy became evident. The experience gained from the administration of Old Age, Survivors, Disability Health Insurance (OASDHI) made it apparent that federal efforts were required in meeting the needs of a growing constituency. The Older Americans Act (OAA) of 1965 and the Administration on Aging (AOA) were born.

What Is the Policy Product?

The OAA clearly affirmed our nation's sense of responsibility toward the well-being of the elderly. The Declaration of Objectives in Title I is a charter of rights for older people. It commits the nation to secure on their behalf an adequate income in retirement, optimum health without regard to economic status, restorative services, suitable housing, opportunity for employment, meaningful activity, and "freedom, independence, and the free exercise of individual initiative in planning and managing their own lives."

Under Title II of the act, the AOA is authorized to serve as a clearing house for information related to problems of the aged and aging; assist the secretary in all matters pertaining to problems of the aged and aging; administer the grants provided in the act; develop plans; conduct and arrange for research and demonstration programs in the field of aging; provide technical assistance and consultation to states and political subdivisions with respect to programs for the aged and aging; prepare, publish, and disseminate educational materials dealing with welfare of older persons; gather statistics in the field of aging that other federal agencies are not collecting; and stimulate more effective use of existing resources and available services for the aged and aging.

Title III provides formula grants to the states to pay part of the cost of planning, developing, and operating a comprehensive social service delivery system in the community. To obtain funding, the designated state agency on aging must divide the state into planning and service areas. The state agency also may elect to designate a local area agency on aging that in turn would be responsible for planning, developing, and operating a social service delivery system for elderly individuals residing in the designated area.

In developing a social service delivery system for the elderly, the state agency has overall responsibility for coordinating and utilizing existing social services available on the local level. Also, the state agency may award grants to public and private nonprofit agencies and organizations for providing services to older people that otherwise would be unavailable.

Title III also awards funds to public or nonprofit private agencies or organizations for paying part or all of the cost of developing and operating statewide, regional, metropolitan, county, city, or community model projects designed to demonstrate new or improved methods of providing needed services to older people.

The 1973 amendments to the Older Americans Act revised this program so that special consideration is given to sponsors who develop projects in one of five areas—housing, transportation, education, preretirement counseling, and special services for older handicapped individuals. Prior to the 1973 amendments, model projects focused on alternatives to institutionalization, outreach activities to identify elderly individuals living in isolated areas, and needed services for elderly individuals living in disaster areas.

Title IV focuses upon training and research. It authorizes grants to public and private nonprofit agencies, organizations, and institutions for training persons employed or preparing for employment in the field of aging. Grants also are awarded to public and private agencies and organizations to publicize available career opportunities in the field of aging and encourage qualified persons to enter or reenter the field of aging. It also authorizes grants to public and private nonprofit organizations, agencies, and individuals for establishing research and demonstration programs in the field of aging. Research and demonstration projects may involve the study of current living patterns and conditions of older persons, methods to improve the standard of living and way of life for older people, and means for improving the coordination of community services designed for older people.

The 1973 amendments to the Older Americans Act authorized the secretary of transportation, the secretary of housing and urban development, and the commissioner on aging to conduct a comprehensive study and survey of the transportation problems of the elderly. In connection with this study, federal grants may be awarded to public and private nonprofit agencies and organizations.

In addition, the 1973 amendments authorized a program of grants to public and private nonprofit agencies, organizations, and institutions to establish or support multidisciplimary centers of gerontology. These centers provide for a wide range of activities such as the recruiting and training of personnel to work in the field of aging. Activities also include research and demonstration projects with respect to the social, economic, and psychological needs of older people. In addition, consultation services are provided to public and voluntary organizations with respect to the needs of older people.

The 1973 amendments added Title V to the act. Title V authorizes the federal government to award grants to or enter into contracts with public and nonprofit private agencies to pay up to 75 percent of the cost of purchasing, leasing, repairing, or altering a facility to serve as a multipurpose senior center. A sponsor must develop the center in an area that is in close proximity to the majority of individuals eligible to use the facility and within walking distance where possible.

In addition, Title V authorizes the federal government to insure mortgages for the acquisition, alternation, or renovation of such facilities. The mortgage insurance is to be financed through a Multipurpose Senior Center Insurance Fund created by the secretary of health, education, and welfare as a revolving fund for carrying out the insurance program.

Title V also authorizes funds for professional and technical staffing required for the initial operation of a multipurpose senior center. The government may award initial staffing grants for three-year periods of up to 75 percent for the first year, 66²/₃ percent for the second year, and 50 percent for the third year.

ADVISORY COMMITTEE

In Title VI, the act provides for the establishment of an Advisory Committee on Older Americans. The commissioner on aging serves as the chairman and fifteen members who are experienced or have demonstrated particular interest in special problems of the aging are appointed by the secretary of health, education, and welfare.

Normally each member is appointed for three years, but, of the first fifteen members, five are appointed for only one year, five for two years, and five for three years.

The secretary is also authorized to appoint such technical advisory committees as he or she deems appropriate, without regard to the civil service laws.

Title VII of the Older Americans Act provides formula grants to the states to pay part of the cost of establishing and operating programs that will deliver low-cost meal programs to older people. The programs must be located in community settings such as schools, senior citizen centers, and churches accessible to the majority of elderly people for whom they are intended. The programs are to provide one hot meal per day on at least five days a week along with services that would introduce the participants to the other social resources in the communities. They also are to provide home-delivered meals to older persons in the community who are unable to leave their homes.

Title IX, the Older Americans Community Service Employment Program provides part-time opportunities in community service activities for unemployed low-income persons who are fifty-five years of age or older and who have poor employment prospects. The secretary of labor is authorized to enter into agreements with public or private nonprofit agencies or organizations to pay up to 90 percent of the costs of establishing and operating a project for the employment of older persons. Up to 100 percent of the costs may be paid for a project located in an emergency or disaster area or in an economically depressed area. Older persons participating in a community service employment project are to be paid a rate equal to at least the federal minimum wage.[5]

1978 AMENDMENTS

The 1978 amendments revised the purpose of the OAA to foster "the development of comprehensive and the coordinated service systems to serve older individuals"—meaning all necessary social services—with an expanded purpose "to provide a continuum of care for the vulnerable elderly." Social services (including multipurpose senior centers), nutrition services (including congregate and home-delivered meals), legal services, and an ombudsman program are consolidated under a new Title III, administered by the state agency for aging. Under the 1978 amendments, three year planning cycles are now required both for area and state agencies on aging. Priorities are set on "access" services, in-home services, and legal services. Fifty percent of each area agency's services allotment are now required to be spent on these three. Training, research, and discretionary projects and programs were consolidated in Title IV, and the commissioner on aging may now make grants to develop comprehensive, coordinated systems of community long-term care.

Revised and expanded authority for community services employment programs for older Americans is provided under a redesignated Title V and a new Title IV authorizes grants to eligible Indian tribal organizations to promote delivery of comprehensive social services for Indians aged sixty and over.

KEY ACTORS AND SOCIOPOLITICAL CONDITIONS

By midcentury, the older adult was a visible sector of the American population that could no longer be ignored with respect to their numbers and their social and economic conditions.

By 1940, the elderly population had increased to 9 million and represented 6.8 percent of the total population, an increase of 2.7 percent since the turn of the century. The formalization of the geriatric society in 1942 and the gerontological society in 1945 established the elderly as a viable policy constituency. In 1950, under the auspices of the Federal Security Agency, a National Conference on Aging was held. A major recommendation of this conference was a "call for all voluntary and government agencies to accept greater responsibility for the problems and welfare of older people in the United States."

In 1956 the Senate Labor Committee established a Special Staff on Aging. The establishment of this group was promoted by the need to attend to the growing problems of low-income levels among the aged, growing numbers reaching retirement age, spiraling rates of inflation and their impact upon relatively fixed retirement income, and growing disabilities among the working aged. Related to this, President Eisenhower created the Federal Council on Aging and attempted to consolidate the efforts among federal departments concerned with the aged. It was also hoped that this move would consolidate planning activities, responsibility, and budgeting allotments and reduce fragmented authority.

Public policy advocacy for the elderly began to be more clearly defined when the U.S. Senate in 1959 created the Special Committee on Aging, and the U.S. House of Representatives created its permanent Select Committee on Aging. Of no small impact upon these developments were the political activities of the elderly. Older people organized themselves into the American Association of Retired Persons (1958), the National Retired Teachers Association (1947), the National Council on Aging (1960), the National Council of Senior Citizens (1962), and the Grey Panthers (1972). Although these groups varied somewhat with respect to each other in style, they all represented a clear notion of the special interests of the elderly and layed expectations upon government officials. In no small part the Kerr–Mills Act of 1962 (Program of Medical Assistance to the Aged), Medicare in 1965, and SSI in 1974 reflected responses to these constituencies.

Perhaps of special relevance to the development of the Older Americans Act were the White House Conferences on Aging.

These were held in 1961 and in 1971. By the end of the 1950s Congress, special interest groups, and individuals began to raise questions as to the lack of direction in the field of aging. Although several states had units on aging dealing with age-related problems, it was apparent that a strong agency operating on the federal level was required. Momentum began to build toward the introduction of legislation that would create an independent agency able to speak with one voice for the interests of older Americans. By the end of the decade, the call for greater action in the field resulted in President Eisenhower's assembling the first federally financed White House Conference on Aging held in 1961.

The final report issued by the conference set the tone for a federal agency in the field of aging to be established with the following provisions: a statutory basis and more independent leadership; adequate funds for coordination and other assigned functions through a line item appropriation; responsibility for formulation of legislative proposals for submittal to Congress; and responsibility for periodic reviews and reports on the various federal programs, departments, and agencies working in behalf of older people to achieve effective coordination and operation (Senate Special Committee on Aging, 1961).

Congressman John E. Fogarty began the long process of introducing legislation, based primarily on these recommendations, to set up an independent agency on aging, namely, H. B. 7957, which strove (1) to provide assistance in developing new or improved programs to help older persons through grants to the states for community planning and services and for training through research, development, or training projects grants and (2) to establish within the Department of Health, Education, and Welfare an operating agency to be designated as the Administration of Aging. Congressman Fogarty along with Congressman McNamara reintroduced the bill, specifically calling for an independent agency within the Department of Health, Education, and Welfare with a commissioner appointed by the president with the advice and consent of the Senate. During the next two years, a good deal of legislative maneuvering culminated in the passage of the Older Americans Act of 1965 and the creation of the Administration on Aging.

Shortly after its establishment, the Administration on Aging came under severe criticism, in part because of the agency's inability to be all things to all of its constituencies. At a hearing in 1967 to extend the Older Americans Act, one witness criticized the agency for its inadequacy in "focal point" roles of policy, leadership, advocacy, and coordination.

In 1967 the agency was placed within the Social and Rehabilitation Service of HEW. This was seen by many as a direct violation of the intent of Congress, but also as a loss of authority and control. The move was also seen by some as evidence of a decline in federal commitment to the problems of older adults. This point of view gained added credence when the Foster Grandparent Program and Retired Senior Volunteers Program were transferred, along with VISTA and the Peace Corps, in 1971 to the newly created ACTION, an umbrella agency. This loss of identity and budgeting independence resulted in problems of morale and a loss of skilled, dedicated personnel.

As a result of these developments plus the complaints of various interests groups promoting the interests of the elderly, a major effort was made at the second White House Conference on Aging (1971) to develop a national policy on aging. Arthur Flemming, commissioner on aging, in the final report on the conference stated:

> The 1971 White House Conference on Aging sought to crystallize in national policy the dimensions of society in which older Americans may "fitly live" while completing the adventure of life with fulfillment and serenity.[6]

In March 1971, President Nixon sent a message to Congress in which he articulated a comprehensive strategy to meet the needs of older Americans. His strategy called for (1) assuring an adequate income, (2) assuring appropriate living arrangements, (3) assuring independence and dignity, and (4) assuring institutional responsiveness and a new attitude toward aging.

FUNDING AND ALLOCATION

The act authorized the secretary of HEW to make allotments to the states for community planning and coordination of pro-

grams for older citizens; demonstration projects; training of
special personnel; and the establishment of new or expansion of
existing programs, including centers providing recreational and
other leisure-time activities and informational, health, welfare,
counseling, and referral services for older persons, assisting
such persons in providing volunteer community or civic services.

The act specifically excluded costs of construction except for
minor alterations and repairs.

For grants to states, $5 million was authorized for the 1966
fiscal year and $8 million for each of fiscal 1967 and 1968.

From the total sum appropriated for a fiscal years, 1.0 percent
could be allotted to each state, the District of Columbia, and
Puerto Rico. The Virgin Islands, Guam, and American Samoa
were allotted 0.5 percent. The remainder of the appropriation
was allotted to the states and other jurisdictions on the basis of
the ratio of the population aged sixty-five or over in each jurisdiction to the national population aged sixty-five and over.

The federal allotment was available for payment of part of the
cost of projects approved by the state in accordance with its state
plan. The federal share from 1965–1973 was 75 percent of the
cost of the project during the first year, 60 percent during the
second year, and 50 percent during the third year. The 1973
amendments changed the ratio to 90 to 10.

A total of 10 percent of each state's allotment, or $15,000
whichever was larger, could be used for paying one-half the cost
of administration of the state plan.

From 1969 until enactment of the 1973 amendments, there
were two separate authorizations for program support. The
1973 amendments provided authorization for fiscal years
1973–1975. Amounts authorized were $103,600,000 for the fis-
cal year ending June 30, 1974, $130,000,000 for fiscal year end-
ing June 30, 1975, and $180,000,000 for the fiscal year ending
June 30, 1976. The 1975 amendments added authorizations for
fiscal years 1976, 1977, and 1978: $231,000,000 for fiscal year
ending September 30, 1977 and $287,000,000 for fiscal year
ending September 30, 1978. Appropriations authority for Title
III grants for state social services and nutrition programs, for
Title V community service employment programs, and for
ACTION agency programs for older Americans (foster

grandparents and RSVP) totaled approximately $1.16 billion for fiscal 1979—a 24.5 percent increase over the year-earlier appropriations authority. Funding authority was increased to $1.32 billion in fiscal 1980 and to $1.55 billion in fiscal 1981. In addition to these specific dollar amounts, "such sums as may be necessary" are authorized for a National Information and Research Clearinghouse; an expanded Federal Council on the Aging, to include a staff; federal administration of the OAA; provision of surplus food commodities for older Americans programs; Title IV research, training, and demonstrations; and Title VI grants to Indian tribal organizations.

The state grant formula continues to be based on population of persons aged sixty and over. Reallocation is authorized, and such reallocated funds remain available through the succeeding program year. Matching funds for Title III grants for services remain at a 90-to-10 rate through fiscal 1980 (matchable in cash or in kind), but the rate is revised to 85 to 15 in fiscal 1981.

Thus the federal government relies upon general sources and makes allocations to states on a grant basis. Allocations over time seem to be growing, and in most recent years (post 1973) require rather minimal matching dollars on the part of states. This stands in marked contrast to funding allocation developments in the field of community mental health. A possible explanation of the difference may be found in the perceived political chart of the elderly in the United States, as well as the acceptance of the elderly as a valued category or group.

PREVENTION AND INTERVENTION

The Older Americans Act is clearly predicated on the premise that the elderly are a valued group that will predictably have problems and needs in our type of society. Such problems and needs are seen as not necessarily leveling themselves to individual and/or family situations. Further, existing organizations and agencies may have to be encouraged to relate more consciously to the needs of older people. In light of this, the Older Americans Act seems to reflect (1) a commitment to offering a

broad range of services to those who are elderly and in need; (2) a recognition that some services should have a developmental focus—that is, keeping the elderly active so as to prevent or delay serious problems from presenting themselves; and (3) a point of view, perhaps best exemplified through funding and allocations patterns, that local organizations and agencies have to be helped to expand services for the elderly. In a sense activities that are related to these different points of view suggest that our country is in the process of developing, in a somewhat disjointed fashion, a system of services and benefits that will be available, and in place, for those of us who become elderly.

Viewed collectively it would appear that the Older Americans Act, and other related legislation, tends to reflect a multilevel perspective of prevention and intervention, with service (tertiary) orientations dominating. However, even the service-level responses do not suggest personal change of the elderly, but rather the provision of benefits tied to the concept of the rights of the elderly, especially their rights to development. Such provision appears to have relation to raising the quality of life of the elderly as well as redistribution of benefits to the elderly.[8]

GENERAL THRUST

The general thrust of the Older Americans Act is to promote the living conditions of the elderly. Basically the act attempts to raise to more acceptable levels the range of activities in which older people may engage and the volume of services and programs that older people often need as a correlate of aging.

Adequacy for the elderly is operationalized within the context of the value of fairness as it is applied to the elderly by our society. Increasingly we as a people are saying that the elderly, by virtue of their age and previous activities, are entitled to services and programs in their more advanced years. Thus our society has moved a long way in institutionalizing the concept of social rights for the aged. Such institutionalization has profound implications on possible redistribution activities within our society.

Implementation—Benefits to People

STRUCTURE AND DISTRIBUTION OF BENEFITS

For a state to be eligible to participate in the programs of grants to states from OAA allotments, the respective states are required to establish designated state agencies on aging as the sole state agency. The state must be divided into area agencies on aging, with each operating under a planning and service area. There must be a state plan approved by the commissioner for the coordination of all state activities and an area plan approved by the state agency.

Basic policy benefits of the OAA are geared to age and problems and conditions of well-being (health, nutrition, social isolation, etc). These benefits are distributed primarily in the form of in-kind essential goods and services (i.e., nutrition programs, transportation, outreach activities, information and referral, social services, work opportunities, etc.).

The federal government assumes responsibility for the administration of these benefits but leaves actual provision in many cases to state agencies and private entrepreneurs and organizations. Many of the benefits to the aged are distributed through such organizations acting on behalf of the aged.

CLIENT CHOICE—AUTONOMY

Under the Older Americans Act, the elderly have a wide range of benefits from which they may choose. Obviously there is no coercion of clients so the elderly have choices in two directions: to participate or not participate in the benefits and to select which one or more of the benefits they want. The elderly also have representatives on the state planning bodies as well as on the area offices on aging. Thus they can influence the range and nature of benefits being distributed within their local areas.

Funds however, as discussed earlier, are distributed to the

organizations and agencies that actually provide services and programs. In this way the Older Americans Act recognizes the clear role of organizations and their staffs as providers, as well as the rights of the elderly to participate actively in the planning of such benefits. Because the range of benefits is rather broad, and not tightly associated with a few professional groups, the chance of benefits collectively being relevant to potential recipients appears relatively high, despite the fact that benefits are not distributed directly to the elderly.

INTERRELATION OF BENEFITS

In addition to the benefits associated with the Older Americans Act, there are many other benefits operating within the society that relate to the elderly. These involve cash payments (OASI and SSI), in-kind payments (medicare, food stamps), and tax exemptions and credits. Further, other legislative enactments that have had a partial focus upon the needs of the elderly are: the Adult Education Act, Age Discrimination Act of 1975, Comprehensive Employment and Training Act of 1973, Economic Opportunity Act of 1964 (as amended), Federal Aid Highway Act of 1973, Higher Education Act of 1965, Housing and Community Development Act of 1974, Library Services and Construction Act (1967), Rehabilitation Act of 1973, Urban Mass Transportation Act of 1964 (as amended), and Vocational Education Act of 1963. Space does not permit a critical examination of this partial list of other benefits to the aged—they are presented more to suggest to the reader the range of recent benefits to the elderly.

One area of benefits worthy of few brief remarks however is the area of health. Congress has responded to the needs of the elderly, particularly in the area of health care, with a wide range of services and programs aimed in part at preserving health in the middle and later years and assuring the availability of medical and restorative care. Notable among these have been the creation of and support given to the National Institutes of Health for research on aging and chronic disease; the Health Facilities Construction Acts of 1946 and 1964 and the National

Housing Acts, particularly the 1959 amendment, with their provisions for financing the construction of diagnostic, treatment, restoration, and long-term care facilities especially designed for older people; the Community Health Facilities Act of 1961; the Community Mental Health Centers Act of 1963 and subsequent amendments; and the Heart, Cancer, Stroke Act of 1965, which provides grants to state and local public and private agencies for studies, experiments, demonstrations, and treatment centers focused on the development of new and improved methods of providing health services, especially services outside of hospitals and institutions. All these programs and services as policy products illustrate an attempt to provide fairly comprehensive care to the elderly.

EVALUATIONS

There has been almost no substantive evaluation of the benefits of Older Americans Act and its amendments because of the limitations inherent in the technology of human services program evaluation. Most human services program evaluation strategies incorporate measures of efficiency and cost-effectiveness or other systems analysis concepts that do not lend themselves to the implicit policy mission of the act. In an ideological sense aging programs respond to value preferences that, for the most part, are couched in terms of "psychic benefits" and domains of social well-being that lend themselves to "soft measures." These measures have limited policy significance because they offer policy analysis almost no reliable data for making decisions about alternative use of scarce resources (allocative efficiency). Aging programs are justified on the basis of the *worthwhileness* of programs, a criterion that can be subjected to various interpretations and value preferences. Moreover, almost each policy benefit derived from the OAA has its own set of beneficiaries. Seldom are the programmatic objectives and clientele served by one program truly substitutable for another. Therefore, alternative use of scarce resources can seldom be measured in such a way as to be cost beneficial.

Focused evaluations have tried to answer such policy questions

as whether the development of a domiciliary care is more efficient than maintaining the elderly in their own homes. Findings for the most part have been inconclusive and have been criticized for methodological deficiencies. Nutrition programs have also been evaluated. However, their findings tend to point up problems of local administration and management rather than policy-related effects.

Critiquing the Problem Perception

UNIT OF ANALYSIS AND SOCIAL SCIENCE CONSTRUCTS

Benefits emanating from the Older Americans Act, as well as other related legislation, are clearly predicated upon a group construct—the elderly. This group is seen as having predictable needs that are the products of age phenomenon interacting with broad living conditions in our society. In approaching this group, our country—especially our legislators—is extremely aware of their substantial representation in the total population and of their strong voting electorate.

It appears that our society approaches the elderly as a valued group—valued because of age and prior productivity—that has difficulties in personally negotiating its advanced years. This condition produces a strain within our society and poses a dilemma to us. On the one hand, we value them as a group, yet on the other hand, our social system affords them a status whereby many of their needs might not be met. It is within this context of socially induced stress that many of the recent benefits for the elderly have been produced as a way to reduce the effects of the strain and to promote their living opportunities. In this regard benefits to the aged are directly tied to not only the needs of the aged but also to a recognition of the role of the society itself in producing such needs.

Implicit in these remarks concerning the status of the elderly in our society, and their needs, is the fact that the elderly is a group whose numbers have grown in our society at a time when

that society appears to not need them for the labor market. This produces still another facet of the strain operating within our society that is experienced by our elderly.

As a result of our thinking about the elderly as a valued entity in group and category terms, and our increasing appreciation of the role of the society impacting upon the elderly, our benefits for them are not only increasing but they presuppose little or no personal change on the part of the elderly. In short we see them as having needs, but we tend not to assume that their needs are tied to personal failure or to personal factors. In short the Older Americans Act, as one major social welfare product relating to the elderly, does reflect an appreciation of the range of needs of the elderly and the demographic patterns and trends of the elderly and suggests in light of these perceptions that our society should relate to individuals affected by these patterns and trends.

CAUSATION

Given our society's increasing use of the group construct, namely, the elderly, our positive valuation of the elderly, and our appreciation of the role our society has in operationalizing the status and needs of the elderly, it is logical to infer that social system processes are perceived as a paramount causal explanation of the problems affecting the elderly. Specifically the social system's inability to adequately provide such benefits as recreation, nutrition, and the like for the aged through normal market mechanisms has encouraged government to provide such necessary social welfare benefits as well as to broaden the options afforded the elderly. In this way social welfare assists the society in reducing its level of strain, minimizes the derived stress and effects felt by the elderly, and attempts to avert the elderly from disengaging from the society.

Cultural-Interest Perspectives

The Older Americans Act clearly reflects a positive extension of the value of work in the sense that its benefits are predicated

upon the public notion of reward for previous work and pro- ductivity. Individualism is only present in the act in the sense that any individual elderly person is entitled to such provisions as senior citizen centers, nutrition, social services, and the like by virtue of their participating in an age group. In short this act, as well as others relating to the elderly, legitimate the notion of individual rights derived from category participation.

The value of collectivism is expressed in terms of society's increasing responsibility to the aggregate older population. Viewed as a social welfare constituency, the aged enjoy wide- spread public sympathy. As Hudson observes, "older persons have done relatively well in the arena of public policy as con- trasted with other population groupings whose aggregate needs can be argued to be equally pressing."[9]

In keeping with other recent developments in social welfare, this value relative to the elderly is operationalized within a fed- eral responsibility/local provision context.

It is perhaps within the area of collectivism that the interest perspective and the political power of the elderly is most pre- sent. The elderly as an interest group have fared relatively well when compared with other social welfare constituencies because of what we have already described as their political legitimacy and utility. As a group, the elderly have been able to maintain an image of "deserving." Moreover, their tradition of active partici- pation in the electoral process has endowed them with political power at the ballot box. Because of their relatively heavy voting record, their influence at the polls is disproportionately greater than their relative ratio in the total population.

Recommendations for Change

This nation has made significant strides toward a national policy on aging since 1965. We have come to accept federal responsibility for assuring our senior citizens relief from the burdens of sickness, mental breakdowns, and social ostracism and assistance in the provision of suitable housing, equal oppor- tunity for gainful employment, and income adequacy.

The Older Americans Act and its amendments have come a

long way toward establishing a framework within which to achieve the goal of creating a society "in which older Americans may 'fitly live' while completing the adventure of life with fulfillment and serenity." But before this goal can be realized the Older Americans Act must give way to some other policy instrument that consolidates the provisions of the OAA, SSI, Medicare, and others into a single approach to old-age benefits. It is hoped that such a consolidation would conform to Binstock's recommendation: "I am suggesting that policies based on observations of people who are old right now . . . are often inadequate because they are not responsive to the needs and experiences of many persons who will be among the aging by the time that implementation is affected."[10]

The elderly as a social welfare constituency is growing. The baby boom of the 1940s will become the geriatric boom of the year 2000. Demographic trends and existing statutory provisions already require that public expenditures for the elderly increase dramatically. The geriatric boom will create new demands from among subgroups of the elderly population housing special needs that have not been addressed by existing benefits. The old–old (seventy-five years and older), economically deprived minorities and women all represent constituencies not adequately addressed. This becomes a major imperative for the future.

Other areas to be addressed by future policy initiatives are improving legal representation for the elderly and the handicapped and setting priorities for regulatory and safety standards to protect the elderly from crimes, health hazards, and abuse.

Summary

Social policy development for the elderly is essentially a twentieth-century phenomenon that began with the enactment of the Social Security Act in 1935 and gained significant impetus with the passage of the Older Americans Act (1965) and the establishment of the Administration on Aging.

The elderly have done relatively well in the arena of public policy as compared with other groups whose aggregate needs, it can be argued, are also very pressing. Critical to these legislative successes have been the elderly's political legitimacy and their political utility.

Moreover, the elderly are the beneficiaries of the Protestant ethic, which views positively those who have worked hard and have been productive. Many of the policy benefits to the elderly are viewed as rewards for past performances.

Finally, the elderly have achieved relative success in public policy because of the indisputability of their needs at the time of the relevant enactments. Hudson suggests that the elderly have reaped great benefits from the Older Americans Act and other policies not only because they are seen as legitimate and deserving recipients but also because executive branch leadership and those favoring an expanded social policy role for the national government have seen it as in their best interest to have such policies in place.[11]

An unanticipated consequence of increasing responsiveness to the needs of the elderly is that such change may be the forerunner of more progressive welfare responses to other segments of the society. As Gold and others have indicated, the "breakthrough" of welfare benefits to the elderly is very much tied to "constituency building" needs of public officials.[12] Once the breakthrough occurs, it might be argued that other groups may also receive benefits at a later point.

Notes

1. Neal E. Cutler, "The Aging Population and Social Policy," in Richard H. Davis, Ed., *Aging: Prospects and Issues* (Los Angeles: University of Southern California, Ethel Purcy Andrus Gerontology Center, 1977), pp. 105–124.
2. Charles Harris, *Fact Book on Aging* (Washington, D.C.: National Council on Aging, 1978), p. 9.
3. Raymond A. Mohl, "Poverty in Early America, A Reappraisal: The Case of Eighteenth-Century New York City." *New York History*, 50 (January 1969), 5–27.

4. Paul A. Kerschner, "Changing Legislation: Its Effects on Programs," in Richard H. Davis, ed., *op. cit.*, pp. 152–171.

5. Titles VI and VIII were repealed. The 1969 amendments added to the act a new Title VI, entitled National Older Americans Volunteer Program. However, this title was repealed by the Domestic Volunteer Service Act of 1973 (PL-93-113, October 1, 1973), which incorporated most of the substance of the repealed Title VI of the Older Americans Act into Title II of that act.

   From 1965 until the 1973 amendments, the last title of the Act was the "General" title. Beginning with the 1965 act it was Title VI. When the 1969 amendments added a new Title VI (National Older Americans Volunteer Program), the "General" title became Title VII. When the 1972 amendments added present Title VII (Nutrition Program for the Elderly), the "General" title become Title VIII. The 1973 amendments repealed Title VIII but added new sections in Title II covering the same subjects as were in the sections of the former Title VIII.

6. Conference on Aging, "Toward a National Policy on Aging," White House/Final Report 1971 (Washington, D.C.: D.H.E.W. Publication No. OHO 74-20911, 1971), vol. 1, p. vii.

7. Walter I. Trattner, *From Poor Law to Welfare State*, 2d ed. (New York: Free Press, 1979), p. 240.

8. Robert B. Hudson, "The 'Graying' of the Federal Budget and Its Consequences for Old-Age Policy," *The Gerontologist*, 18 (October 1978), 430.

9. *Ibid.* p. 430.

10. Robert A. Binstock, "Social Goals in Contemporary Society," in Carter C. Osterbind, ed., *Social Goals, Social Programs, and the Aging*, (Miami: University Presses of Florida, 1975), p. 33.

11. Hudson, *op. cit.*, p. 430.

12. Byron Gold, Elizabeth Kutza, and Theodore Marmor, "United States Social Policy on Old Age: Present Patterns and Predictions," in Bernice Neugarten and Robert Havighurst, eds., *Social Policy, Social Ethics, and the Aging Society* (Washington, D.C.: National Science Foundation, 1976), pp. 9–20.

Chapter 14

Reflections on and Proposals for Social Welfare

WE INTEND THIS CONCLUDING CHAPTER to capture our personal reflections concerning social welfare in the American society. In no way do we assume that our thoughts, our values, and biases should become those of the reader. Rather, we offer our ideas so that they may serve as a frame of reference, in the hope that they will assist the social welfare-oriented person in positively contributing to the society and its social welfare arrangements. We are assuming that people concerned with social welfare should have normative expectations concerning what constitutes the good society and what constitutes appropriate personal and professional behavior. Without certain normative expectations, we believe that the evolution of progressive, humanistic thought and behavior is not linear, necessarily determined, or even probable. In any case, we feel that clear expectations concerning people's social nature and social rights are central to the ability to become more and more socially responsible.

In operationalizing the notion of normative expectations as they can affect our thought and behavior, we would like to stress two interrelated points: (1) the focal concerns that should be stressed within society relative to social welfare and (2) the intervention strategies appropriate for people concerned with social welfare.

229

Focal Concerns

We suggest that a major concern for social welfare personnel should be the promotion of social change within the society. As a concept, social change speaks to change in structural components, that is, statuses, roles, and membership patterns within society and its respective units.[1] In examining this concept relative to "deprived" or "disadvantaged" groups, it would appear that such groups are produced precisely because they have been relegated to inferior role statuses without adequate opportunities to participate in the major institutions within society; whether such groups or individual members have diminished motivation, or are "sick," are secondary considerations. If social welfare personnel are to maximize social functioning, then basic structural issues associated with the goal of social change must become paramount agenda items. Admittedly, people in our society have a range of psychological problems that constitute real and present concerns, but social welfare personnel should at least explore the possible relations between prior structural factors and subsequent personal effects.

We are not suggesting that people in current pain and need should not be helped; nor are we suggesting that there should be a moratorium on clinical services. On the contrary, we are suggesting that people in this field should critically examine how much of their efforts should be directed to structure and how much to effects. It appears to us that our field has become increasingly unbalanced so that little emphasis is given to structural issues. We are asking for more concern with structural phenomena, and that means more concern with the policy and benefit responses in our society and in our agencies.

Intervention Strategies

Once the issues of social change and personal adjustment are examined, there appear to be several problems and issues facing the structurally oriented welfare worker. These issues and problems speak to the interrelated topics of levels of change (where it should occur), how they should occur, and who should be the objects or targets of intervention.

At the highest level, that is, at the dominant society and the federal government level, our activity should focus on goals and objectives related to guaranteed income and supports that reflect appreciation for the concepts of true adequacy and greater equality. Similarly, we should vigorously advocate comprehensive, universal health programs as well as benefits that upgrade the amount, type, and location of housing opportunities for low- and moderate-income people. Harrington says that structural reform at the national level might even relate to increased social ownership, tax reform, and socialization of investment.[2]

In reflecting on these goals, the individual worker within the social welfare institution may feel powerless. It is true that activity at the macro level presupposes politically orchestrated behavior and power—not just well-meaning efforts by individuals. We feel that the National Association of Social Workers has been correct in allocating resources for political activity at the national level in recent years. Such activities must be supported; in fact we are asking that they be increased. Strong coalitions with labor, gays, blacks, and women's groups among others have to be forged as all these groups in varying ways want their interests met through some modification and/or change of the existing structures within society.

What we are suggesting is that people who share the common denominator of being oppressed by structure should come together within specific issue arenas and support each other. In this regard, Flacks has spoken of multiple issues leading to change in various aspects of our society. In his view, "Fundamental political change occurs only after a prolonged period of ferment and conflict within the principle cultural, social, and economic institutions."[3] Not only is the chance of social change heightened when political activity occurs, but the concern of social change itself becomes institutionalized. As this process builds, a possible outcome is that more people might get more benefits. Although this strategy does not guarantee immediate payoffs, this should not lead to the false conclusion that the only "real" welfare activity is direct service work. That conclusion, though perhaps reducing the anxiety of workers about delayed payoffs and lack of current concrete results, helps ensure the continued need for direct service workers as well as the possible maintenance of problems over time.

Admittedly, many people within social welfare now might say that they cannot act out a commitment to change at the national level within the scope of their current occupational positions. Such a judgment would be basically correct. Our reflections lead us to the conclusion that change efforts at the national policy level should be made, but they have to be made through national lobbying groups and often in the context of the role of concerned citizen and professional rather than as agency employee. We ought to be honest with ourselves in recognizing that there is often a fundamental bifurcation between our professional aspirations and goals in the policy area and many of our work activities. Thus, bifurcation should logically lead to a more appropriate understanding of the many ways in which our professional identity has to transcend our current work roles.

In addition to political activity at the national level, social welfare personnel, while recognizing the relation between structure and change, may be quite correct in focusing on helping minorities in the context of the concept of "due process." In writing this book, one issue that periodically confronted us was the rights of the majority (democracy) relative to the rights of the minority. The confrontation has led us to the judgment that in many situations the principle of "due process" has to take precedence over the collective feelings of the majority. This confrontation is especially relevant for social welfare personnel who have to deal with minorities within the context of local communities and states. Our feeling is that true appreciation of the complex, and often subtle, issues associated with "due process" and minorities leads to a consideration of the evolving relationship of the law, social welfare, and the courts. It appears that the courts and quasi-judicial arenas may be still another level at which we should direct our policy concerns. To participate in these arenas social welfare personnel will have to become more familiar and comfortable with adversary relationships and the use of "test cases."

Obviously, there have been developments in recent years—courses offered in social work and the law and universities that grant joint degrees in social work and law—that indicate a growing recognition of the relevant interplay of these two professions. Although we are encouraged by these developments, we believe that has not been sufficient concern with fusing these two fields within a social welfare policy perspective. Rather, there has been an infusion of a humanistic base within the case practice of law. It seems that the relationship has to be examined and that a policy focus should be stressed more heavily. In a sense, what we are asking for is a new professional role that takes as its dependent variable the study, analysis, and change of policy within a legal framework and with a clear value commitment to the concept of due process.

Discussion of the possible relations between law and social welfare leads us to our third level of change, namely, the social welfare organization. The reader may have concluded that little or no social change is possible within the context of work roles and formal organizations. This is simply not true. We have attempted to suggest in Chapter 8 that many decisions within the context of benefits meeting client/consumer are not totally determined. We would like to enumerate some of the things that a social welfare worker, especially those with legitimacy derived from administrative positions, might be able to pursue:

1. Exploring possible biases in the choice of populations served. This would often require changes in the ways in which information on cases is collected and interpreted. Examination of ecological and demographic data on a group level could facilitate such exploration. If examination showed biases, existing policies might not preclude giving special attention to areas and populations not served adequately.

2. Looking for patterns in cases relative to discrimination and/or lack of appropriate service responses from other agencies. This might lead to adversary postures on the part of some workers and agencies relative to other workers and agencies, or at least aggressive strategies of planning and service integration.

3. Consciously promoting case manager roles in service networks to ensure that organizations and workers receive clients and to provide services that they are capable of giving.
4. Promoting expanded resources for social welfare by facilitating and organizing former consumers of services to work for changes in service responses and types of services being offered people.
5. Being at least willing to experiment with new roles in practice such as teacher and consultant to benefit groups as they try to procure services from agencies and organizations.
6. Accepting the possibility that the social welfare worker may be part of the problem, as well as part of the solution, and hence that the worker may become the target of client or group discontent and change efforts.
7. Recognizing that the formal organization within which welfare workers are employed may have a decision-making process, relative to policy, that has inadequate information concerning client needs and/or client discontent. The worker may be able to influence the nature and process of policy making by providing compensatory information (this relates especially to point 1).
8. Being attuned to the possibility that the professional worker and his/her colleagues may be able to identify gaps in service networks relative to types of clients. If such gaps are detected, this will necessitate fairly aggressive compensatory communication with program personnel in social welfare agencies.
9. Being less inclined to utilize referral processes when workers might be able to "extend" themselves and their agencies a bit more and when referrals are made, ensuring that the worker act out the role of linker and advocate.
10. Reverting, where possible, to geographical social orientations wherein identification of particular populations or needs can lead to particular service responses. This approach is compatible with developments in public health, epidemiology, and anthropology.
11. Pursuing more vigorous and more comprehensive evaluations of social welfare programs. This would involve build-

ing in evaluation components that focus on effect of benefits and consumer satisfaction.

12. Being less rigid about professional self-interests that can impede imaginative use of more available and cheaper resources to get to certain objectives.

In examining these types of activities within a social welfare organization, certain considerations have to be kept in mind. First, if social welfare personnel do not have expectations relative to their activity areas, they might not see or seize opportunities for change within their oganization and its service network. Second, the worker should understand that activity in any of these areas may be somewhat difficult to initiate and that there may be few material rewards and inducements emanating from the organization relative to doing these activities. Again, normative expectations that transcend organization are relevant to supporting the professional's work.

To conclude this chapter and the book, we would like to emphasize the need for all of us to stress the special interests and needs of the people we serve, to understand that many problems in our society emanate from the structure of our society and even the structure of our caring responses, and to be mindful of the political implications inherent in concept selection and utilization in problem-policy and benefit program processes.

Notes

1. Robert R. Mayer, *Social Planning and Social Change* (Englewood Cliffs, N.J.: Prentice-Hall, 1972).
2. Michael Harrington, *Socialism* (New York: Saturday Review Press, 1970), pp. 291–307.
3. Richard Flacks, "Strategies for Radical Change," *Social Policy*, 1 (March–April 1971), 10.

Bibliography

ADAMS, DWIGHT. "Fund Executives and Social Change" 17 (January 1972): 68–77.

AIGNER, STEPHEN, AND ROLAND L. SIMMONS. "Social Work and Economics: Strange Bedfellows," *Social Work* 22 (July 1977): 305.

ANDERSON, C. H. *Toward a New Sociology: A Critical View.* Homewood, Ill.: Dorsey Press, 1971.

ATHERTON, CHARLES A. "The Social Assignment of Social Work," *Social Service Review* 43 (December 1969): 421–429.

AXINN, JUNE AND HERMAN LEVIN. *Social Welfare: A History of the American Response to Need.* New York: Dodd, Mead, 1975.

BAKKE, E. WIGHT. *The Mission of Manpower Policy.* Kalamazoo, Mich.: W. E. Upjohn Institute for Employment Research, 1969.

BARD, RAY, MICHAEL L. LAUDERDALE, AND JAMES PETERSON. *Planning for Change.* Washington, D.C.: Education, Training, and Research Sciences, 1971.

BINSTOCK, ROBERT A. "Social Goals in Contemporary Society," in R. Oesterbind, ed., *Social Goals, Social Programs and the Aging.* Miami: University Presses of Florida, 1975.

BERMAN, MARSHALL. *The Politics of Authenticity: Radical Individualism and the Emergence of Modern Society.* New York: Atheneum, 1970.

BLAU, PETER. "Orientation Toward Clients in a Public Welfare Agency," in Blau, ed., *On the Nature of Organizations.* New York: John Wiley, 1974.

236

———, AND MARSHALL MEYER. *Bureaucracy in Modern Society.* New York: Random House, 1971.

BLAU, ZENA SMITH. *Old Age in a Changing Society.* New York: Franklin Watts, 1973.

BOLIN, DAVID C., AND LAWRENCE KIVENS. "Evaluation in a Community Mental Health Center," *Evaluation Quarterly* 2 (June 1974): 28–35.

BORENZWEIG, HERMAN. "Social Work and Psychoanalytic Theory: A Historical Analysis," *Social Work* 16 (January 1971): 7–16.

BOSKIN, MICHAEL J. *The Crisis in Social Security: Problems and Prospects.* San Francisco: Institute for Contemporary Studies, 1977.

BOTTOMORE, T. B. *Classes in Modern Society.* New York: Random House, 1968.

BRAUDE, LEE. *Work and Workers: A Sociological Analysis.* New York: Praeger, 1975.

BREAK, GEORGE, AND JOSEPH PECHMAN. *Federal Tax Reform: The Impossible Dream.* Washington, D.C.: The Brookings Institution, 1975.

BREMNER, ROBERT H. *From the Depths.* New York: New York University Press, 1956.

BRINKER, PAUL ALBERT, AND JOSEPH J. KLOS. *Poverty, Manpower, and Social Security.* Austin, Tex.: Austin Press, 1976.

BROOM, LEONARD, AND PHILLIP SELZNICK. *Sociology.* New York: Harper & Row, 1977.

BURNS, EVELINE. "The Financing of Social Welfare," in Cora Kasius, ed., *New Directions in Social Work.* New York: Harper, 1954.

BUTLER, ROBERT N. *Why Survive? Being Old in America.* New York: Harper & Row, 1975.

BUTTRICK, SHIRLEY. "On Choice and Services," *Social Service Review* 44 (December 1970): 427–433.

CAMERON, JAMES M. "Ideology and Policy Termination: Restructuring California's Mental Health System," *Public Policy* 26 (Fall 1978): 533–570.

CAPLAN, GERALD. "Community Psychiatry: Introduction and Overview," in S. E. Goldstone, ed., *Concepts of Community Psychiatry.* Washington, D.C.: Government Printing Office, 1951, pp. 3–18.

———. *Principles of Preventive Psychiatry.* New York: Basic Books, 1964.

CHAMBERS, CLARKE A. "Social Service and Social Reform: A Historical Essay," *Social Service Review* 37 (March 1963): 76–90.

CLAGUE, EWAN. *The Aging Worker and the Union; Employment and Retirement of Middle-Aged and Older Workers.* New York: Praeger, 1971.

CLARK, J. M., et al. *Adam Smith, 1776–1926.* Chicago: University of Chicago Press, 1928.

COHEN, HENRY. "Poverty and Welfare: A Review Essay," *Political Science Quarterly* 87 (December 1972): 631–652.

COHEN, WILBUR J. "The First Twenty-Five Years of the Social Security Act, 1935–1960," *Social Work Year Book.* New York: National Association of Social Workers, 1960, pp. 49–61.

————. *Social Work Year Book.* New York: National Association of Social Workers, 1960.

COLL, BLANCHE D. "Perspectives in Public Welfare: The English Heritage," *Welfare in Review* 4 (March 1966): 1–12.

COWHERD, RAYMOND. *Political Economists and the English Poor Laws: A Historical Study of the Influence of Classical Economics on the Formation of Social Welfare Policy.* Athens, Ohio: Ohio University Press, 1978.

CUTLER, NEAL E. "The Aging Population and Social Policy," in Richard H. Davis, ed., *Aging: Prospects and Issues.* Los Angeles: The Ethel Purcy Andrus Gerontology Center, University of Southern California, 1977.

DAHRENDORF, RALF. *Class and Class Conflict in Industrial Society.* New York: Free Press, 1963.

DICKSON, PAUL. *The Future of the Workplace: The Coming Revolution in Jobs.* New York: Weybright and Talley, 1975.

DOERINGER, PETER B., AND MICHAEL J. PIORE. *Internal Labor Markets and Manpower Analysis.* Lexington, Mass.: Heath Lexington Books, 1972.

DURKHEIM, EMILE. "The Normal and Pathological," in *The Rules of the Sociological Method.* New York: Macmillan, 1966.

DURMAN, EUGENE. "Have the Poor Been Regulated? Toward a Multivariate Understanding of Welfare Growth," *Social Service Review* 47 (September 1973): 339–359.

DYCKMAN, JOHN. "Social Planning, Social Planners, and Planned Societies," *American Institute of Planners Journal* 32 (March 1966): 66–76.

DYE, THOMAS. *Understanding Public Policy.* Englewood Cliffs, N.J.: Prentice-Hall, 1978.

EDWARDS, RICHARD C., MICHAEL REICH, AND THOMAS E. WEISSKOPF, eds. *The Capitalist System.* Englewood Cliffs, N.J.: Prentice-Hall, 1972.

————. "Emptying the Mental Wards: New Treatment Stirs a Controversy," *U.S. News and World Report,* February 24, 1975.

Encyclopedia of Social Work. New York: National Association of Social Workers, 1971.

FEAGIN, JOE R. *Subordinating the Poor: Welfare and American Beliefs.* Englewood Cliffs, N.J.: Prentice-Hall, 1975.

FINCH, WILBUR A., JR. "Social Workers Versus Bureaucracy," *Social Work* 21 (September 1976): 370–376.

FLACKS, RICHARD. "Strategies for Radical Change," *Social Policy* 1 (March–April 1971): 7–14.

FRIEDLANDER, WALTER A. *Introduction to Social Welfare.* Englewood Cliffs, N.J.: Prentice-Hall, 1966.

FRIEDMAN, MILTON. "The Role of Government in a Free Society," in Edmund Phelps, ed., *Private Wants and Public Needs.* New York: W. W. Norton, 1962, 104–117.

GALPER, JEFFREY. *The Politics of Social Services.* Englewood Cliffs, N.J.: Prentice-Hall, 1975.

GANS, HERBERT. *The Urban Villagers.* New York: Free Press, 1962.

GETTLEMAN, MARVIN E. "Philanthropy as Social Control in Late Nineteenth Century America," *Societas* 5 (Winter 1975): 49–59.

GILBERT, NEIL. "The Transformation of Social Services," *Social Service Review* (December 1977): 624–641.

———, AND HARRY SPECHT. *Dimensions of Social Welfare Policy.* Englewood Cliffs, N.J.: Prentice-Hall, 1974.

———, AND HARRY SPECHT. *The Emergence of Social Welfare and Social Work.* Itasca, Ill.: Peacock, 1976.

GLASSCOTE, RAYMOND, DAIRD SANDERS, H. M. FORSTENZER, AND A. R. FOLEY. *The Community Mental Health Center.* Baltimore: Goramowe/ Predemark Press, 1964.

GLINER, ROBERT. *American Society as a Social Problem.* New York: Free Press, 1973.

GOLD, BYRON, ELIZABETH KUTZA, AND THEODORE MARMON. "United States Social Policy on Old Age: Present Patterns and Predictions," in Bernice Neugarten and Robert Havighurst, eds., *Social Policy, Social Ethics and the Aging Society.* Washington, D.C.: National Science Foundation, 1976, pp. 9–20.

GOODMAN, PAUL. *Growing Up Absurd!* New York: Random House, 1960.

GOODWIN, LEONARD. *Do the Poor Want to Work? A Social–Psychological Study of Work Orientations.* Washington, D.C.: The Brookings Institution, 1972.

GORDON, DAVID. *Theories of Poverty and Underemployment.* Lexington, Mass.: D. C. Heath and Company, 1972.

GORDON, MARGARET, ed. *Poverty in America.* San Francisco: Chandler, 1965.

GREEN, A. S. "The Professional Worker in the Bureaucracy," *Social Service Review* 40 (March 1966): 71-77.

GROB, GERALD. *Mental Institution in America: Social Policy to 1875.* New York: Free Press, 1973.

GROSS, BERTRAM, AND JEFFREY SSTRAUSSMAN. "Full-Employment Growthmanship and the Expansion of Labor Supply," *Annals* 418 (March 1975): 1-11.

GROSS, RONALD, AND PAUL OSTERMAN. *Individualism: Man in Modern Society.* New York: Dell Publications, 1971.

HARRINGTON, MICHAEL. *The Other America: Poverty in the United States.* New York: Penguin Books, 1962.

———. *Socialism.* New York: Saturday Review Press, 1970.

HARRIS, CHARLES. *Fact Book on Aging.* Washington, D.C.: National Council on Aging, 1978.

HARRIS, ROBERT. *Welfare Reform and Social Insurance: Program Issues and Budget Impacts.* Washington, D.C.: Urban Institute, 1977.

HAVEMAN, ROBERT. "Poverty, Income Distribution, and Social Policy: The Last Decade and Next," reprint ser. 252. Madison: University of Wisconsin, Institute for Research on Poverty, 1977.

HAWKINS, CHARLES E. "The Welfare and Child Health Provisions of the Social Security Amendments of 1967," *Welfare in Review* 6 (May–June 1968): 1-34.

HEFFERNAN, JOSEPH W., *Introduction to Social Welfare Policy.* Itasca, Ill.: Peacock, 1979.

HOFFMAN, WAYNE, AND TED MARMOR. "The Politics of Public Assistance Reform: An Essay Review," *Social Service Review* 50 (March 1976): 11-22.

HOFSTADTER, RICHARD. *Social Darwinism in American Thought.* Boston: Beacon Press, 1955.

HOROWITZ, IRVING L. *Power, Politics and People.* New York: Ballantine Books, 1965.

HORTON, JOHN. "Order and Conflict Theories of Social Problems as Competing Ideologies," *American Journal of Sociology* 71 (May 1966): 701-713.

HOSHINO, GEORGE. "Britain's Debate on Universal or Selective Social Services: Lessons for America," *Social Service Review* 43 (September 1969): 245-258.

HUBER, JOAN, AND PETER CHALFANT. *The Sociology of American Poverty.* Cambridge, Mass.: Schenkman, 1974.

HUDSON, ROBERT B. "The 'Graying' of the Federal Budget and Its Consequences for Old-Age Policy," *The Gerontologist* 18 (1978): 430.

JAMES, DOROTHY BUCKTON. "The Limits of Liberal Reform," *Science and Society* 2 (Spring 1972): 311–312.

KAHN, ALFRED J. *Planning Community Services for Children in Trouble.* New York: Columbia University Press, 1963.

————. "Social Services in Relation to Income Security," *Social Service Review* 39 (December 1965): 381–389.

————. *Social Policy and Social Services.* New York: Random House, 1973.

————. *Theory and Practice of Social Planning.* New York: Russell Sage, 1969.

————, ed. *Shaping the New Social Work.* New York: Columbia University Press, 1973.

KALLEN, DAVID S., AND DOROTHY MILLER. "Public Attitudes Toward Welfare," *Social Work* 16 (July 1971): 83–90.

KAMERMAN, SHELIA B., AND ALFRED J. KAHN. *Social Services in the United States: Policies and Programs.* Philadelphia: Temple University Press, 1976.

KANTER, ROSABETH MOSS. *Work and Family in the United States: A Critical Review and Agenda for Research and Policy.* New York: Russell Sage, 1977.

KERSCHNER, PAUL A. "Changing Legislation: Its Effects on Programs," in Richard H. Davis, ed., *Aging: Prospects and Issues.* Los Angeles: The Ethel Percy Andrus Gerontology Center, University of Southern California, 1977.

KINGSLEY, DAVIS. "Mental Hygiene and the Class Structure," in Patrick Mullahey, ed., *A Study of Interpersonal Relations.* New York: Hermitage, 1949.

KIRK, STUART A., AND JAMES R. GREENBY. "Denying or Delivering Services?", *Social Work* 19 (July 1974): 439–447.

KIRKLAND, EDWARD C. *A History of American Economic Life.* New York: Appleton-Century-Crofts, 1951.

KNICKMEYER, ROBERT. "A Marxist Approach to Social Work," *Social Work* 17 (July 1972); 58–65.

KRAMER, RALPH M. "Public Fiscal Policy and Voluntary Agencies in Welfare States," *Social Service Review* 53 (March 1979): 1–15.

KUHN, THOMAS S. "Reflections On My Critics," in Imre Lakatos and Alan Musgrave, eds., *Criticism and the Growth of Knowledge.* Cambridge: Cambridge University Press, 1970.

242BIBLIOGRAPHY

———. *The Structure of Scientific Revolutions.* Chicago: University of Chicago, 1970.

LAMPMAN, ROBERT J. "Changing Patterns of Income, 1960–1974," reprint ser. 235. Madison: University of Wisconsin, Institute for Research on Poverty, 1977.

———. "Comments on Taxes, Equity and Income Distribution," reprint ser. 247. Madison: University of Wisconsin, Institute for Research on Poverty, 1977.

LANDAU, MARTIN. "Redundancy, Rationality, and the Problem of Duplication and Overlap," *Public Administration Review* 29 (July 1969): 346–358.

LANTZ, JAMES E. "Referral-Fatigue Therapy," *Social Work* 21 (May 1976): 239–241.

LASZLO, ERWIN. *Individualism, Collectivism, and Political Power: A Relational Analysis of Ideological Conflict.* The Hague: M. Nijhoff, 1963.

LEE, ALFRED McCLUNG. "What Kind of Sociology Is Useful to Social Workers?", *Journal of Sociology and Social Welfare* 4 (September 1976): 4–13.

LEVITAN, SAR A. *The Great Society's Poor Law: A New Approach to Poverty.* Baltimore: Johns Hopkins University Press, 1969.

———, AND GARTH MANGUN. *Federal Training and Work Programs in the Sixties.* Ann Arbor, Mich.: Institute of Labor and Industrial Relations, 1969.

———, AND ROBERT TAGGART, III. *Social Experimentation and Manpower Policy: The Rhetoric and Reality.* Baltimore: Johns Hopkins University Press, 1971.

———. *The Promise of Greatness.* Cambridge, Mass.: Harvard University Press, 1975.

LOWRY, RITCHIE. *Social Problems: A Critical Analysis of Theories and Public Policies.* Lexington, Mass.: D.C. Heath, 1976.

LUBOVE, ROY. *The Professional Altruist: The Emergence of Social Work as a Career, 1880–1930.* Cambridge, Mass.: Harvard University Press, 1965.

———. *The Struggle for Social Security, 1900–1935.* Cambridge, Mass.: Harvard University Press, 1968.

LURIE, IRENE. "Work Requirements in Income-Conditioned Transfer Programs," *Social Service Review* 52 (December 1978): 551–567.

McCONNELL, CAMPBELL. *Economics: Principles, Policy, and Problems.* New York: McGraw-Hill, 1976.

McEwen, William P. *The Problem of Social-Scientific Knowledge.* Totowa, N.J.: Bedminster Press, 1966.

MacDonald, Maurice. "Food Stamps: An Analytical History," *Social Service Review* 51 (December 1977): 642-658.

Mangum, Garth L. "Perspectives on a Positive Manpower Policy," in George F. Rohrlich, ed., *Social Economics for the 1970s.* New York: The Dunellen Co., 1970.

Marmor, Theodore. *The Politics of Medicare.* Chicago: Aldine, 1973.

Martin, John M., and Joseph P. Fitzpatrick. *Delinquent Behavior: A Redefinition of the Problem.* New York: Random House, 1966.

Mayer, Robert R. *Social Planning and Social Change.* Englewood Cliffs, N.J.: Prentice-Hall, 1973.

Mechanic, David. *Mental Health and Social Policy.* Englewood Cliffs, N.J.: Prentice-Hall, 1969.

Meenaghan, Thomas M. "Role Changes for the Parents of the Mentally Retarded," *Journal of Mental Retardation* 12 (June 1974): 48-49.

————. "Clues About Community Power Structures," *Social Work* 21 (March 1976): 126-132.

————. "Specifying Sociological Options and Sociological Strategies," *Journal of Sociology and Social Welfare,* forthcoming.

————, and Michael Mascari. "Consumer Choice, Consumer Control in Service Delivery," *Social Work* 10 (October 1971): 50-57.

Mencher, Samuel. *Poor Law to Poverty Program.* Pittsburgh, Penn: University of Pittsburgh, 1967.

Merton, Robert, and Robert Nisbet, eds. *Contemporary Social Problems.* New York: Harcourt Brace Jovanovich, 1976.

Mills, C. Wright. *The Sociological Imagination.* New York: Oxford University Press, 1959.

Mitchell, William C. *The Popularity of Social Security: A Paradox in Public Choice.* Washington, D.C.: American Enterprises Institute for Public Policy Research, 1977.

Mogulof, Martin. "Future Funding of Social Services," *Social Work* 19 (September 1974): 607-613.

Mohl, Raymond A. "Poverty in Early America, A Reappraisal: The Case of Eighteenth-Century New York City," *New York History* 50 (January 1969): 5-27.

Mott, Paul E. *Meeting Human Needs: The Social and Political History of Title XX.* Columbus, Ohio: National Conference on Social Welfare, 1976.

MOYNIHAN, DANIEL P. "Memo from Daniel Moynihan to Richard Nixon," *The Wall Street Journal*, March 13, 1970.

————. *The Politics of a Guaranteed Income.* New York: Random House, 1973.

MURDRICK, NANCY. "The Use of AFDC by Previously High- and Low-Income Households," *Social Service Review* 52 (March 1978): 107–116.

MYERS, ROBERT JAMES. *Social Security.* Homewood, Ill.: Irwin, 1975.

MYRDAL, ALVA. *Nation and Family.* Cambridge, Mass.: M.I.T. Press, 1968.

NATIONAL MANPOWER POLICY TASK FORCE. *The Nation's Manpower Programs.* Washington, D.C.: National Manpower Policy Task Force, 1969.

NEUGARTÉN, BERNICE, ed. *Middle Age and Aging.* Chicago: University of Chicago Press, 1968.

NEW YORK RESEARCH BUREAU. "Evaluating a Reform: Welfare," *Catalyst* 2 (Spring 1978): 18–34.

NIEBUHR, REINHOLD. *The Contribution of Religion to Social Work.* New York: Columbia University Press, 1932.

OFFE, CLAUSS. "Advanced Capitalism and the Welfare State," *Politics and Society* 2 (Summer 1972): 479–488.

OFFENBACHER, DEBORAH D., AND CONSTANCE H. POSTER. *Social Problems and Social Policy.* New York: Appleton, 1970.

OSSOWSKI, STANSILAU. *Class Structure in the Social Consciousness.* New York: Free Press, 1964.

OWEN, DAVID. *English Philanthropy, 1660–1960.* Cambridge, Mass.: Harvard University Press, 1964.

OZAWA, MARTHA. "Issues in Social Welfare Reform," *Social Service Review* 52 (March 1978): 37–56.

PAGE, ALFRED N. "Economics and Social Work: A Neglected Relationship," *Social Work* 22 (January 1977): 48.

————. "Points and Viewpoints: The Myth of Professional Purity," *Social Work* 22 (July 1977): 308.

PARADIS, ADRIAN A., AND ROBERT H. WOOD. *Social Security in Action.* New York: Messner, 1975.

PARKER, RONALD, AND JANE KNITZER. *Day Care and Preschool Services: Trends and Issues.* Atlanta, Ga.: Avatar, 1972.

PARSONS, TALCOTT. *The Social System.* New York: Free Press, 1951.

———. "Definitions of Health and Illness in the Light of American Values and Social Structure," in E. Gartley Jaco, ed., *Patients, Physicians, and Illness.* Glencoe, Ill.: Free Press, 1963.

———. *Societies: Evolutionary and Comparative Perspectives.* Englewood Cliffs, N.J.: Prentice-Hall, 1966.

———, EDWARD SHILS, et al. *Theories of Society,* vol. 1. New York: Free Press, 1961.

PASCAL, ANTHONY. "New Departures in Social Services," *Social Welfare Forum.* New York: Columbia University, 1969.

PAWLAK, EDWARD J. "Organizational Tinkering," *Social Work* 21 (March 1976): 376–381.

PECHMAN, JOSEPH A., et al. *Social Security: Perspectives for Reform.* Washington, D.C.: Brookings Institution, 1968.

PERLMAN, HELEN HARRIS. "Freud's Contribution to Social Welfare," *Social Service Review* 31 (June 1957): 192–202.

PILIAVIN, IRVING, AND ALAN E. GROSS. "The Effects of Separation of Services and Income Maintenance on AFDC Recipients," *Social Service Review* 51 (September 1977): 389–406.

PIORE, MICHAEL J. "The Dual Labor Market: Theory and Implications," in D. M. Gordon, ed., *Problems in Political Economy: An Urban Perspective.* Lexington, Mass.: Heath Lexington Books, 1972.

PIVEN, FRANCES FOX, AND RICHARD A. CLOWARD. *Regulating the Poor: The Functions of Public Welfare.* New York: Pantheon, 1971.

———. *Regulating the Poor: The Functions of Public Welfare.* New York: Random House, 1971.

———. "Reaffirming the Regulation of the Poor," *Social Service Review* 48 (June 1974): 147–169.

POLLAK, WIILIAM. *Costs of Alternative Care Settings for the Elderly.* Washington, D.C.: Urban Institute, 1973.

PRATT, HENRY J. *The Gray Lobby.* Chicago: University of Chicago Press, 1977.

REDER, MELVIN. "A Partial Survey of the Theory of Income Size Distribution," in Lee Soltow, ed., *Six Papers on the Size Distribution of Wealth and Income.* New York: National Bureau of Economic Research, 1969, pp. 224–239.

REID, NELSON. "Reforming the Service Monopoly," *Social Work* 17 (November 1972): 44–54.

REIN, MARTIN. *Social Policy: Issues of Choice and Change.* New York: Random House, 1970.

————. *Social Science and Public Policy.* New York: Penguin Books, 1976.

————, AND LEE RAINWATER. "Patterns of Welfare Use," *Social Service Review* 52 (December 1978): 511-535.

REJDA, GEORGE E. *Social Insurance and Economic Security.* Englewood Cliffs, N.J.: Prentice-Hall, 1976.

RIVLIN, ALICE. *Systematic Thinking for Social Action.* Washington, D.C.: The Brookings Institution, 1971.

ROBY, PAMELA. *Child Care—Who Cares?* New York: Basic Books, 1973.

ROMANYSHYN, JOHN. *Social Welfare: Charity to Justice.* New York: Random House, 1971.

RUTTENBERG, STANLEY, AND JOSELYN GUTCHESS. *Manpower Challenge of the 1970s: Institutions and Social Change.* Baltimore: Johns Hopkins University Press, 1970.

SCHNEIDER, HERBERT W., ed., *Adam Smith's Moral and Political Philosophy.* New York: Hafner, 1948.

SCHORR, ALVIN L., ed. *Jubilee for Our Times: A Practical Program for Income Equality.* New York: Columbia University Press, 1977.

SCHRAM, SANFORD E. "Elderly Policy Particularism and the New Social Services," *Social Service Review* 53 (March 1979): 75-91.

SCHUMPETER, JOSEPH. *Capitalism, Socialism, and Democracy.* New York: Harper & Row, 1942.

SEELEY, JOHN. "Social Science? Some Probative Problems," in Maurice Stein and Arthur Vidich, eds., *Sociology on Trial.* Englewood Cliffs, N.J.: Prentice-Hall, 1963.

SELEGMAN, BEN B. *Permanent Poverty.* Chicago: Quadrangle Books, 1968.

SHATTUCK, GERALD, AND JOHN MARTIN. "New Professional Work Roles and Their Integration into a Social Agency Structure," *Social Work* 14 (July 1969): 18-19.

SIMMONS, LEONARD. "Agency Financing and Social Change," *Social Work* 14 (January 1972): 62-68.

SMITH, ADAM. *The Wealth of Nations.* New york: Modern Library, 1973.

SMITH, BERT KRUGER. *Aging in America.* Boston: Beacon Press, 1973.

SPECHT, HARRY. "Disruptive Tactics," *Social Work* 14 (April 1969): 5-16.

STEINER, GILBERT. *The State of Welfare.* Washington, D.C.: The Brookings Institution, 1971.

————. "Reform Follows Reality: The Growth of Welfare," *Public Interest* 34 (Winter 1974): 47-65.

STEINFELS, MARGARET O'BRIEN. *Who's Minding the Children?* New York: Touchstone Books, 1973.

STEVENS, ROBERT AND ROSEMARY. *Welfare Medicine in America: A Case Study of Medicaid.* New York: Free Press, 1974.

SUCHMAN, EDWARD. *Evaluative Research.* New York: Russell Sage Fn, 1967.

TAWNEY, R. H. *Religion and the Rise of Capitalism.* New York: Mentor Books, 1954.

TERRELL, PAUL. "Private Alternatives to Public Human Services Administration," *Social Service Review* 53 (March 1979): 56–75.

THACKERAY, MILTON G., REX A. SKIDMORE, AND WILLIAM FARLEY. *Introduction to Mental Health: Field and Practice.* Englewood Cliffs, N.J.: Prentice-Hall, 1979.

THEOBALD, ROBERT, ed. "The Guaranteed Income: Next Step in Economic Evolution?", Garden City, N.Y.: Doubleday, 1966.

THUROU, LESTER C. *Poverty and Discrimination.* Washington, D.C.: The Brookings Institution, 1969.

———. *Investment in Human Capital.* Los Angeles: Wadsworth, 1970.

———. *Generating Inequality.* New York: Basic Books, 1975.

TITMUSS, RICHARD. *Essays on the Welfare State.* New Haven, Conn.: Yale University Press, 1959.

———. "The Role of Redistribution in Social Policy," *Social Security Bulletin* 23 (June 1965): 1–7.

———. *Commitment to Welfare.* New York: Pantheon, 1968.

———. "Equity, Adequacy and Innovation in Social Security," *International Social Review* 2 (1970): 250–267.

TOLLEY, G. S., AND RICHARD BURKHAUSER, eds. *Income Support Policies for the Aged.* Cambridge, Mass.: Ballinger Publishing, 1977.

TRATTNER, WALTER I. *From Poor Law to Welfare State: A History of Social Welfare in America.* New York: Free Press, 1979.

U.S. Department of Commerce, Bureau of the Census. *Current Population Reports,* ser. P-60. Washington, D.C.: Government Printing Office.

VISWANTHAN, NARAYAN. "The Role of American Public Welfare Policies in the United States, 1930–1960," unpublished Ph.D. dissertation. New York: Columbia University, 1961.

WASHINGTON, ROBERT O. *Program Evaluation in the Human Services.* Milwaukee: Center for Advanced Studies in Human Services, University of Wisconsin, 1975.

WEBER, MAX. *The Protestant Ethic and the Spirit of Capitalism,* trans. Talcott Parsens. New York: Scribner, 1958.

————. *Basic Concepts in Sociology.* New York: Citadel Press, 1966.

WEISBROD, BURTON A. "Benefits of Manpower Programs: Theoretical and Methodological Issues," in G. G. Somers and W. D. Wood, *Cost–Benefit Analysis of Manpower Programs.* Kingston, Ont.: Queen's University, 1969.

WEISS, CAROLE H. *Evaluation Research.* Englewood Cliffs, N.J.: Prentice-Hall, 1972.

WILCOX, CLAIRE. *Toward Social Welfare.* Homewood, Ill.: Irwin, 1969.

WILENSKY, HAROLD. *The Welfare State and Equality.* Berkeley: University of California Press, 1975.

————, AND CHARLES LEBEAUX. *Industrial Society and Social Welfare.* New York: Free Press, 1967.

WILLHELM, SIDNEY M. *Who Needs the Negro?* Garden City, N.Y.: Doubleday, 1971.

WILLIAMS, ROBIN, JR. *American Society.* New York: Knopf, 1970.

WINOUER, STANLEY. "A Political View of the United Way," *Social Work* 20 (May 1975): 223–230.

WITTE, EDWIN E. *The Development of the Social Security Act.* Madison: University of Wisconsin, 1962.

WOOD, ELLEN MERKSIN. *Mind and Politics: An Approach to the Meaning of Liberal and Socialist Individualism.* Berkeley: University of California Press, 1972.

ZALD, MAYER. "Demographics, Politics and the Future of the Welfare State," *Social Service Review* 51 (March 1977): 88–125.

ZIMBALIST, SIDNEY. "Recent British and American Poverty Trends: Conceptual and Policy Contrasts," *Social Service Review* 51 (September 1977): 419–433.

————. "Absolute and Relative Poverty," *Social Service Review* 52 (March 1978): 132–133.

Name Index

Subject Index

261

Subject Index